Marketing and Design in the Service Sector

Marketing and Design in the Service Sector: Enhancing Customer Experience

EDITED BY

SALOOMEH TABARI

Cardiff University, UK

WEI CHEN

Sheffield Hallam University, UK

AND

STELLA KLADOU

Hellenic Mediterranean University, Greece

United Kingdom – North America – Japan – India – Malaysia – China

Emerald Publishing Limited
Emerald Publishing, Floor 5, Northspring, 21-23 Wellington Street, Leeds LS1 4DL

First edition 2024

Reprints and permissions service
Contact: www.copyright.com

British Library Cataloguing in Publication Data
A catalogue record for this book is available from the British Library

ISBN: 978-1-83797-277-7 (Print)
ISBN: 978-1-83797-276-0 (Online)
ISBN: 978-1-83797-278-4 (Epub)

Printed and bound by CPI Group (UK) Ltd, Croydon, CR0 4YY

INVESTOR IN PEOPLE

I dedicate this book with love to my best friends and confidante, Daniel, and my parents Sarah and Mohsen, thank you for your constant love and support. You all have been my inspiration, and my world is a better place because of you all...
Saloomeh Tabari

Thanks to everyone who helped me so much during this very special time in my life. Special thanks to Jinping and the kids; your love makes me strong.
Wei Chen

To Stavros, Eleni, Magda, Murat, Alex Ege and Alina, for making our shared experiences so memorable.
Stella Kladou

Contents

List of Figures and Tables   *ix*

About the Editors   *xi*

About the Contributors   *xiii*

Acknowledgements   *xix*

Introduction   *1*
Saloomeh Tabari, Wei Chen and Stella Kladou

**Chapter 1   The Role of Industrial Design in the Designscape
Development Based on the Marketing and Customer Experience
Design**   *7*
Hassan Sadeghi Naeini and Mahdiyeh Jafarnejad Shahri

**Chapter 2   Independent Coffee Shops and Cafes: Creating Unique
Environments and Servicescapes**   *21*
Saloomeh Tabari, Dave Egan and Helen Egan

**Chapter 3   Intangible but Effective: The Role of Hotel Lobby Music
Background on Customer Satisfaction**   *35*
Yuyuan Wu and Saloomeh Tabari

**Chapter 4   Hotel Design and Its Impact on the Customer's Booking
Decision**   *51*
Minhan Wang, Saloomeh Tabari and Wei Chen

**Chapter 5   Innovative Services, Processes and Product Design
Crucial for Enhancing Customer Experience**   *63*
Hassan Ali Khan

Chapter 6   Opportunities and Possibilities for Online Marketing Innovation   *83*
Agnieszka Nawrocka, Aleksandra Borowicz and Joanna Kuczewska

Chapter 7   Virtual Design in the Digital Age – Reshaping Hospitality Landscape   *101*
Hassan Ali Khan

Chapter 8   Tourist Experience in Digital Detox Tourism   *119*
İsmail Uzut and Serap Özdemir Güzel

Chapter 9   Customer Experience Design in Sportswear Retail Stores   *137*
Sardar Mohammadi, Abed Mahmoudian and Manuel Alonso Dos Santos

Chapter 10   Applying the Strategic Model of Customer Experience in the Field of Sports: The Customer Experience Model in Sports and Recreation Complexes   *153*
Sardar Mohammadi, Abed Mahmoudian and Mike Rayner

Chapter 11   How Marketing and Design can Enhance Customer Experience in Hospitality by Meeting Their Evolving Needs   *175*
Michael Donald and Ashleigh Donald

Index   *187*

List of Figures and Tables

Figures

Fig. 1.1.	Ergonomic Product Place.	16
Fig. 1.2.	The Place of Ergonomics in Marketing.	17
Fig. 2.1.	Conceptual Framework.	25
Fig. 3.1.	Conceptual Framework, the Relationship Between Background Music in Hotel Lobbies and Customer Satisfaction.	45
Fig. 4.1.	The Chi-Square Test of Customer Preference.	56
Fig. 4.2.	The Chi-Square Test of Customer Choice.	57
Fig. 4.3.	The Chi-Square Test Between Colours and Gender.	57
Fig. 4.4.	The Chi-Square Test Between the Local Characteristic and Gender.	58
Fig. 4.5.	The One-Way Analysis of Variance.	58
Fig. 8.1.	Information on Theme and Sub-codes.	130
Fig. 8.2.	Word Cloud of Comments by Users Participating in Digital Detox Tourism.	131
Fig. 8.3.	Code Co-occurrence Model.	133
Fig. 9.1.	Customer Experience Model in Sportswear Retail Stores	144
Fig. 10.1.	Customer Experience Model in Sports and Recreation Complexes.	164

Tables

Table 2.1.	The Final Template Below Summarises the Key Themes Identified.	31

Table 3.1.   The Impact of Four Musical Variables on
             Customer Satisfaction.   42
Table 3.2.   Chi-Square Test Relationship Between Age and
             Musical Variables.   43
Table 6.1.   Characteristics of Interviewed Companies.   87
Table 6.2.   Selected Key Extracts From Interviews With
             Companies.   89
Table 8.1.   Activities Preferred by Tourists to Participate in
             Digital Detox Tourism.   125
Table 8.2.   Descriptive Profile of Analysis Unit.   129
Table 9.1.   Demographic Characteristics of the Interviewees.   143
Table 9.2.   Customer Experience Coding in Sports Stores.   145
Table 10.1. Demographic Characteristics of the Interviewees.   162
Table 10.2. Customer Experience Coding for Sports and
             Recreational Complexes.   165

About the Editors

Dr Saloomeh Tabari is a Lecturer in Marketing at Cardiff Business school. She has served as a Senior Lecturer in Huddersfield University prior to joining Cardiff University. Her research mainly centres on consumer behaviour, intercultural communication, cultural intelligence and marketing. She has edited a few books in the area of consumer behaviour and marketing. She has published in prominent academic journals and books and presented at international conferences. She is an Associate Editor for the *Journal of Islamic Marketing* and is on the scientific and editorial board of international conferences and journals.

Dr Wei Chen is a Senior Lecturer in Strategic Management at Sheffield Hallam University. He has wide experiences in cross-culture management in the hospitality and tourism industry. His book *International Hospitality Management* with Professor Alan Clarke has been published in English, French and Portuguese, and he has translated books such as *Trade Show and Event Marketing* into different languages. He is the chief overseas editor for 'Finance and Economy', a business magazine, in China. Wei Chen is also a Senior Business Advisor of a renowned sport company in England.

Dr Stella Kladou (PhD, MBA, FHEA) is an Assistant Professor at the Hellenic Mediterranean University (Greece). Her international experience started with her PhD, which involved field research in Greece, Italy and Turkey and was supported by national funding bodies, Istanbul Bilgi University and the University of Rome La Sapienza. Upon its completion, her academic experience first developed in the United Kingdom (Sheffield Hallam University), Turkey (Boğaziçi University) and their international partners. Stella's research revolves around place branding and specifically the heritage-culture and tourism dimensions of the place brand. She has co-edited books, published in prominent academic journals and books of international publishers and presented at well-esteemed international conferences. She is an International Place Brand Specialist for The Place Brand Observer, a jury member for the International Place Brand Impact Story Competition, the Associate Editor for Europe and Africa Region of the Journal of Foodservice Business Research, in the editorial review board of the Annals of Tourism Research, in the editorial board of the Journal of Qualitative Research in Tourism and the Journal of Destination Marketing and Management and in the organising and/or scientific board of international conferences, such as the Advances in Tourism Marketing Conference (ATMC).

About the Contributors

Aleksandra Borowicz is an Assistant Professor at the Department of International Economics and Economic Development at the Faculty of Economics at the University of Gdansk. Aleksandra Borowicz specialises in international economics, with the focus on international trade, foreign direct investment and the economics of European integration. She has experience in applying for and implementing projects co-financed by the European Union. Member of the Team Europe network at the European Commission in Poland. She is a member of the board of Polish European Community Studies Association (PECSA). Aleksandra Borowicz also holds a seat at the editorial boards of two journals *Review of European Affairs* published by PECSA and *European Integration Studies* published by Kaunas University of Technology.

Dr Wei Chen is a Senior Lecturer in Strategic Management at Sheffield Hallam University. He has wide experiences in cross-culture management in the hospitality and tourism industry. His book International Hospitality Management with Professor Alan Clarke has been published in English, French and Portuguese, and he has translated books such as Trade Show and Event Marketing into different languages. He is the chief overseas editor for 'Finance and Economy', a business magazine, in China. Wei Chen is also a Senior Business Advisor of a renowned sport company in England.

Ashleigh Donald has over 40 years of experience working in the hospitality service industry. Specialising in operations, customer experience, marketing and communications, they have each led teams in luxury hotels around the world, including The Goring, Turnberry Hotel, Shanghai-La at The Shard, Hilton, Luxury Collection and Sheraton. In 2019, they co-founded Halo Business Consulting to support clients around the globe to drive customer loyalty through tailored marketing plans, process improvement and bespoke retention strategies.

Michael Donald has over 40 years of experience working in the hospitality service industry. Specialising in operations, customer experience, marketing and communications, they have each led teams in luxury hotels around the world, including The Goring, Turnberry Hotel, Shanghai-La at The Shard, Hilton, Luxury Collection and Sheraton. In 2019, they co-founded Halo Business Consulting to support clients around the globe to drive customer loyalty through tailored marketing plans, process improvement and bespoke retention strategies.

Manuel Alonso Dos Santos holds a PhD in Marketing and Consumer Behaviour. His areas of interest are family entrepreneurship, entrepreneurship in marketing and sponsorship marketing. He currently works at the Universidad Católica de la Santísima Concepción in Chile, and his research articles have been published in international journals on the subject of entrepreneurship, family firms, education, digital marketing and sport management. To this day, Alonso has worked on more than 50 papers (e.g. *Psychology & Marketing, Engineering Economics, Journal of Business Research, Industrial Management and Data System*) and has participated in 50 international conferences (e.g. GIKA, AMS).

Dave Egan was a Senior Lecturer in Hospitality Management at Sheffield Hallam University until his recent retirement. He has written extensively in the field of hospitality management and in the field of café research. A recent publication was Egan, H., Elsmore, I. and Egan, D. (2022), 'Café Tribes: A Typology of Café Customers', Tabari, S. and Chen, W. (Ed.) *Global Strategic Management in the Service Industry: A Perspective of the New Era*, Emerald Publishing Limited, Leeds, pp. 153–162. https://doi.org/10.1108/978-1-80117-081-920221012

Helen Egan was a Senior Lecturer in Sheffield Business School until her recent retirement. She has researched into cafes and café culture, and this has been reported in various conferences and the book chapter referenced above.

Serap Özdemir Güzel, Istanbul University-Cerrahpaşa, graduated from Dokuz Eylul University, Faculty of Business, Department of Tourism Management (English) (2010). Received an MA degree from Dokuz Eylül University Institute of Social Sciences, Department of Tourism Management (2013), a PhD degree from Istanbul University, Institute of Social Sciences, Department of Tourism Management. She currently works as an Assoc Prof at Istanbul University-Cerrahpasa, Tourism and Hotel Management programme. She has also been involved in more than one national project. She is currently a Researcher and an Expert of Erasmus + KA227, and in two KA220 projects. She has studied especially on the development of tourism, tourism management, destination marketing, rural development, heritage tourism and sustainability. Also, her recent paper on smart technology received an award.

Hassan Ali Khan is currently serving as the Head of Learning and Development and Group AGM Customer Services at The Monal Group & A-Cube Pvt Ltd, Pakistan. He served as a Senior Lecturer of Hospitality & Business Management and led International Industrial and Academics Linkages at Hashoo School of Hospitality Management (HSHM) Islamabad, Pakistan. A dynamic Hospitality Management Professional and Academician with more than 18 years of managing Hospitality, delivered Corporate Trainings at Yum! Brands, Lola Event Productions UK and globally. Equipped with strong philosophy of Academic Research, Training and Development and Transferring Knowledge to motivate business executives and students to develop their expertise in specific areas of business and hospitality management. Other areas of interests are Value Co-creation, ESG, Sustainability, Ecotourism and Digitisation of hospitality and tourism industry.

Joanna Kuczewska is an Associate Professor at the Department of Finance and Banking at the WSB Merito University in Poznań. She specialises in company competitiveness research, benchmarking method, effects of cooperation in clusters, project management, economics of European integration and international management. A team member of numerous research projects carried out in the Department of International Economics and Economic Development at the Faculty of Economics at the University of Gdańsk. Member of the Polish European Community Studies Association (PECSA) and the Polish Economic Society (PTE). Author of evaluation reports of projects financed from EU funds. Manager of a nationwide project co-financed from the EU funds. Expert in Foundation Future Industry Platform.

Abed Mahmoudian is a PhD of Sport Marketing Management in the Department of Physical Education and Sport Sciences, University of Kurdistan, Sanandaj, Iran. His research interests are focused on consumer behaviour, fan behaviour, branding, team identification and social media. He has authored or co-authored over eight refereed research manuscripts. His studies have been published in top-tier peer-reviewed sport and non-sport management and marketing journals (e.g. *European Sport Management Quarterly*, *Journal of Sport Management*, *Journal of Business and Industrial Marketing*, *Corporate Reputation Review* and *Journal of Science and Technology Policy Management*).

Sardar Mohammadi is a PhD of Sport Marketing Management in the Department of Physical Education and Sport Sciences, University of Kurdistan, Sanandaj, Iran. His research interests are focused on consumer behaviour, fan behaviour, branding, team identification and social media. He has authored or co-authored over eight refereed research manuscripts. His studies have been published in top-tier peer-reviewed sport and non-sport management and marketing journals (e.g. *European Sport Management Quarterly*, *Journal of Sport Management*, *Journal of Business and Industrial Marketing*, *Corporate Reputation Review* and *Journal of Science and Technology Policy Management*).

Hassan Sadeghi Naeini, Associate Prof, Iran University of Science and Technology (IUST), Tehran, Iran. He is an Associate Professor at the Industrial Design Dept, School of Architecture and Environmental Design, Iran University of Science and Technology (IUST). His scientific field is ergonomics in design, and most of his research and didactic are focusing on ergonomics and sustainability. Journal papers publishing, books, book chapters writing and attending several international conferences as a Presenter or Keynote Speaker are some of his scientific works in the field of human-centred design. He is a referee in some international journals and a referee team member in some national industrial design competitions and exhibitions. He has some international experiences in both field of research and didactic in some universities, i.e. School of Design, Politecnico di Milano (POLIMI)-Italy, KTH University-Sweden, UPM University – Malaysia.

Agnieszka Nawrocka is a graduate of Master's degree studies in Economics, with a specialisation in Innovation in Economy from the Department of International Economics and Economic Development at the Faculty of Economics, University of Gdansk. Graduating with a strong grounding in market principles and business mechanisms. Co-Founder of Visioner company and the owner of the LunaSky brand has equipped her with the ability to proficiently manage a business and adeptly execute marketing strategies and innovative solutions. Exploring emerging trends in marketing, new technologies and social media has evolved from a personal passion into a dedicated profession that spans several years. Her expertise has been further honed through participation in various business training programs focused on enterprise management, internet marketing and social media promotion.

Mike Rayner is a Reader (Associate Professor) and Associate Head (Global Engagement and Education Partnerships) in the School of Sport, Health and Exercise Science. Dr Mike Rayner is a National Teaching Fellow of the Higher Education Academy, Fellow of The Institute of Leadership and Management, Fellow of the Chartered Institute for the Management of Sport and Physical Activity, a Senior Fellow of the Higher Education Academy and a registered Practitioner with the Chartered Management Institute and the Chartered Institute of Marketing. Mike is currently the Section Editor for the Sport Section of the Cogent Social Sciences Journal and sits on the editorial boards of Managing Sport and Leisure, Business and Management and The International Journal for Business and Social Science Journals. He is a Reviewer for the Newton Fund, Sports Management Review, Managing Sport and Leisure and The International Journal for Sport and Society.

Mahdiyeh Jafarnejad Shahri, Industrial Design Department, School of Architecture and Environmental Design, Iran University of Science & Technology (IUST), Tehran, Iran. She is a PhD candidate in industrial design. She as a designer has already developed some conceptual designs in both product and service design. She also got some design awards. The main fields of her research and study are sustainable, ergonomics and aesthetics in design for enhancing UX for end users.

Dr Saloomeh Tabari is a Lecturer in Marketing at Cardiff Business school. She has served as a Senior Lecturer in Huddersfield University prior to joining Cardiff University. Her research mainly centres on consumer behaviour, intercultural communication, cultural intelligence and marketing. She has edited a few books in the area of consumer behaviour and marketing. She has published in prominent academic journals and books and presented at international conferences. She is an Associate Editor for the Journal of Islamic Marketing and is on the scientific and editorial board of international conferences and journals.

İsmail Uzut, Istanbul University-Cerrahpaşa, is currently working as a Lecturer at Tourism and Hotel Management Programme at İstanbul University-Cerrahpaşa in Istanbul. His PhD thesis examined gastronomy and the tourism competitiveness of İstanbul. His research interests focus on gastronomy, strategic management, marketing, management and sustainability.

Minhan Wang is a Business Administration Master's student at the University of Amsterdam. She received a Bachelor's degree in Hospitality Business Management from Sheffield Hallam University and completed a Master's degree in International Hotel Management at the University of Surrey. Now she is continuing her studies in the business field, and she is interested in hotel management, sustainability and customer behaviour.

Yuyuan Wu received a Bachelor of Science degree in Hospitality Management from Sheffield Hallam University in 2020 and a Master of Science degree in International Hotel Management from Surrey University in 2021. Her research interest in her Bachelor's degree includes the impact of atmosphere on guest experience in luxury hotels, mainly focusing on one of the varieties – music. For her Master's paper research, the highlight is to investigate the way to promote women employees' career progression in international luxury hotels in China. After finishing her studies, she came back to her hometown, and she is currently working towards Digital Marketing in Rosewood Beijing, China.

Acknowledgements

We would like to thank the contributors to the book for their forbearance in the face of a protracted editorial process; special thanks to the reviewers, especially Professor Hadyn Ingram for their positive and encouraging comments, and the support of Goodfellow Publishing. We are grateful to our future readers for showing interest in our edited book.

Saloomeh, Wei and Stella

Introduction

Saloomeh Tabari[a], Wei Chen[b] and Stella Kladou[c]

[a]Cardiff University, UK
[b]Sheffield Hallam University, UK
[c]Hellenic Mediterranean University, Greece

Customer experience has long been central in the pursue of a sustainable competitive advantage, leading to numerous explorations and reviews of the concept in scholarly research (e.g., Becker & Jaakola, 2020; Rose et al., 2011). Customer experience research develops in services marketing, consumer research, service-dominant logic, online marketing, branding, experiential marketing and service design, as either responses to managerial stimuli or responses to consumption processes (Becker & Jaakola, 2020). The ultimate objective remains progressing the research agenda in a way that will facilitate businesses, organisations and institutions to better understand how customers process and evaluate their experiences. In this manner, managers obtain a roadmap on how to establish long-term relationships with their customers and customers benefit from a memorable, rewarding experience (e.g., Kim, 2010; Rose et al., 2011).

This book contributes towards this direction by looking through the spacescape and designscape to improve service performance to better address customer needs and desires. In specific, this edited volume aims to provide a practical, evidence-based vision of how to enhance and enrich customer experience through tangibles, exterior and interior design and space within the service industry.

In doing so, the book focuses on the new perspective of design in marketing within the service sector and explores how the spacescape and designscape impacts on customer experience. We look at fresh and recent research to provide a new perspective on design, offline and online spaces in customer-oriented services, such as retail, healthcare, sports, restaurants, cafes and hotels. The book explores new ideas and approaches on the importance of the internal and external environment as seen from the customers' experience.

A key characteristic of experience-centric services is that they are designed to engage customers, that is to enable the customer to connect with the service in a personal, memorable way (Beltagui & Candi, 2018; Pine & Gilmore, 1998; Pullman & Gross, 2004). A context consists of the physical and relational elements in the experience environment. It includes the physical setting, the social

Marketing and Design in the Service Sector, 1–6
doi:10.1108/978-1-83797-276-020241001

actors and any social interactions with other customers and/or service facilitators (Gupta & Vajic, 2000; Kumar et al., 2019). The context can be used to intensify engagement and emotional connections and is the primary concern of experience design (Pullman & Gross, 2004; De Keyser et al., 2020). The context of a service sends cues to customers that create and influence their experience. Bitner (1992), in her first approaches to the servicescape, distinguishes among people, processes and physical evidence that send cues to customers.

The importance of internal and external environment (interior and exterior) and the product design have been discussed by many researchers in the past as part of designscape; however, the COVID-19 pandemic brought unprecedented changes to the service industry. As a result, the product design, delivery design and setting of the sector faced a holistic change. The service sector tries to provide customers with comfort and, in the process, we witness innovative ways to meet the demand, including, for instance, contactless delivery or robots for delivery even in the healthcare industry. Even before the pandemic, the hospitality, travel and tourism industry had started attracting attention for innovations in terms of designing spaces, with the introduction of the spacescape and an enhanced experiencescape which provided a unique stress-free experience for their customers (e.g., silent airport). The pandemic outbreak has impacted on the industry, leaving destinations and relevant businesses struggling for the resilience of the sector and exploring their options through intense focus on the customer experience and the designscape on offer.

The experiences gained from service digitalisation during the recent pandemic crisis offer fruitful learning for digital innovation, transformation and service design and development. The easy access to services without waiting in a queue (e.g., e-banking, takeaway and remote working) changed customer perspective towards the spacescape and designscape. In the meantime, the pandemic served as a reminder to both businesses and consumers that we ought to be more sustainable and aware of our environment. This edited volume contributes towards the challenges hereby set, by collecting chapters which bring theory and practice together as well as relevant and fresh case studies.

The Structure of Edited Book

The book begins with an exploration of the role of industrial design in developing the designscape. In Chapter 1, Hassan Sadeghi Naeini and Mahdie Jafarnejad Shahri discuss the importance of service design for industrial design. According to the authors, as customer experience becomes increasingly more important in order to inspire loyalty and boost performance, focus moves from the physical characteristics of products to memorable, holistic service experience. The conceptual approach of this chapter helps the reader to build one's understanding by step-by-step navigating from one concept to the next one and their in-between relationship. Industrial design helps enhance customer experience by creating products, systems and services that can foster emotional engagement and user experience in order to boost loyalty. Taken the complexity and interdependency of products and services, industrial designers need to employ design thinking, product–service system (PSS) approaches and sustainability principles. Design thinking hereby develops as a problem-solving approach to grasp customers' needs and emotions in order to develop innovative products and services. Similarly, the PSS reflects a business innovation on its own, by embracing approaches that take the complete service experience into consideration in order to design interconnected products and services as part of a cohesive system. Service design prioritises the complete service experience. Thus, incorporating its principles into industrial design facilitates positive customer experience beyond the level of experience with a physical product, which is important in terms of developing and maintaining a competitive advantage and for the success of marketing and branding strategies.

The conceptual approach of Chapter 1 smoothly passes the baton to Chapter 2 in which Saloomeh Tabari, Dave Egan and Helen Egan take on board the aspect of servitisation of the modern business landscape of the previous chapter to discuss the challenges of creating unique environments and servicescapes in the café industry. The authors used an auto-ethnographic approach as café flaneurs to report on how dimensions such as the place identity and its welcoming character, along with safety perceptions relate with their café experience and decision-making. Reporting back to three case studies and their experiences at Manchester's Northern Quarter, Gainsborough and Lincoln in the United Kingdom (UK) reveal that, next to the food and beverage, perceived authenticity of the café and its genius loci were the most important elements contributing to the café experience. Thus, Egan, Egan and Tabari recommend to independent coffee shop businesses to focus on both the external (e.g., architecture and street art) and the internal environment (e.g., music, crockery, furniture, dishes and blends of tea and coffee) in order to attract and satisfy the café flaneurs.

Chapter 3 then takes us to another part of the hospitality industry (i.e., accommodation), picks up specifically the element of music and explores its role to emotional reactions and memory. Yunyan Wu and Saloomeh Tabari follow a mixed methods approach to investigate the connection of musical variables (musicscape, as they name it) in hotel lobbies to enhance customer satisfaction. Data collected at a hotel in the South of the UK, through a structured questionnaire and online interviews, reveal that background music has a significant impact on customer satisfaction and the time customers wish to spend at the lobby. Additional analysis suggests this impact changes according to customers' age and gender. Thus, practitioners are advised to consider the findings of this study, adjust lobby background music according to their targeted segments and harvest the benefits of sound marketing.

Chapter 4 delves into physical attributes of hotel interior and exterior design to evaluate their effect on customer satisfaction and hotel choice. In specific, Minhan Wang, Saloomeh Tabari and Wei Chen adopt a mixed methodology design to survey and interview customers on the influence of hotel design on their selection process and satisfaction. Wang et al. hereby look into a variety of aspects, such as the hotel room design, but also the geographical location and the local cultural landscape of the hotel. Analysis reveals that hotel design stimulates guests' visual experience to some extent and boosts satisfaction. Yet, in line with Lo (2010), design should be people-oriented and place customer needs in the centre. Thus, hotels should continue to pay increased attention to facilities and services in order to make sure that design, customer needs and psychological integration are considered holistically when designing and delivering the hotel experience.

Chapter 5 then moves on to innovative service, processes and product design in the accommodation industry. Hassan Ali Khan hereby looks into how the aforementioned types of design help create engaging and custom-made customer experiences. In-depth interviews with experts, guest surveys and case studies employed highlight the importance of a variety of elements, such as market research and intelligence in order to stay tuned with guests' expectations and wants, employee training and development, the adoption of emerging technologies, and timely response to sustainability requirements.

Chapter 6 looks more into online marketing innovation. In this chapter, Joanna Kuczewska, Agnieszka Nawrocka and Aleksandra Borowicz seek to unearth pioneering solutions within the domain of online marketing and discern relevant opportunities. Focussing on three small companies located in Poland, the authors investigate whether these companies utilise innovative marketing tools on Instagram to fulfil their business objectives. Instagram emerges as an important platform for these companies, not simply as a platform used for promotion but also as a facilitator of co-creation opportunities, an image enhancer and a relationship builder for the companies with their customers.

Hassan Ali Khan acknowledges the importance of virtual design to create memorable experiences. Therefore, in Chapter 7, he examines how virtual reality, augmented reality and other digital technologies are implemented in other facets of the hospitality experience, such as room and restaurant decoration and staff responsiveness to customer needs. Interviews with experts, guest surveys and in-depth analysis of the virtual design of hotels put in the scope help investigate the potential outcomes and advantages of virtual design on the hotel and its clientele and confirm its importance in the pursue of customised services, customer loyalty and competitive advantage.

Chapter 8 then introduces digital detox and the act of intentionally disconnecting from digital devices in order to more fully engage with the physical environment. Serap Özdemir Güzel and Ismail Uzut particularly focus on digital detox tourism experiences and their potential to promote mindfulness and enhance the overall travel experience. The thematic analysis of Tripadvisor posts reveals the experiential focus and health philosophy of digital detox tourism, as well as the importance of digital detox to connect and relax during the travel experience. Building on these findings, the authors invite tourism stakeholders to concentrate on such conscientious consumers and factors these travellers appreciate, namely novelty, technostress, well-being and health, relaxation, social bonding and self-expression.

The following two chapters shift the interest from the hospitality and tourism industry to the sports industry. First, Sardar Mohammadi, Abed Mahmoudian and Manuel Alonso Dos Santos in Chapter 9 focus on the consumption experience of in sportswear retail stores. Qualitative research carried out in Iran with sports marketing experts reveal that sports stores consider aspects of human resources, products, interior design, exterior space, technology and interaction and communication in their marketing strategies. In fact, the authors confirm that the priority of sportswear retail stores is to inspire purchase but also boost satisfaction and loyalty by creating a unique experience for their customers.

Chapter 10 acknowledges limited research on the design of sports customer experience. In response, Sardar Mohammadi, Abed Mahmoudian and Mike Rayne attempt to identify the areas of creating customer experience in sports and recreational environments by focussing on the case of the Engelab sports and recreational club in Iran. The content analysis of interview data reveal the use of functional, comprehensive, human, physical, performance, aesthetic, sensory, social, emotional and sharing aspects in the marketing strategies of sports and recreational clubs. According to the authors, such aspects provide a memorable customer experience and may lead to satisfaction and loyalty.

The final chapter of the book, Chapter 11, takes us back to the hospitality industry to investigate how customer experience drives innovation and how changing values, precipitated by social, economic and behavioural flux, mean that hospitality and tourism brands are creating new systems and processes. Michael Donald and Ashleigh Donald in this chapter present the findings of their interviews with four hospitality leaders from various sectors of the hospitality industry based in the UK. According to these data, the COVID-19 pandemic has accelerated trends, and technology has been leveraged to meet customers' expectations for instantaneous service. Personalised marketing, omnichannel experiences, sustainability, ethical practices and customer feedback emerge as key performance metrics for the future of the hospitality industry.

References

Becker, L., & Jaakola, E. (2020). Customer experience: Fundamental premises and implications for research. *Journal of the Academy of Marketing Science, 48,* 630–648.

Beltagui, A., & Candi, M. (2018). Revisiting service quality through the lens of experience-centric services. *International Journal of Operations & Production Management, 38*(3), 915–932.

Bitner, M. J. (1992). Servicescapes: The impact of physical surroundings on customers and employees. *Journal of Marketing, 56*(2), 57–71.

De Keyser, A., Verleye, K., Lemon, K. N., Keiningham, T. L., & Klaus, P. (2020). Moving the customer experience field forward: Introducing the touchpoints, context, qualities (TCQ) nomenclature. *Journal of Service Research, 23*(4), 433–455.

Gupta, S., & Vajic, M. (2000). The contextual and dialectical nature of experience. In J. A. Fitzsimmons & M. J. Fitzsimmons (eds), *New Service Development* (pp. 33–51). Sage Publications.

Kim, J.-H. (2010). Determining the factors affecting the memorable nature of travel experiences. *Journal of Travel & Tourism Marketing, 27*(8), 780–796.

Kumar, V., Rajan, B., Gupta, S., & Pozza, I. D. (2019). Customer engagement in service. *Journal of the Academy of Marketing Science, 47*, 138–160.

Lo, K. P. Y. (2010). *Emotional design for hotel stay experiences: Research on guest emotions and design opportunities* Doctoral dissertation. The Hong Kong Polytechnic University.

Pine, B. J., & Gilmore, J. H. (1998). *Welcome to the experience economy* (Vol. 76, No. 4, pp. 97–105). Harvard Business Review Press.

Pullman, M. E., & Gross, M. A. (2004). Ability of experience design elements to elicit emotions and loyalty behaviors. *Decision Sciences, 35*(3), 551–578.

Rose, S., Hair, N., & Clark, M. (2011). Online customer experience: A review of the business-to-consumer online purchase context. *International Journal of Management Reviews, 13*, 24–39.

Chapter 1

The Role of Industrial Design in the Designscape Development Based on the Marketing and Customer Experience Design

Hassan Sadeghi Naeini and Mahdiyeh Jafarnejad Shahri

School of Architecture and Environmental Design, Iran University of Science and Technology (IUST), Iran

Abstract

Nowadays, product and service design play a crucial role in people's daily life and marketing settings; however, both of the product and service design process have always been affected by various factors, including the growth of technology, economic tensions and endemic and pandemic health challenges. Undoubtedly, the importance of service and product design is increasing in the near future, and these changes are also associated with customers' experience. In this regard, some factors have a prominent place such as customer preferences, marketing improvement, technology push-marketing pull and different aspects of sustainability. Since the development of product–service systems (PSSs) should be based on the requirements and needs of users on the one hand, and environmental and technological considerations on the other hand, the role of product and service designers in the context of presenting creative and innovative ideas is important. The mentioned features are known as the main pillars of industrial design. Industrial design as an integrated science of art and technology concerns customers' experience, user experience (UX) design, innovative design, customer-oriented service development and so on. Industrial design make value not only for customers but also for producers. Besides, some new designscape may develop by industrial design considerations. In this chapter, authors explain the industrial design scope towards customer experience orientation in service design, enhance the experiencescape, design thinking (DT), PSS approaches and sustainability.

Marketing and Design in the Service Sector, 7–20
Copyright © 2024 by Emerald Publishing Limited
All rights of reproduction in any form reserved
doi:10.1108/978-1-83797-276-020241002

Keywords: Marketing; service design; customer experience; industrial design; designscape; ergonomics

Introduction

In the modern business landscape, customers seek more than just products or services; they desire a complete experience. Companies that can deliver exceptional customer experiences have a distinct advantage in today's competitive market. This chapter delves into the integration of industrial design into service design, aiming to enhance the overall customer experience. Industrial design encompasses creating aesthetically pleasing, functional and user-friendly products, systems and services. Traditionally, the focus has been on physical products, but with the emergence of service design, industrial designers must shift their attention to the holistic service experience. Service design involves crafting every aspect of the service journey, from initial customer contact to post-service follow-up. This chapter explores how industrial designers can employ DT, PSS approaches and sustainability principles to create customer-centric service designs. Additionally, it delves into the significance of emotional and UXs in industrial design and how technology can be leveraged to elevate the overall customer experience. The modern business landscape is constantly changing, driven by various influences and shorter innovation cycles. This also affects traditional manufacturing companies that historically focused on developing, producing and selling physical products. However, these companies are now facing increasing pressure as customers' expectations shift from just products to the overall value they provide. As a result, these companies are exploring new business models that combine products and services, offering customers unique utility and value while fostering loyalty. Developing these product–service combinations in a modular and customisable way is key to delivering this new value proposition. This transformation towards offering services alongside products, known as servitisation, can be facilitated through PSSs. However, systematically developing these combinations poses significant challenges, which existing literature addresses through various PSS process models (Richter et al., 2019). A successfully crafted PSS can effectively address uncertainties associated with both products and services, such as product deterioration speed, ultimately leading to enhanced value creation. Designing a PSS is a more intricate task compared to designing its individual product component. This complexity arises not only from the integration of services but also from the interdependencies between products and services. Previous empirical research has highlighted the challenges faced by manufacturers, particularly in harnessing these dependencies, especially during the synthesis stage of PSS design (Sakao et al., 2022).

The Importance of Customer Experience in Industrial Design

The impact of the customer experience on customer loyalty and repeat business cannot be underestimated. Industrial designers play a pivotal role in cultivating a positive customer experience by designing aesthetically pleasing, functional and user-friendly products, systems, and services. By prioritising customer-centric design, industrial designers can create intuitive and user-friendly products, contributing to a positive customer experience. Furthermore, they can utilise design elements to establish an emotional connection with customers, evoking positive emotions and leaving a lasting impression. This emotional connection fosters increased customer loyalty and repeat business. Understanding the correlation between a positive customer experience, loyalty, and repeat business is crucial. The emotional and subjective responses to beauty are an integral aspect of human experience, where art emerges from a love and longing for aesthetics. Design, often referred to as "art with a purpose", can be employed to distinguish products and services. It is crucial for designers and business leaders to collaborate in order to develop strategies that promote a more sustainable, visually appealing and ultimately more profitable future, whether directly or indirectly (Alfakhri et al., 2018). As per the Industrial Design Society of America (IDSA), a crucial responsibility of design consultants is to create product specifications that are visually appealing, easily manufacturable and functional (Chung, 2019). This entails operating in various domains, including production engineering, aesthetics and ergonomics, to develop a blueprint that aligns with client requirements. Design is a multidimensional process involving innovation, change, invention and creativity, aiming to introduce new products or improve existing ones. The consumer is the central focus for designers, considering their needs and preferences in the design and production process. Fierce market competition necessitates prioritising customer requirements and finding innovative ways to engage them. Advanced tools and technologies are vital for product success and consumer engagement. Industrial designers create products that cater to diverse demographics, encompassing humans, pets, and all races and genders. Empathy and creativity are fundamental attributes for designers, enabling them to understand clients' perspectives. Thorough research plays a crucial role, providing insights that inform the aesthetic and functional aspects of the design. Designers incorporate historical, present and future elements in their design concepts. Understanding the target consumer is essential, requiring research on similar existing products, prototyping and testing. Designers need to critically connect with consumers, utilising objective data and conscious reflections, including demographics and observation of end-user issues (Iheme et al., 2018).

Design Thinking and Customer Centricity

DT is a problem-solving method based on users' needs and requirements in which the customer-centric approach is followed. The origin of design thinking concept defined by IDEO, a design company in Palo Alto, California USA, and then when the Stanford Design Centre was founded in 2006, it was changed as a popularised issue in educational centres. DT is known as a prominent context for innovation based on the concept of human-centred approach (Kleber, 2018; Ramanujam et al., 2021) and revolves around deeply grasping the customer's needs and exploring multiple possibilities before arriving at a preferred solution. DT has an iterative process in which some phases will be done such as analysing the problem and experimenting with various designs. The ultimate solution is then developed based on several experimental designs. DT is an approach to problem-solving that prioritises human needs and emotions. It combines analytical thinking with creative intuition to address business constraints while considering customer requirements. DT involves an iterative and non-linear process, translating observations into insights and ultimately leading to innovation. One key advantage of DT is its focus on user perspectives, which enhances the UX and adds value to products. Moreover, DT facilitates the integration of managers' perceptions, rational analysis and technical, cultural and commercial factors to create value for customers and identify market opportunities. While there are various DT models, they typically involve three phases: inspiration, ideation and implementation. It's important to view the DT process as overlapping spaces rather than a linear sequence of steps. DT has proven successful in developing products and services across different markets (B2B, B2C and B2G). Notable examples of companies utilising DT include P&G, Pfizer, Intel and Nokia (Scherer et al., 2016).

Product–Service System (PSS) Approaches in Industrial Design

PSS approaches refer to designing interconnected products and services that form a cohesive system. These approaches are particularly suitable for service design, as they consider the complete service experience rather than solely focussing on the physical product. PSS approaches find applications in industrial design, enabling the creation of seamless service experiences. The adoption of PSS approaches offers numerous advantages, such as heightened customer satisfaction and a diminished environmental footprint. A PSS focuses on customers' needs meeting and users' satisfaction in which customer experiences in human-centred design approaches will be achieved. Furthermore, smart PSS, which are characterised by context awareness and specificity, strong human centration, reconfigurable product and service elements and co-creative value provision of ecosystem stakeholders, is receiving a lot of attention in PSS research (Kim, 2022). Besides, PSS is known as a business model innovation strategy that aims to integrate products and services, allowing businesses to break away from relying solely on product sales for success and economic growth, in this regard PSS is related to marketing (Dewi et al., 2023). PSS-based business models are considered essential in driving the circular economy transition as they have the potential to generate economic growth while minimising resource consumption (Frederiksen et al., 2021). Also, there is a firm association between PSS and the logic of Industrial 4.0 approach. Both the mentioned issues play a crucial role in sustainability and enhancing the customer's experiences (Kim et al., 2023). In recent years, there has been an increasing focus on sustainability in manufacturing, with organisations seeking to develop new business models aligned with sustainability requirements from manufacturers, consumers and governments. This has led to the exploration of PSS as a means to meet these demands. PSS offers a framework that goes beyond traditional business models, enabling the creation of sustainable models centred around fulfiling users' needs through dematerialization. Instead of selling tangible products, PSS focuses on offering the use of products or delivering results. This represents a shift towards a leasing society and a change in consumers' attitudes from product ownership to a service-oriented approach (Chávez et al., 2019). A PSS is a combination of products and services that provides greater value compared to traditional offerings, and manufacturing companies need to strategically design their PSS offerings to effectively meet customer needs while also driving sustainability improvements (Sarancic et al., 2022).

Service Design in Industrial Design

Oxford English Dictionary defines service as "helping or doing work for another." Furthermore, a service is described as "a public system or private organisation responsible for a specific type of activity or for providing a specific thing that people need" by the Cambridge Dictionary. An infrastructure of functional systems with clearly defined policies, guidelines and processes is referred to as a service. It refers to acting as a systemic entity, such as how the scientific community, the health system, or organisational knowledge arranges procedures and activities. Marketing-related concerns are essentially the origin of the term "service design" (NAEINI et al., 2023). Service design involves designing the complete service experience, spanning from the first customer interaction to the after-service follow-up. It is particularly relevant to industrial design since it considers the holistic service experience, going beyond the physical product itself. By employing service design principles in industrial design, a positive customer experience can be crafted. This comprehensive approach to service design can lead to enhanced customer loyalty and repeat business. The term "service design" arose when the importance of services in economic activities became apparent and the necessity to effectively structure service-related activities became evident (Morelli et al., 2021).

Enhancing Customer Experience Through Industrial Design

Industrial design plays a crucial role in improving the customer experience by incorporating various design elements that contribute to a positive experience, including aesthetics, usability and functionality. One way to achieve a positive customer experience is through emotional design, which utilises emotions to create a positive impact. Emotional design in industrial design involves using storytelling and different design elements like colour, shape and texture to evoke specific emotions. By strategically applying these elements, industrial design can enhance the customer experience and elicit positive emotional responses (Yusa et al., 2023). Design aesthetics, as its name suggests, primarily explores the relationship between design and aesthetics. Its scope is wide, encompassing various aspects of life in society. The main focus of research is how to creatively combine elements in a unique way to portray a distinct form of beauty, largely relying on people's subjective perception. As the economy continues to advance, innovation becomes crucial in almost every industry, raising the demand for design to higher levels. As a result, the significance of design aesthetics has been progressively recognized as it offers solutions to challenges encountered in numerous industries (Wei, 2022).

Industrial Design for Sustainable Customer Experience

Sustainability is gaining significance in the field of industrial design, as customers increasingly seek products and services that have minimal environmental impact (Mosaddad et al., 2022; NAEINI et al., 2023). Industrial design can contribute to creating sustainable customer experiences by employing various strategies. For instance, eco-design focuses on minimising the ecological footprint of products and services, while cradle-to-cradle design aims to create products that can be recycled and reused in a closed-loop system. By embracing these sustainable design approaches, industrial designers can meet the demands of environmentally-conscious customers and contribute to a more sustainable future. Customers' satisfaction or dissatisfaction with products or services is influenced by their prior experiences. Their assessment of these experiences determines their satisfaction levels. This assessment is often explained using the "disconfirmation paradigm", which suggests that satisfaction arises when there is a perception of meeting or exceeding expectations, while dissatisfaction emerges from a perceived performance shortfall. Customers form expectations based on their needs and past experiences with similar products/services, and these expectations are shaped by both word-of-mouth communications within their social circles and information provided by the company through various media, including direct advertising (Stauss et al., 2019).

Industrial Design for User Experience (UX)

The significance of UX in industrial design is on the rise. UX emphasises the creation of products that are not only user-friendly but also engaging to interact with. Industrial design can play a crucial role in crafting a positive UX. There are various design elements that can enhance the UX, including user interface design and user testing (Fleury & Chaniaud, 2023). UX refers to an individual's perceptions and responses resulting from using or anticipating the use of a product, system or service. This definition acknowledges the subjective nature of UX, but some clarification is needed regarding the specific factors that influence it. UX is closely related to usability, which includes qualities like efficiency, effectiveness and satisfaction. Satisfaction, in turn, encompasses factors such as likeliness, pleasure and trust. From this perspective, UX can be seen as an extension of usability. The key difference between usability and UX lies in their focus on objective and subjective measures, respectively. Usability is assessed using objective methods, while UX relies on subjective measures. It's important to note that these two concepts have different qualities and cannot be measured interchangeably. UX serves as an umbrella term that encompasses both objective and subjective measurements of users' perceptions, aligning with the ISO 9241-210 definition (Hashim et al., 2021).

Measuring and Evaluating Customer Experience in Industrial Design

In modern market economies, it is important to assess the economic and social advantages of competition from both financial and non-financial perspectives. Among these perspectives, customer satisfaction measurements have emerged as a widely accepted non-financial performance indicator. A high level of customer satisfaction is believed to contribute to a positive company image, protection of market share, improved customer loyalty, reduced customer complaints and enhanced financial performance. Consequently, it is vital to comprehend the factors that drive changes in customer satisfaction over time. This understanding is crucial for businesses in order to adapt and meet customer needs effectively (Hallencreutz & Parmler, 2021). When designing products, utilitarian value is a key criterion. However, research on holistic design identifies parameters like elegance, functionality and social importance that influence user satisfaction. Products serve utilitarian and symbolic purposes, with appeal beyond aesthetics alone. Product hedonic value is influenced by elements like form, texture, experience and presence. Aesthetic experience holds personalised value and is vital in product appreciation. In design, trade-offs between functionality and hedonic value attract customer attention, satisfaction and pleasure. Achieving a balance between functionality and aesthetics is considered good design, impacting consumer perceptions and intentions. The balance achieved in product design holds importance for consumers' purchasing intentions and usage behaviour. With the increasing use of wearable devices, designers face the challenge of satisfying users with an optimal product experience that balances utilitarian and hedonic values (Iftikhar et al., 2020).

The Importance of Industrial Design in Marketing and Branding

Industrial design plays a crucial role in the success of a product or brand in the market. It involves creating and refining products that are practical, visually appealing, comfortable to use and ergonomic. In today's consumer-driven era, where customers expect more than just functionality, industrial design is increasingly important in marketing (Chitale & Gupta, 2023). Examining the components of influence on consumer behaviour and its impact on branding in industrial design is very important, and designers can use it to create successful products and brands by being aware of it. Design should include technology, business and creativity, and it is essential for achieving Sustainable Development Goals. It requires time, research, analysis, knowledge of trends, materials, manufacturing processes and an understanding of limitations. Social and environmental impact must also be considered (Burke et al., 2023). Industrial designers should incorporate knowledge from various fields, such as marketing strategies, research and development, production, integration management and communication. The visual appearance of consumer goods often determines market success, and understanding consumer behaviour and engagement is facilitated by big data. Monitoring post-purchase consumption patterns through product ecosystems provides valuable insights into design, and considering social impact is also crucial. Marketing and product design significantly contribute to a company's performance. Social impact assessments and social life cycle assessments are commonly discussed processes for evaluating social impact. Processes should be developed to help designers incorporate social impact considerations into their products (David et al., 2021).

Industrial Design: A Competitive Advantage

Design has gained popularity in business and marketing, as both managers and marketers recognise its potential to enhance meaningful customer and organizational experiences. However, design in marketing goes beyond being a passing trend. It has a substantial presence demonstrated by decades of theoretical development and offers a three-fold perspective on design with relevance to marketing and consumer research. Design outcomes showcase its relevance through performance perspectives, while design processes incorporate various tools and practices that can directly apply to marketing strategy and consumer contexts. Additionally, the philosophical aspect of design, often overlooked in marketing, deserves greater attention. Embracing a designer philosophy can establish a conceptual foundation for decision-making and action in the field of marketing (Beverland et al., 2017). In today's competitive commercial market, customer expectations for products are increasing. Customers not only seek functional features but also desire affective features such as attractive design, ergonomic structure and tactile appeal. Customers are willing to pay for product affective features, as seen with the popularity of the deep green colour option for the iPhone 11. Understanding customer affective needs helps generate effective design ideas and enhance the customer experience. In customer-driven product design, collecting customer opinions is crucial for understanding their needs and preferences. While traditional methods like questionnaires are useful, they may overlook distinctive and innovative customer preferences. Leveraging information technology and e-commerce allows customers to express their opinions based on their experiences, and potential customers rely on reviews to make informed purchase decisions, avoiding unnecessary expenses (Jin et al., 2022).

The Future of Industrial Design for Customer-Centric Service Design

Emerging trends in industrial design, such as the Internet of Things (IoT) and artificial intelligence (AI), have the potential to enhance various aspects discussed previously, including DT, PSS approaches, sustainability, emotional design and UX. By leveraging these technologies, designers can accelerate and amplify these methods as valuable tools to create products and services that cater to the needs and desires of customers. This, in turn, can lead to increased customer loyalty and repeat business, further emphasising the importance of staying aligned with these advancements in industrial design. Digital technologies create opportunities for novel services, enhancing interactions between companies and customers (Jafarnejad & Sadeghi Naeini, 2020). This shift brings challenges and new ways of working (Vaidyanathan & Henningsson, 2023), furthermore, AI and deep learning (DL) are known as the effective fields in design. Also, AI plays an effective role in different aspects of sustainable development (Walk et al., 2023). In this regards, industrial design considerations should be involved these new technologies. This raises questions about what industrial designers should create in the information and digital age, how to innovate for new types of products and how to improve industrial design education to prepare future designers for their careers (Qian et al., 2011). Customer satisfaction refers to the point at which the perceived performance of a product aligns with a customer's expectations. When the performance of a product falls significantly below customer expectations, the buyer is dissatisfied. Conversely, if the performance meets or exceeds expectations, the buyer is satisfied or even delighted. Customer satisfaction is thus contingent upon the alignment between perceived product performance and customer expectations (Ummi et al., 2021). Moreover, customer satisfaction is greatly impacted by the reliability of service quality. As a result, service providers can enhance their competitive advantage and preserve their market position by offering value-added services with key quality attributes. By prioritising the reliability of service quality, companies can differentiate themselves, meet customer expectations and ultimately achieve higher levels of customer satisfaction (Chen et al., 2019).

The Significance of Ergonomics in Customer-Centred Marketing

A successful product is one that has control over its target market and has loyal customers. This success is achieved when users and customers are satisfied with the commodity and believe that the desired product meets a significant portion of their physical or psychological needs (Chung-Herrera, 2007). The phase of discovering customer needs and striving to meet them is one of the most important activities of industrial designers in the process of design and DT. In this regard, ergonomics has a very special place. Ergonomics is a multidisciplinary and human-centred science that provides methods and principles to designers so that they can develop products that align with customer needs (Karwowski & Zhang, 2021).

Ergonomics considers safety, security and customer satisfaction on the one hand and productivity and efficiency on the other hand. An ergonomic product provides conditions for appropriate communication and interaction between the user and the product; undoubtedly, this process is closely related to the success of the product in the market. A good customer experience with the product indicates customer satisfaction and leads to product promotion. Additionally, considering ergonomic considerations aligns with sustainable DT (Fischer et al., 2021). To create a good experience, physical and behavioural needs of individuals must be discovered and fulfiled, and ergonomic considerations precisely examine both of these aspects. From the perspective of customers' physical needs, creating dimensional compatibility between the product and the user's body is one of the most important associated factors. In this regard, anthropometric measurements are considered (Sadeghi Naeini et al., 2023). This section of measurements falls under the sub-group of micro-ergonomics. In fact, ergonomics can be categorised into five sub-groups, including micro-ergonomics, macro-ergonomics, environmental ergonomics, cognitive ergonomics, and cultural ergonomics. Micro-ergonomics concerns users' physical needs; therefore, the physical features and dimensions of products are considered. For example, anthropometric designs aim to create a logical fit between the product's body and the user's dimensions (Panjaitan et al., 2020, p. 12078). After considering micro-ergonomics rules, cognitive ergonomic needs must be fulfiled (e.g., designing user interfaces for customers to understand the product's messages), followed by cultural ergonomics if necessary. However, it should be noted that not only should these five sub-groups of ergonomics not be distinguished, but the prioritisation of applying various ergonomics considerations depends on the nature of the different products. Considering the micro- and cognitive ergonomics in a product provides conditions where the customer is satisfied with the product and enjoys using it. This interaction creates a positive experience, which is a strong point for maximising product sales (Alfeb & Salim, 2024). Ergonomics in product design is of special importance for three key individuals involved in the design, manufacturing and selling processes, i.e., industrial designers, production managers and end customers. Therefore, ergonomic product design is considered to be a common understanding and language among designers, employers, and product customers (Fig. 1.1).

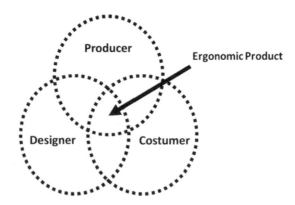

Fig. 1.1.   Ergonomic Product Place. *Source:* Sadeghi et al. (2022).

It is also essential to mention that regardless of the application of ergonomics in product design, by implementing ergonomic considerations in the design of production line stations, suitable conditions can be provided for workers' activities in the production lines, which also helps industrial efficiency and business; furthermore, there is an association between ergonomics design and industry 5.0 approaches (Sadeghi Naeini et al., 2022). The application of ergonomics in product design can also lead to the development of new experiences in using the product. This characteristic is crucial in the competition between different products and market development. Ergonomics also plays a role in the development of a product or market in accordance with what is mentioned in the Ansoff model (Sadeghi Naeini, 2020; Suzianti et al., 2023).

As seen in the Fig. 1.2., both the development of a new product and the redesign of existing products should be based on customer needs, and ergonomics has a role in all four parts of the Ansoff model for matching the product with the market.

Conclusion

Industrial design concerns enhancing the overall customer experience by creating products, systems and services in which some features are critical, i.e. aesthetically pleasing, functional and user-friendly based design. Moreover, industrial design can foster emotional and UXs that strengthen customer loyalty and repeat business. However, there are some challenges for industrial designers, especially when designing PSSs and combination of products and services should be considered. These difficulties stem from the complexity and interdependency of products and services, requiring a systematic and holistic design process. To overcome the mentioned challenges, industrial designers can employ DT, PSS

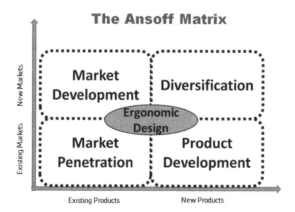

Fig. 1.2.   The Place of Ergonomics in Marketing. *Source:* Sadeghi (2020); Suzianti et al., (2023).

approaches and sustainability principles to create customer-centric service designs. By doing so, industrial designers can contribute to the servitisation of the modern business landscape, offering customers unique value and utility through products and services.

References

Alfakhri, D., Harness, D., Nicholson, J., & Harness, T. (2018). The role of aesthetics and design in hotelscape: A phenomenological investigation of cosmopolitan consumers. *Journal of Business Research, 85*, 523–531.

Alfeb, N. V., & Salim, M. (2024). The influence of product quality and brand image on consumer loyalty is mediated by customer satisfaction. *Gema Wiralodra, 15*(1), 87–98.

Beverland, M. B., Gemser, G., & Karpen, I. O. (2017). Design, consumption and marketing: Outcomes, process, philosophy and future directions. *Journal of Marketing Management, 33*(3–4), 159–172.

Burke, H., Zhang, A., & Wang, J. X. (2023). Integrating product design and supply chain management for a circular economy. *Production Planning & Control, 34*(11), 1097–1113.

Chávez, C. A. G., Romero, D., Rossi, M., Luglietti, R., & Johansson, B. (2019). Circular lean product-service systems design: A literature review, framework proposal and case studies. *Procedia CIRP, 83*, 419–424.

Chen, Mu-C., Hsu, C.-L., & Lee, Li-H. (2019). Service quality and customer satisfaction in pharmaceutical logistics: An analysis based on Kano model and importance-satisfaction model. *International Journal of Environmental Research and Public Health, 16*(21), 4091.

Chitale, A. K., & Gupta, R. C. (2023). *Product design and manufacturing.* PHI Learning Pvt. Ltd.

Chung, W. C. (2019). *The praxis of product design in collaboration with engineering.* Springer.

Chung-Herrera, B. G. (2007). Customers' psychological needs in different service industries. *Journal of Services Marketing, 21*(4), 263–269.

David, J. -V., Ana, M. -R., Santiago, F. -B., & Faustino, A. -V. (2021). Aspects of industrial design and their implications for society. case studies on the influence of packaging design and placement at the point of sale. *Applied Sciences, 11*(2), 517.

Dewi, D. R. S., Budi Hermanto, Y., Tait, E., & Sianto, M. E. (2023). The product–service system supply chain capabilities and their impact on sustainability performance: A dynamic capabilities approach. *Sustainability, 15*(2), 1148.

Fischer, K., Thatcher, A., & Zink, K. J. (2021). Human factors and ergonomics for sustainability (Chapter 57). In W. Karwowski (Ed.), *handbook of human factors and ergonomics* (pp. 1512–1527). John Wiley & Sons, Inc.

Fleury, S., & Chaniaud, N. (2023). Multi-user centered design: acceptance, user experience, user research and user testing. *Theoretical Issues in Ergonomics Science, 25*, 1–16.

Frederiksen, T. B., Pieroni, M. P. P., Pigosso, D. C. A., & McAloone, T. C. (2021). Strategic development of Product-Service Systems (Pss) through archetype assessment. *Sustainability, 13*(5), 2592.

Hallencreutz, J., & Parmler, J. (2021). Important drivers for customer satisfaction–from product focus to image and service quality. *Total Quality Management and Business Excellence, 32*(5–6), 501–510.

Hashim, W., Mkpojiogu, E. O. C., Hussain, A., & Abdul-Aziz, S. N. (2021). A product pain-pleasure framework for software product design in the usability and user experience domains. *Webology, 18*(SI01), 1–31.

Iftikhar, H., Shah, P., & Luximon, Y. (2020). Exploring the balance between utilitarian and hedonic values of wearable products. In *Advances in physical ergonomics and human factors: Proceedings of the AHFE 2019 international conference on physical ergonomics and human factors*, July 24–28, 2019, Washington DC, USA 10 (pp. 407–416). Springer International Publishing.

Iheme, M. F., Egiri, Y. O., & Kwasu, I. A. (2018). Entrepreneurship strategies in achieving aesthetic and functional products through industrial design practices. *International Journal of Innovative Research and Development, 7*(9), 1–4.

Jafarnejad, M., & Sadeghi Naeini, H. (2020). The effectiveness of smart furniture in urban development and social sustainability (Case Study: Metropolises of Iran). *Quarterly Journals of Urban and Regional Development Planning, 5*(12), 137–156.

Jin, J., Jia, D., & Chen, K. (2022). Mining online reviews with a Kansei-integrated Kano model for innovative product design. *International Journal of Production Research, 60*(22), 6708–6727.

Karwowski, W., & Zhang, W. (2021). The discipline of human factors and ergonomics. In *Handbook of human factors and ergonomics* (4th ed., Vol. 1, pp. 1–37). John Wiley & Sons, Inc.

Kim, Y. S (2022). Customer experience design for smart product-service systems based on the iterations of experience–evaluate–engage using customer experience data. *Sustainability, 15*(1), 686.

Kim, M., Lim, C., & Hsuan, J. (2023). From technology enablers to circular economy: Data-driven understanding of the overview of servitization and product–service systems in industry 4.0. *Computers in Industry, 148*, 103908.

Kleber, D. M. -S. (2018). Design thinking for creating an increased value proposition to improve customer experience. *Etikonomi: Journal Ekonomi, 17*(2), 265–274.

Morelli, N., de Götzen, A., & Simeone, L. (2021). An approach to service design. In *service design capabilities springer series in design and Innovation* (Vol. 10, pp. 9–26). Springer. https://doi.org/10.1007/978-3-030-56282-3_2

Mosaddad, S. H., Sadeghi Naeini, H., Shahri, M. J., & Karuppiah, K. (2022). Product design process in the context of sustainable development: An approach to waste reduction. *Iran University of Science & Technology, 32*(3), 0.

Naeini, H. S., Conti, G. M., Motta, M., Karuppiah, K., Koleini Mamaghani, N., & Jafarnejad, M. (2023). Sustainable workplace: An integrated approach to industrial ergonomics and service design. *Rivista Italiana Di Ergonomia, 25*, 13–27.

Panjaitan, N., Ali, A. Y. B., & Samat, H. A. (2020, December). Ergonomic research trends in the health. In *IOP conference series: Materials science and engineering* (Vol. 1003, No. 1, p. 012078). IOP Publishing.

Qian, Z. C., Visser, S., & Chen, Y. V. (2011). Integrating user experience research into industrial design education: The Interaction Design Program at Purdue. *VentureWell. Proceedings of Open, the annual conference.* (p. 1). National Collegiate Inventors & Innovators Alliance.

Ramanujam, H., Ravichandran, B., Nilsson, S., & Ivansen, L. (2021). Barriers and opportunities of implementing design thinking in product development process of a business to business company. *Proceedings of the Design Society, 1*, 551–560.

Richter, A., Glaser, P., Kölmel, B., Waidelich, L., & Bulander, R. (2019). A review of product-service system design methodologies. *ICETE, 1*, 121–132.

Sadeghi, N., Hassan, G. M. C., & Mosaddad, S. H. (2022). Industrial design evolution in the context of ergonomics and industry 5.0. *Journal of Design Thinking, 3*(2), 165–172.

Sadeghi Naeini, H. (2020). Basics of ergonomic product design based on psychology: An integrated approach to art & manufacturing. *Theoretical Principles of Visual Arts, 4*(2), 75–84.

Sadeghi Naeini, H., Jafarnejad Shahri, M., Koleini Mamghani, N., & Karmegam, K. (2023). Work-satisfaction throughout workplace design: An approach on ergonomics and hedonomics for office design. *Journal of Design Thinking, 4*(1), 32–42.

Sakao, T., Neramballi, A., & Matschewsky, J. (2022). Avoid service design trap by guiding product/service system design with product-service dependency knowledge base. *Proceedings of the Design Society, 2*, 1955–1964.

Sarancic, D., Pigosso, D. C. A., & McAloone, T. C. (2022). Designing industrial Product-Service System (PSS) pilot projects in manufacturing companies: A proposed process for product and customer selection. *Proceedings of the Design Society, 2*, 1119–1128.

Scherer, J. O., Paula Kloeckner, A., Ribeiro, J. L. D., Pezzotta, G., & Pirola, F. (2016). Product-Service System (PSS) design: Using design thinking and business analytics to improve PSS design. *Procedia Cirp, 47*, 341–346.

Stauss, B., & Seidel, W. (2019). The behavior of dissatisfied customers. In *Effective complaint management. Management for professionals* (pp. 35–54). Springer. https://doi.org/10.1007/978-3-319-98705-7_3

Suzianti, A., Devi Amaradhanny, R., & Fathia, S. N. (2023). Fashion heritage future: Factors influencing Indonesian Millenials and generation Z's interest in using traditional fabrics. *Journal of Open Innovation: Technology, Market, and Complexity, 9*(4), 100141.

Ummi, N., Wahyuni, N., & Apriadi, I. (2021). Analysis of service quality on customer satisfaction through importance performance analysis and KANO model. *Journal Industrial Services, 6*(2), 174–183.

Vaidyanathan, N., & Henningsson, S. (2023). Designing augmented reality services for enhanced customer experiences in retail. *Journal of Service Management, 34*(1), 78–99.

Walk, J., Kühl, N., Saidani, M., & Schatte, J. (2023). Artificial intelligence for sustainability: Facilitating sustainable smart product-service systems with computer vision. *Journal of Cleaner Production, 402*, 136748.

Wei, N. (2022). On the application and development of design aesthetics in product packaging design. *Learning & Education, 10*(5), 99–100.

Yusa, I., Ketut Ardhana, I., Nyoman Darma Putra, I., & Pujaastawa, I. B. G. (2023). Emotional design: A review of theoretical foundations, methodologies, and applications. Nyoman and Pujaastawa, Ida Bagus Gde, Emotional design: A review of theoretical foundations, methodologies, and applications (April 19, 2023). Yusa, IMM, Ardhana, IK, Putra, IND and Pujaastawa, IBG 1–14.

Chapter 2

Independent Coffee Shops and Cafes: Creating Unique Environments and Servicescapes

Saloomeh Tabari[a], Dave Egan[b] and Helen Egan[b]

[a]Cardiff University, UK
[b]Sheffield Hallam University, UK

Abstract

This chapter will explore how independent coffee shops and cafés are creating unique servicescapes to meet the needs and desires of their clientele. Using the model of servicescape, the authors report on several micro-case studies in which the researchers play the role of customers and explore their own feelings and preferences when choosing and visiting an independent coffee shop or café. In each case, the researchers noted their feelings and experiences of the environment under the headings of ambience; arrangement and function with reference to the furnishings and crockery; the signs, symbols and artefacts were considered in relation to the name of the business and the marketing message of the business.

Keywords: Coffee shop; servicescape; flaneur; authentic; template analysis

Introduction

The café is becoming a ubiquitous part of the street scene in towns and cities across the globe. Visiting a café has become a daily ritual for many people. However, the context of this ritual varies from person to person. For many, the cafe is an essential part of their daily life, meeting the need for a third 'place' Oldenberg (1997) – a meeting place for friends, a meeting place for strangers or even a place to be amongst, but not necessarily with, people.

An area that is under-recorded is the role that the café plays in the experience of a visitor new to the area. Several articles do refer to cafes as part of the tourist

Marketing and Design in the Service Sector, 21–33
doi:10.1108/978-1-83797-276-020241003

experience (Sims, 2009). However, our research is investigating what factors influence a visitor to choose a particular café when visiting an area that is unknown to them. The research study specifically investigates the independent café as an alternative to the large chains such as Starbucks, Costa and Coffee Republic which tend to be viewed as the safe option as whatever the requirements of the visitor – a place to eat and drink, a place to sit or a place to take a toilet break – the experience will be very similar whether in Bakewell, Manchester, New York or Hong Kong.

The starting point of this research is the concept of the servicescape, introduced by Bitner (1992). In a study by Waxman (2006), the characteristics of the coffee shop have been highlighted as an important element for the customers, together with the ability to socialise, either with employees or other customers. She also identified that physical factors could provide a feeling of 'place attachment' (e.g., feeling part of community, trust and respect).

Place attachment has been defined by Altman and Low (1992, p. 58) as 'the bonding of people and place' which includes emotions and geographic setting and holds deep meaning for the individual. In this regard, several studies stated that the feeling of attachment is a result of both physical and social imperatives (Burley, 2007; Waxman, 2006).

Furthermore, ambience is affected by the physical space. Ambience includes numerous factors, such as social and physical surroundings, sound, temperature, duration and colour of environment, smell and time of consumption (Stroebele & De Castro, 2004). As Kotler (1973, p.52) argued 'in certain situations, the ambience of a location can be more important than the product'. A major factor influencing the ambience will be the physical environment.

Very much linked to the concept of servicescape is the perception of authenticity, a concept which is well developed in the tourism literature; in particular, a number of authors have noted the importance that the sensations of taste, touch, sound and smell, in addition to sight, can play in a visitor's experience of a place (Boniface, 2003; Eastham, 2003; Mitchell & Hall, 2003). A number of researchers have looked specifically at the significance of local food to the visitor experience (Cohen & Avieli, 2004; Long, 2004; Torres, 2002). Visitors' desire for authenticity is perceived as a major driver in the demand for 'traditional' and 'local foodstuffs'. However, minimal research appears to have been carried out into the experience of the authenticity of an area to be obtained from a visitor's use of the local cafes. Although there is a considerable debate in the tourism literature regarding the increase, and even the validity, of authenticity, Taylor (2001, p. 8) suggests that 'there are as many definitions of authenticity as there are those who write about it'.

In this chapter, we do not intend to revisit the debate about what 'authenticity' actually means but rather we accept that authenticity should be viewed as a social construct (Hughes, 1995). Wang (1999) views authenticity as being based on an 'existential' understanding that relates to the response to the visitor experience; thus, visitors can construct their identity to experience a more authentic sense of self and, we would suggest, of place. For the purpose of this research, Taylor

(2001) provides the necessary insights to distinguish between the chains, such as Costa and Starbucks, and the local independent cafes:

> Authenticity is valuable only where there is perceived inauthenticity. Such is the "plastic" world of the consumer. Enamoured by the distance of authenticity, the modern consciousness is instilled with a simultaneous feeling of lack and desire erupting from a sense of loss felt within "our" world of mass culture and industrialisation and giving rise to possibilities of redemption through contact with the naturally, spiritually and culturally "unspoilt" (Taylor, 2001, p.10).

Barnett et al. (2005) and Clarke et al. (2007) suggest that consumerism is moving beyond the self-interested, egotistical viewpoint and that there is now a perception of consumerism as involving the independent, individual, local and ethical (i.e. 'non-big business'), thus underpinning the authors' concept of 'existential authenticity' as part of their identity and their quest for an authentic experience as visitors in their search for local independent café experiences. This can be described as 'authentic-seeking', a process which describes 'consumers searching for authenticity from a range of products, services and experiences, and looking for it within themselves' (Yeoman et al., 2006).

This research adopts the concept of the flaneur, which is the French term for a stroller or urban observer. Benjamin (2007) cited in Del Rio (2016) uses the concept of the flaneur as an urban observer and explorer of the modern urban experience. He views the flaneur as an analytical tool: 'the observer-participant'.

The authors propose that, as cafes are such an important aspect of modern urban life, the concept of the flaneur is a valid one for the purpose of this research. It gives the research a different perspective to that of traditional participant observation, which focuses on ethnographic research, on learning the culture or subculture of the people being studied (Punch, 2014). In this research, the role of the flaneur is simply to look at a particular aspect of the urban spectacle. As stated by Wilson (1995), the researcher takes visual possession of the city simply by looking at the urban spectacle, thus vision prevails in studying and recording the urban experience.

A key aspect of a café is its sense of place. In order to understand that sense of place it is necessary to position the café in its local urban environment, considering how it interacts and engages with that surrounding environment. The authors propose that the 'authenticity' of a particular café experience is dependent on its location and position within the urban landscape. These all add to the character of a café. What the researchers are trying to unpick is the concept of the 'genius loci' of a particular café and to see if there are common themes underlying the 'genius loci' of different cafes. In this research, we are using the concept of the 'genius loci' as defined by Jiven and Larkham (2010) in their review of sense of place, character and authenticity within the urban context. Their focus is on the intangible 'atmosphere of a place', taking into account all the elements that create an environment. In support of the methodology adopted, Jakle (1987) suggested that the best person to experience and describe the genius loci of a place is the tourist, the visitor, as tourism 'involves the deliberate searching out of a place experience' (Jakle, 1987, p. 8). The concept of genius loci is implicitly used by other researchers to perceive and to describe which is perceived holistically, through the senses (Walter, 1988). Thus, the café flaneur as defined here is an appropriate, if novel, methodological approach to identifying, describing and evaluating the genius loci and, hence, authenticity of a café.

Methodology

In broad methodological terms, the approach of the café flaneur/s, who are the authors in this instance, fits into the approach of sociological impressionism presented by Lynch (2005) as an appropriate methodological approach for undertaking research into the hospitality context. In particular, the value and role of personal experiences is recognised, by sociological impressionism, and has been for a considerable period of time (Ridley & Love, 1999). Lynch (2005) 'notes that sociological impressionism has a resonance with a critical theory perspective, but what impressionism provides is an 'island of subjectivity':

> It is preoccupied with the subjective experience, the spiritual, emotional self. It may be a difficult concept to grasp, but is best thought of here as a focus on the intangibles that arise from the hospitality experience, a search for non-cultural objectifications (Lynch, 2005, p. 530).

Ethnographic research has seen a massive increase in tourism and hospitality research in recent years. A report by O'Gorman et al. (2014) notes the increase but also discusses the challenges of the use of ethnographic research. In particular, they suggest that the 'significance of the personal is often ignored in practice and ethnographies are, in effect, reified as representations of generality' (O'Gorman et al., p. 47). Although the research reported here is not ethnographic, its focus on the personal perspectives of the authors means it is open to similar criticisms as those identified by O'Gorman et al. (2014):

> The significance of the personal is often ignored in practice and ethnographies are, in effect, reified as representations of generality. In effect, users of tourism ethnographies are over-privileging certain studies by using individual interpretations or infrequently questioned "truths" (O'Gorman et al., 2014, p. 47).

To overcome, or at least minimise, these criticisms of the sociological impressionism, the authors visited the cafes reported here together, made their own individual notes at the first opportunity, shared a coffee and discussed their observations and then came back to their notes after a period of time in order to objectively reflect on these observations/impressions.

So, who are our café flaneurs? The first and third authors of this chapter took part in data collection. Obviously, we are university lecturers, so we are middle class. We are a married couple with a taste for the unusual, proponents of counter culture in that we avoid, where possible, the clinical experience of the chain coffee shops. We must admit to being middle-aged and financially comfortable. We visit cafes and tea rooms together on an almost daily basis as part of our non-academic lives. Indeed, our behaviours in undertaking this research have been very similar, if not the same, as in our normal lives. If on holiday, we walk round looking for a café that looks interesting and welcoming. Indeed, it was walking around a historic town deciding which café to choose that generated the idea for this research.

It is interesting to reflect on the process of entering a café, deciding where to sit and interacting with the café experience. For example, the female member of the party always looks at the crockery in some detail, for her the crockery is an important part of the café experience. The male researcher cannot remember a time when a visit to a new café has not included a comment on the crockery. This in itself is an important element. It reflects that we are all individuals and that we are all perceiving the café experience differently; therefore, the key drivers of the experience are individuals. Thus, the flaneur, as defined here, is an appropriate, if novel, methodological approach to understanding this research.

The field work approach is summarised here in Fig. 2.1.

Case Studies

For this chapter, we chose to present only three case studies of our research as follows:

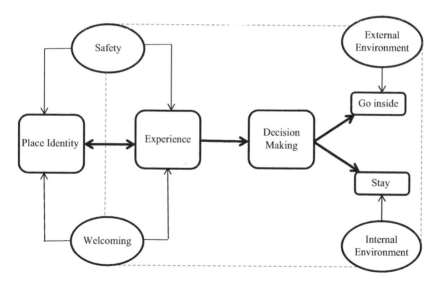

Fig. 2.1.   Conceptual Framework. *Source:* Authors.

Manchester's Northern Quarter

A visit to the Northern Quarter of Manchester provided the initial thoughts that this research arose from. As we wandered past, a myriad of café bars looking for somewhere to have our lunch; the question arose as to why there were so many of these 'unattractive' (in our perception) places around? We realised that this was because the impression they gave us was that they were too 'hipster-ish', not places we, personally, would feel comfortable in. The café bars were authentic, however, in that they reflected the area in which they were situated – edgy, the home of gentrification where the youngish, well-heeled brush shoulder to shoulder with the homeless and where the 'rough' pubs from a previous era are still in evidence. This whole area speaks 'loft living'. It contains a wealth of retro/vintage shops, infilled by relicts from the past – the takeaways and sex shops. The charity shops in the area epitomise the gentrification taking place as they tend to be upmarket, with a focus on vintage.

The Northern Quarter constitutes a small area but is extremely cosmopolitan. The trendy café bars, serving alcohol and open throughout the day and night, are very representative of the 'genius loci' of the area, true to the spirit of the place and authentic in terms of the gentrification taking place. However, as a middle-aged couple looking for a non-alcoholic environment, we find ourselves visiting a café in the converted market, an area which now possesses a number of interesting craft shops. Although still a café bar, with alcohol on sale, the focus is on food and tea/coffee.

So, what are the impressions that attract us to this place? Initially, it is the environment, crafty, arty, safe and refined, very different from the edginess of the surrounding streets. The café area is open to the old market, and you can see immediately what is on offer; it is part of this 'safe', arty/crafty experience. The café is simple and retro but clean, the décor simple and background music is 1970s middle of the road (not too loud). The overall impression is of 'shabby chic' and comfort. The other clientele are similar to ourselves – browsers in the craft shops.

As we approach the counter to order, our first impressions are reinforced by the menu, the cakes on display and the refined quality of the dining offer. When we sit at the table, the impression of shabby chic is augmented by the crockery, which is a mix of vintage items. As we relax and chat, sipping our tea and coffee and eating our lunch, there is the definite feeling of a comfortable, refined café experience; the café mirrors the craft gallery it sits in, and it feels 'right' – its food and beverage offer, its décor and its furniture all feel authentic to its location. It feels safe and welcoming to these café flaneurs, and we will return here. Why? Because the 'genius loci' – the atmosphere, the spirit of the place – is right for us: individual, shabby chic, comfortable, safe, a place to eat drink and chat and a place to relax.

During another visit to the Northern Quarter, our intrepid flaneurs decided to visit one of the many café bars. After walking the street for an hour, no particular venue entices us in although independent they all seem to have the same 'hipster-ish' offer. Eventually, we settle for one which is a bar, eatery, coffee spot and this lunchtime the clientele are, on the whole, young, well-heeled people – hipsters! It is open all day and evening, and alcohol is a key part of the beverage offer.

Our first impressions are of a streetscape that is edgy and is gentrifying fast. The café bar is large, several shop fronts' worth and when we look through the windows, the bar and alcohol products figure large in our impressions. Some of the tables and chairs are wooden and basic – modernist – and there are also tatty sofas, armchairs and red metals chairs, a real mixed bag. The walls are plain except for large lithographs, statement pieces in bright, primary colours. Unusual background music is playing – music that is hard to compartmentalise, but definitely not modern. The overall impression is of industrial chic, a place to drink beer with your friends or to be on your own with just your laptop company. The menu, the furniture, the presentation of the food and the prices all combine to give the impression that this is the playground of the "loft livers", the people who live in the trendy flats. It is the home of the hipsters, and it constitutes a key part of the gentrification taking place, one of the many islands of prosperity that are materialising as graffiti-covered, boarded up shop fronts are consumed by the café bar culture. It is an authentic experience, but we are outside our comfort zone; it would not be our choice.

As we walk around the area, there are many similar café bars, all independent, all 'cool', each different, but at the same time very much of the same ilk. All appear to offer an authentic hipster experience. The genius loci, the spirit of the place, is hipster, but it could be part of a hipster chain, as it feels very much 'manufactured'.

Gainsborough

Our second round of visits is centred on Gainsborough, a free-standing town in Lincolnshire and somewhere we haven't visited before. Gainsborough was chosen as, being a small town, it is feasible to walk around the area in our search for cafes. On walking around, the first impression is that there is a predominance of 'greasy spoon' type establishments and chains. However, a sign for a church café catches our attention. Our expectation is that this will be a community-style cafe, and we are not disappointed in this belief.

Walking into the café space, we see that it is basic, but spacious and clean – utilitarian. The menu is very traditional and the prices are low, thus reinforcing the message as to the target market. The staff are clearly volunteers. Customers appear to be a mix of church members, elderly people and people who are financially challenged or have special needs. Every aspect of the café proclaims the message that all are welcome there, not just the well-heeled. There is also a real 'community spirit', the community being composed of the staff volunteers and the 'regulars'. There is a definite feeling of hospitality in a non-commercial setting.

Our second café is housed in a heritage building. The building is very impressive, and the comparison with our previous destination could not be more pronounced. Once again, the café area is spacious, but modern and functional, unlike the building it is housed in. The clientele appear to be predominantly middle class, comprising visitors to the hall and locals. Indeed, the majority of the clientele could be described as 'ladies who lunch'. This is reflected in the menu, which is basic – soups/salads/quiches – but well-presented. Overall, this appears to be a very 'safe' environment, but lacking in any real character, particularly taking into account the building in which it is housed. Indeed, our 'fieldwork' notes record that the overall impression is that the café is not in keeping with the historic hall. There is a lack of authenticity, which is disappointing in that the café does not reflect the historic grandeur, the atmosphere, the 'sense of place' of the host building. The church café, on the other hand, appears to be perfectly in keeping with the building in which it is situated and the ethos of its community; all expectations are met. By contrast, the historic house café is a 'safe bet' but doesn't reflect the context of its heritage building.

Our final venue is down on the riverside, an area of gentrification, a place where warehouses have been turned into trendy residences. Our riverside café is in the modern 'coffee shop' style, with armchairs and wooden tables, all a bit worn but functional and clean. Everything has an element of minimalism – prints on bare walls and staff dressed in simple black uniforms. This is a place to sit and chat with friends, and probably attracts a younger clientele. Overall, it feels clean and safe – even 'safe' prices – almost like an independent Costa. Does it provide an authentic experience? Yes and no. Yes, when considering the experience of a middle-class flat dweller in a small town – minimalistic and functional above all else. No, in that, as stated previously, it could almost be part of a chain, with its emphasis on a clean, safe experience. And if we consider its authenticity in the context of the area in which it is situated, again the result would be ambiguous as there are two layers visible here – both the modern refurbishment and also the historic remnants of the important port that was once Gainsborough.

On reflection, the overall impression of the cafes we chose to visit is that the authenticity of the experience is nuanced by one's expectations and life experiences. The most authentic experience was the church café, where everything about it was what you would expect from a church community in that all are welcome, particularly the disadvantaged, and we were happy to support such a genuine offer.

Lincoln

On the train en route for our third visit, we decide to enter the 21st century and use Trip Advisor to identify a café to visit in our destination, Lincoln, a historic city with a significant tourist presence. Scanning the list of the '10 Best Cafes in Lincoln' (TripAdvisor, 2018), one immediately catches our eye – the name is intriguing and the description even more so: it is located between two churches. The reviews look good.

We would not have found this particular café without Google maps. It is positioned between two churches, but they so dominate the streetscape that it would be easy to overlook the café. First impressions, gleaned from the outside, are that this is going to be a social café and basic. However, on entering we discover an unexpected world – it is large and airy, and the senses are almost overwhelmed by the sense of space and the vintage feel. It has a 'USA' brashness, and yet it is very British, sporting Union Jacks, and also pictures and prints of film stars – Hollywood, but with a UK focus; these are the actors who would have been popular in Britain in their era. The menu, too, features such items as 1940s Super Star Salads, each named after a particular star such as Ginger Rogers, or Bing Crosby. There are other vintage-themed menu items such as Babe Ruth, Churchill, The American Alliance and so forth. There is an immediate vibrancy as you enter – conversations, no music. The café is full of groups of people talking and there is a wide mix – young, old, couples, families and groups of friends. There is a counter culture feel, Bohemian. These are not the customers of Star-bucks; they *are* of the social classes that populate Starbucks, requiring a safe, clean environment and able to afford Starbucks prices, but these customers want an individual experience, an authentic experience.

This is a place for locals, those in the know, not a place for tourists. It's away from the tourist tracks. The offer of 15% student discount confirms our initial impressions – this café is the type of place inhabited by university lecturers and counter culture students.

You order at the counter, the food looks good and there is a wide range of food. It is not cheap, but it is clearly quality. The furniture comprises much 'industrial stuff', upcycled, for example ladders on the ceiling, and shouts 'Bohemian'. There are plenty of staff, and they sport an informal uniform of striped T shirts. The uniforms epitomise the atmosphere of the place – casual, individual but with a very definite underlying structure and order. The toilets are clean – industrial and distressed – and are very well-equipped.

What we have here is the best of both worlds, the cleanliness and safety of the large chains, together with the individuality of the independent café. We felt comfortable from the moment we walked in and if we lived in Lincoln this would be our 'local'. It is exactly the 'third place' (Oldenberg, 1997) that would meet our requirements – somewhere to meet, talk or sit in peace on your own. The expe-rience is one of authentic bohemianism, a place for writers, a place to talk and put the world to rights; it has the authenticity of a Bohemian space and would appear to be more a place for the regular visitor than the visiting tourist.

The second café we visit in Lincoln is once again linked to a church, in fact it occupies a small corner of a church and includes a churchyard where you can sit out to partake of your tea and cake. We anticipate another social enterprise, but in fact this turns out be a commercial operation. Inside it is light and airy, but a little 'soulless' – bare tables, a number of 'campers' on their PCs, rather loud background music – not a place for quiet conversation or solitude. Indeed, the existing customers are all interacting with their PCs or mobiles, even when in couples, although there is a predominance of individuals. Staff are young and casually dressed. The overall impression is utilitarian, the steady trade of tourists and of people buying lunchtime sandwiches making it clear that the main business is the provision of food and beverage; the tables are there to eat or 'camp' at, not to hold conversations. The crockery – white enamel with a blue rim – says that this is place of minimalism. For us, it is a place to keep out of the rain and to eat lunch, but not a place for a 'café experience'. It is neither hospitable nor inhospitable. There is a neutrality of experience. The inside is not authentic to the outside, either in terms of place or experience.

Data Analysis

The authors' notes were written up and then analysed by a second author as an independent researcher to identify the underlying themes using Template Analysis (TeA). This approach provides a holistic view of themes to the researchers and ability to identify key points to address the key findings in discussion to liaise to the research questions and research aim (Tabari et al., 2020). Furthermore, the flexibility of the TeA technique and template help to provide clearer and more robust analysis towards developing a model and understanding of the role of physical elements on customers' decision-making. The template went through three stages before it reached the final coding. First, a priori themes have been identified and compared with the aims and objectives of the research and second, an initial template developed with a few sub-levels. After going through all the text one more time, the final template has been confirmed with some sub-levels. The other two authors individually checked the codes and final template for quality before writing up to ensure that the themes made sense (King et al., 2018; Tabari et al., 2020). Following this, minor changes were made to the order of some sub-levels to provide a better link between themes. The final template (Table 2.1) is used as the basis for interpretation of the data.

Discussion and Conclusion

Reflecting on our 'strollings' as café flaneurs of the independent café, it is clear that concepts of authenticity, or genius loci, underlie the café experience. Yes, the food and beverage offer is an important part of the total experience, but the genius loci is interwoven into that experience. The food and beverage offer does contribute to the authenticity of a cafe but is only a small part of this authenticity. Underlying our café flaneur journey was the search for an authentic café experience rather than the sanitised safety of, say, a Starbucks. For us, our starting point is that sanitised safety of Starbucks, that lack of authenticity in the café experience, whilst the antithesis of this, the authenticity, we found to be epitomised in the concepts of 'naturalness', 'spirituality' and 'culture' underlying some of the cafes visited. Our perceptions determined the expected and actual authenticity of the experience.

Many of the cafes that we felt provided an authentic experience for us were very different from each other that experience being influenced by a myriad of factors, including the crockery, the menu, the food and beverage offer, the furniture and the surrounding streetscape. How these variables interact creates the genius loci, the spirit and the atmosphere, of a place.

Table 2.1. The Final Template Below Summarises the Key Themes Identified.

Final Template	
Place identity	*Classification*

Place identity

- Trendy
- Rough
- Community
- Mixed range
- Urban
- Cosmopolitan

Experience

- Food and beverage
  - Trendy drink
  - Trendy food
  - Alcohol
- Opening and closing time
- Entertainment
  - Event
  - Theatre
- People
- Fancy shops/little surprizes

External environment

- Artefact
  - Street art
  - Art shops/Gallery/sex shops/ tattoo
- Architecture
  - Modern building
  - Old building
- Clean/Dirty
- Edgy

Internal environment

- Design
  - Modern
  - Classy
  - Artefact
- Music
  - Background
  - Live band
- Cosy

Classification

- Luxury area
- Modern area
- Casual area
- Formal area
- Pricy
- Affordable

Safety of area

- Feeling safe
- Looks safe to walk around

Welcoming

- From host
- From other customers
- Community
- Couples and friends
- Tourist
- Business women/men (working on laptop)

Connection with outside

- Windows
- First floor

Invisible to outside

- No window
- Under ground

Source: Authors.

The genius loci was strongest, felt the most authentic, in the cafes that purveyed a strong message as to what they were about. These tended to be the Bohemian, social enterprises whereas the hipster and minimalistic, for us, lacked the café *experience*, they fell short on atmosphere and authenticity; they were the independent versions of Starbucks. To us, they felt inauthentic. However, our suspicion is that these impressions of authenticity, or lack of it, in the cafes visited reflects our own individual response to the café experience, reflected in the 'social construct' of our sense of self and then deconstructed by the TeA.

What does this mean for prospective or existing independent coffee shop businesses? Essentially, it suggests that not only do you need to identify your prospective customers, but that you need to design a coffee shop environment which also provides an authentic feel to the café atmosphere. To do this, you need to consider all aspects of the offer, from the general environment, including background music, to the crockery, furniture, staff uniforms, presentation of the food and even the names given to the dishes and blends of tea and coffee. Lastly, don't forget the external environment as it sends a strong message to passing trade, and the effectiveness of the ubiquitous chalk board should not be ignored.

References

Altman, I., & Low, S. M. (1992). *Place attachment*. Plenum Press.

Barnett, C., Cloke, P., Clarke, N., & Malpass, A. (2005). Consuming ethics: Articulating the subjects and spaces of ethical consumption. *Antipode, 37*, 23–45.

Benjamin, W. (2007). *Passagens. (Brazilian edition of the German original Das Passages-Werk)*. Editora da Universidade Federal de Minas Gerais.

Bitner, M. J. (1992). Servicescapes: The impact of physical surroundings on customers and employees. *Journal of marketing, 56*(2), 57–71.

Boniface, P. (2003). *Tasting tourism: Travelling for food and drink*. Ashgate.

Burley, D. (2007). Place Attachment and Environmental Change in Coastal Louisiana. *Organization & Environment, 20*(3), 347–366.

Clarke, N., Cloke, P., Barnett, C., & Malpass, A. (2007). Globalising the consumer: Doing politics in an ethical register. *Political Geography, 26*, 231–249.

Cohen, E., & Avieli, N. (2004). Food in tourism: Attraction and impediment. *Annals of Tourism Research, 31*, 755–778.

Del Rio, V. (2016). Urbanity, the flâneur, and the visual qualities of urban design: A walk in Lisbon, Portugal. *Focus, 12*(1), 16.

Eastham, J. (2003). Valorizing through tourism in rural areas: Moving towards regional partnerships. In C. Hall, L. Sharples, R. Mitchell, N. Macionis, & B. Camborne (eds), *Food tourism around the world: Development, management and markets*. Butterworth-Heinemann.

Hughes, G. (1995). Authenticity in tourism. *Annals of Tourism Research, 22*, 781–803.

Jakle, J. A. (1987). *The visual elements of landscape*. University of Massachusetts Press.

Jiven, G., & Larkham, P. J. (2010). Sense of place, authenticity and character: A commentary. *Journal of Urban Design, 8*(1), 67–81.

King, N., Brooks, J., & Tabari, S. (2018). Template analysis in business and management research. In M. Ciesielska & D. Jemielniak (Eds.), *Qualitative methodologies in organization studies: Volume II: Methods and possibilities* (pp. 179–206). Palgrave Macmillan.

Kotler, P. (1973). Atmospherics as a marketing tool. *Journal of Retailing, 49*(4), 48–64.

Long, L. (2004). Introduction. In L. Long (ed.), *Culinary tourism*. The University Press of Kentucky.

Lynch, P. A. (2005). Sociological impressionism in a hospitality context. *Annals of Tourism Research, 32*(3), 527–548.

Mitchell, R., & Hall, C. (2003). Consuming tourists: Food tourism consumer behaviour. In C. Hall (Ed.), *Food tourism around the world: Development, management and markets*. Butterworth-Heinemann.

O'Gorman, K., Lochrie, S., & Watson, A. (2014). Research philosophy and case studies. *Research methods for business & management*, 152–172.

Oldenburg, R. (1997). *The great good place: Cafés, coffee shops, community centres, beauty parlours, general stores, bars, hangouts and how they get you through the day*. Marlowe and Co.

Punch, K. F. (2014). *Introduction to social research: Quantitative and qualitative approaches* (3rd ed.). Sage.

Ridley, R., & Love, L. (1999). The state of qualitative tourism research. *Annals of Tourism Research, 27*, 164–187.

Sims, R. (2009, May). Food, place and authenticity: Local food and the sustainable tourism experience. *Journal of Sustainable Tourism, 17*(3), 321–336.

Stroebele, N., & De Castro, J. M. (2004). Effect of ambience on food intake and food choice. *US National Library of Medicine National Institutes of Health, 20*(9), 821–838.

Tabari, S., King, N., & Egan, D. (2020). Potential application of template analysis in qualitative hospitality management research. *Hospitality and Society, 10*(2), 197–216.

Taylor, J. (2001). Authenticity and sincerity in tourism. *Annals of Tourism Research, 28*, 7–26.

Torres, R. (2002). Towards a better understanding of tourism and agriculture linkages in the Yucatan: Tourist food consumption and preferences. *Tourism Geographies, 4*, 282–307.

TripAdvisor. (2018). *The 10 best cafes in Lincoln*. Accessed 30th July 2018. https://www.tripadvisor.co.uk/Restaurants-g186336-c8-Lincoln_Lincolnshire_England.html

Walter, E. V. (1988). *Placeways: A theory of the human environment*. University of North Carolina Press.

Wang, N. (1999). Rethinking authenticity in the tourist experience. *Annals of Tourism Research, 26*, 349–370.

Waxman, L. (2006). The coffee shop: Social and physical factors influencing place attachment. *Journal of Interior Design, 31*(3), 35–53.

Wilson, E. (1995). The Invisible *Flaneur*. In S. Watson & K. Gibson (eds), *Postmodern cities and spaces*. Blackwell.

Yeoman, I., Brass, D., & McMahon-Beattie, U. (2006). Current issues in tourism: The authentic tourist. *Tourism Management, 28*, 1128–1138.

Chapter 3

Intangible but Effective: The Role of Hotel Lobby Music Background on Customer Satisfaction

Yuyuan Wu[a] *and Saloomeh Tabari*[b]

[a]Surrey University, UK
[b]Cardiff University, UK

Abstract

Background music is considered an intangible element but has a close attachment to emotional reaction and memory. Background music is constantly present in our everyday lives, whether for distraction, recreation or mood enhancement. It can be heard in the supermarket, in lifts, cafés or hotels. Music has been identified as important in the construction of auto-biographical memories and emotions of individuals. Many premises use music to enhance customers' emotions, and hoteliers try to use music in their lobby to increase the likelihood of customer experience. The purpose of this chapter is to examine the impact of background music as an intangible element in hotel lobbies on customer satisfaction. More specifically, this study aims to draw a connection between the musical variables (musicscape) in hotel lobbies with regard to the gender and age of guests and how hotel businesses can make use of this intangible element to enhance their guest's satisfaction. Sound marketing is an overlooked area in hospitality and tourism research. A mixed-method approach has been employed in this study, including a questionnaire and online interviews. The result shows that background music in hotel lobbies has a significant impact on customer satisfaction and the time they are willing to spend in the lobby. Moreover, different musical variables have obvious influences on the experience of guests of different ages and genders. The results of this study provide theoretical and managerial recommendations on the importance of sound marketing in a hotel lobby setting.

Marketing and Design in the Service Sector, 35–50
Copyright © 2024 by Emerald Publishing Limited
All rights of reproduction in any form reserved
doi:10.1108/978-1-83797-276-020241004

Keywords: Customer satisfaction and experience; background music; musicscape; hotel lobbies; sound marketing; atmosphere

Introduction

The hotel lobby provides a boundary between the street and the inner spaces of the hotel (Short, 2019). Lobbies have a great influence on customers' first impressions of the hotel, and background music is one of the important factors that affect customer satisfaction. The hotel lobby represents the overall image of the hotel and often attracts the initial attention of customers (Kilburn, 2018). In order to generate greater profits and meet the needs of more customers, hotel operators now pay a larger amount of attention to the ambiance of the lobby (Manley, 2018). According to Durst (2018), the lobby constitutes the centre of all hotel activities, such as reception, gathering and waiting, etc., which will be one of the main reasons why most tourists tend to choose traditional accommodation instead of modern one like Airbnb (Nagy, 2018). In recent years, hoteliers show more interest to provide better atmosphere and enhance their ambiance to increase customer experience and satisfaction. The previous study stated that physical environments have a significant impact on guest satisfaction (Han & Back, 2009). The guest in the hotel evaluates their experience based on the five senses (e.g. sight, smell, taste, touch and hearing) that are stimulated by the tangible and intangible factors in each service environment (Bitner, 1992; Chang, 2000).

Customer satisfaction is a judgement of the level of satisfaction of products or services that provide pleasant consumption, including above or below the level of satisfaction. In a service environment, the evaluation of overall customer satisfaction is mainly determined by customers throughout the entire process of their service experience. It is determined by the accumulated judgement of the service encountered. In order to create a satisfactory and memorable hotel experience, combinations of three elements of service; hotel staff, physical hotel environment and service process (Ariffin et al., 2013) are needed. Servicescape by Bitner, primarily to point out that the service environment is composed of many elements, such as colour, music, scent, temperature and design (Harrington et al., 2015). In addition, previous studies indicated that the pleasant physical environments in a hotel will increase customer satisfaction (Ariffin et al., 2013; Chang, 2000; Lam et al., 2011). Studies on music background in the restaurant showed that among all physical environments, background music was identified as one of the most critical determinants of the atmosphere of the space (Stroebele & Castro, 2006; Su. 2011; Wilson, 2003a, 2003b). Music has been identified as important in the construction of autobiographical memories and emotion of individuals (Jancke, 2008). Music, in particular, has a great influence on the behaviour and perception of customers. Several studies highlighted the important role of background music on purchasing and decision-making of customers (Jacob, 2006). For instance, Yalch and Spangenberg (1990) study stated that the different type of music in store and spending time of customer with regard to their age. Wilson (2003a, 2003b) stressed that customers in wines shop intended to buy more expensive wine when the store was playing classical music, and they intend to spend more time in the shop. Furthermore, research by Schubert (2007) found that background music played in the waiting areas decrease customers' tension and anxiety. Furthermore, Vida et al. (2007:478) in their study found that 'shoppers' liking of the music in the retail setting and the perceived music fit with the store image has a positive effect on the length of shopping time which indirectly influences customers' expenditure'. In the past decade, music has become a major element in the design of atmospherics; music appears to be a central strategic marketing and integral components of the environment in the store and retail setting because of its proven effects on customer emotion and behaviour (Garlin & Owen, 2006; Levy & Weitz, 2004; Machleit & Mantel, 2001; Turley & Milliman, 2000). Sound marketing plays an important role on customer satisfaction, and various research studies noted this effect on consumer in retail and shopping and restaurant settings, but little attention has been paid to the impact of music background on customer satisfaction in hospitality and tourism research, especially in the context of hotel lobbies. In order to bridge this gap in the literature, this research intends to examine the effect of background music in hotel lobbies and the importance of sound marketing on consumer satisfaction by answering to the following questions: Why is background music important in the hotel lobby? How does background music affect customer satisfaction in the hotel lobby? What is the relationship between musicscape and customer satisfaction?

Musicscape

The musicscape framework of Oakes (2000) is more widely known and has become an important reference for many studies. Musicscape draws on Bitner's servicescape model and focuses on the impact of specific music variables on the behaviour of customers and employees (Oakes, 2000). This visual framework emphasised that music is only one of many factors that affect the service environment and focused on the specific characteristics of music including tempo, volume, genre and preferences, which can influence consumer behaviour in different service environments (Harrington et al., 2015). Moreover, these musical variables could be used in combination with each other or interact with other physical environmental factors in the servicescape to create an appropriate atmosphere to promote consumer behaviour and improve customer satisfaction. For example, a young man may think that the warm air, bright colour and cheerful music created a comfortable service environment that can stimulate his consumption (Oakes et al., 2013).

The Impact of Musical Variables on Customer Satisfaction

Tempo

Many studies have shown that musical tempo can influence the consumer experience of guests. Musical tempo represents the speed of music playback, and it is a variable that is relatively easy to control and adjust (Jain & Bagdare, 2011). For example, Caldwell and Hibbert (2002) noted that customers eat more slowly in a slow tempo music restaurant, which makes them stay longer than in a fast tempo music restaurant. Slow tempo music also stimulated consumer behaviour, allowing customers to buy extra food and drinks. Fast music may encourage customers to buy more products rather than more expensive ones, thereby lessening the negative impact of a crowded environment on consumer spending (Knoeferle et al., 2017). In addition, the cheerful tempo of house music may easily drive the mood of guests. Customers in their thirties may prefer to go to the cocktail bar or lobby of a boutique hotel where the music is played (Rogers, 2004).

Volume

High-volume music is exciting, while low-volume music is relaxing. Studies have shown that the relaxing effects of music can improve the performance of different activities. For example, consumers exposed to a low-volume environment reported greater self-efficacy in resisting temptation and unhealthy foods than those exposed to a high-volume environment (Biswas et al., 2019).

Beverland et al. (2006) demonstrated that beyond the acceptable music volume range, customers may shorten their stay duration and reduce shopping consumption. In particular, loud music promoted consumption among young people compared to the older people. According to Oakes (2000), Stipp claimed that the effect of volume also varied in different genders. Women preferred slow and soft music while men preferred fast and loud music (Mest, 2013).

Genre

With respect to the musical genre, its consistency with the service environment and selling products will have a great impact on customers' consumption behaviours and attitudes (Oakes et al., 2013). According to the survey conducted by Areni (2003), managers were more likely to play jazz and classical music in the consumption environment of high-end hotels and restaurants. For example, customers may spend more time dining in restaurants where the background music is jazz rather than classical music. Customers were also more willing to spend more money in restaurants where the background music was jazz rather than lighter music (Wilson, 2003a, 2003b).

Furthermore, through playing different types of music in various areas, time could create a unique customer experience in the hotel. Hertzfeld's (2010) argued that using a variety of customised music in the hotel can reflect the brand culture of the hotel. Choosing appropriate music according to different times and seasons in the functional area of the hotel can provide customers with a special consumption experience, so as to improve customer satisfaction. In the lobby of Montreal's ALT Hotel, every day from 4:00 p.m. to 8:00 p.m., the DJ constructed the unique atmosphere of the hotel by playing different music to guests, which brought a wonderful experience to guests, and, subsequently, attracted more guests (Forsey, 2010).

Liking

Musicscape pointed out that musical preference also has a great impact on consumer behaviour (Oakes & North, 2008). The music that customers like can make them feel pleasure and enjoyment. Therefore, this resulted in an increase in their consumption, the intention to return and recommendation of the restaurant (Caldwell & Hibbert, 2002). Michon and Chebat (2004) also discussed the music that guests like can increase their positive evaluations of the service environment and make them willing to wait longer.

Physical Environment

Through years of research, it has become evident that the ambiance of the service environment has a great influence on the consumer experience (Nanu et al., 2020). Bitner created a conceptual framework called servicescape that describes the impact of an artificial physical environment on the behaviour of customers and employees within a service environment (Oakes, 2000). 'Bitner's servicescape model explores the broader domain of non-verbal communication within service environments, and portrays the way in which environmental dimensions can have an effect on the cognitive, emotional and physiological responses of both customers and employees' (Oakes, 2000, p. 539).

According to Ariffin et al. (2013), three related complicated dimensions that make up the servicescape: ambient conditions; space/function; signs, symbols and artefacts. Ambient conditions related to the background features of the environment, such as lighting, temperature, colour, sound (noise and music) and scent. Eiseman (2017) argued that different colours will trigger different personal emotions. Especially in indoor environments, colours could produce a strong visual effect. Kim and Moon (2009) proposed that space refers to the arrangement of machinery, equipment and furniture. The function represented the capabilities of all of these items during the service exchange process. For example, in a restaurant, space meant planning and arranging tables, chairs, corridors and service queues for waiters to serve food. In addition, signs, symbols and artefacts referred to the physical signals about the location, direction, warnings and rules that managers convey to guests during the service (Rosenbaum & Massiah, 2011).

The Importance of Music Within the Service Environment

The Customer's Point of View

As an ambience factor, music plays an important role in many aspects of the service environment. Jain and Bagdare (2011) illustrated the cognitive effect of music on customers, which influences their expectations, perceptions, attitudes and quality evaluation of the service environment. For example, the Toronto Shangri-La Hotel lobby used the sound of a Fazioli piano to attract customers and increase their expectations of hotel service standards and the environment (Marrin, 2013).

Furthermore, this sense of ceremony can make guests feel the hospitality of the hotel and more willing to choose the hotel (Ariffin & Maghzi, 2012).

In terms of emotional responses, music will affect the moods, feelings and emotions of guests. The previous research studies showed that customers prefer to listen to music while shopping in supermarkets (Oakes et al., 2013). Music can enhance customer satisfaction and make customers more happiness when shopping (Yi & Kang, 2019). In addition, when customers experience a high degree of pleasure from music consistency, they will give higher comments on the quality of services and the quality of environment (Demoulin, 2011). Moreover, it has been proposed that the behavioural responses by customers are reflected in the length of stay, the amount of money spent and the speed of waiting (Jain & Bagdare, 2011). Sullivan (2002) pointed out that compared to restaurants without music, customers spend more time in restaurants with any type of music and spend more money on food and drinks. In addition, music can enhance customer satisfaction, stimulate and promote their desire to buy (Yi & Kang, 2019). Good perception of the service environment will also increase the willingness of customers to visit the restaurant again (Demoulin, 2011).

Employees' and Service Providers' Point of View

Magnini and Parker (2009) concluded that music can increase the interaction between employees and customers and actively collect feedback from customers on their service experience. Second, playing music has an effect upon employees; they could potentially increase their love for work and motivate them to work harder. Because pleasant music can improve employees' work efficiency while sad music can reduce employees' attention performance and even increase the frequency of mistakes. It is worth noting that music with lyrics had a more negative effect on employees' attention than music without lyrics (Shih et al., 2016).

Sweeney and Wyber (2002) suggested that music can be seen as an effective marketing tool. Music can help service providers build unique brand image and clarify their market position. For example, some Chinese restaurants offer multilingual menus to their guests, and these restaurants build an atmosphere by continuously playing Chinese music. However, guests in some countries do not like this type of music, which would reduce the satisfaction of the consumer experience. Therefore, managers should be cautious when using music to create or enhance the image of a service provider (Ariffin et al., 2013). Meanwhile, music could reflect the culture of the service place. Various types of music are played in different public areas of the hotel, and the type of music is adjusted according to the change of time so that the hotel can better show its culture to the guests. For example, different music was played in the lobby, restaurants and swimming pool area of the Portofino Bay Hotel (Hertzfeld, 2010). In addition, Areni (2003) claimed that playing appropriate music in the business place will have a positive impact on the cognition and emotion of guests, so as to attract more guests and increase the income and interests of the business place.

Methodology

This study is designed through a mixed methodology, which is mainly based on quantitative research and supplemented by qualitative research, in order to better improve the research results (Morse, 2016). Due to the advantages of quantitative research, many studies on the effect of music on hotel customer satisfaction have adopted this approach. For example, Areni's (2003) study used quantitative research to investigate the impact of atmospheric music on customer consumption experience, employee performance and corporate interests. Jain and Bagdare (2011) also explored the relationship between different music variables and customer response in the context of retailing through quantitative research.

Data for this study were collected from customers who stayed in a hotel in the South of the UK. On the basis of research questions and literature review, the questionnaire has been designed with 19 items reflecting the impact of music background in the hotel lobby on customer satisfaction and willingness to spend time in the lobby. In order to ensure the reliability of the questionnaire, the authors randomly selected 10 people for a pre-test and improved the content of the questionnaire according to the pilot results. Out of 160 questionnaires distributed, only 147 questionnaires were answered and only 100 of them were fully answered, with more than half of these participants saying that the background music in the hotel lobby had a great influence on their consumption behaviour and mood and the length of spending time in the lobby.

The authors used a purposive sampling method to distribute questionnaires in chosen hotels. Purposive sampling provides the opportunity for the researcher the selection of research objects with special destinations according to the judgement of researchers (Sharma, 2017). To examine the influence of background music in the hotel lobby on different customers, the participants selected by the researchers are customers who are staying at one of the hotels in the South of the UK. Furthermore, online interviews were conducted with six participants who had stayed in the hotels in this area, including three men and three women. They were all between 19 and 29 years old. The online interview was conducted via Zoom and Skype, the use of computers allows researchers to access potential participants, erasing boundaries of time and space (Bowden & Galindo-Gonzalez, 2015), and each interview lasted around 20 to 30 minutes. The purposes of the online interviews were to obtain more in-depth information and explore specific music variables that affect the customer's experience.

Findings and Discussion

The researchers collected a total of 147 questionnaires, of which 100 were valid. Data in different genders are similar, which are males (51.47 %) and females (48.53%) in the study. However, the most common age group among participants was 30 to 45 years old (28.56%), followed by 46 to 55 years old (24.56%) and 19 to 29 years old (23.56%), 56 to 65 years old (14.02%), and finally above 65 years old (9.3%).

The findings of this study showed that 28.97% of the participants believed the lobby temperature had a great impact on customer satisfaction, followed by sound (noise and music), accounting for 26.17%. Similarly, the research carried out by Jain and Bagdare (2011) found that music has a positive effect on customers' cognitive and behavioural responses. For example, enjoyable music can make guests stay longer and spend more (Sullivan, 2002). In addition, it also supports Areni's (2003) research showing that music can make customers feel relaxed and comfortable, thus, to improve the consumption experience.

Moreover, the results in the research indicate that musical tempo, volume, genre and preference could have an obvious effect on customer behaviours (see Table 3.1). Particularly, women and men respond very differently to different tempos and volumes of music. It was supported by the study of Hunter et al. (2011) that women prefer slow and soft music, while men prefer fast and loud music.

It can be seen from Table 3.2 that the goodness of fit test has no significance (chi = 1.400, $p = 0.706 > 0.05$), which means that the selection ratio of each item is relatively uniform without any significant difference. However, it can be seen that the genre of music has the greatest impact on participants' satisfaction, followed by tempo and volume, and finally liking.

As far as the musical genre is concerned, the findings of this research highlight that 65.42% of participants thought that the music in the hotel lobby should be different from that in other parts of the hotel. This supports Hertzfeld's (2010) research stating that playing customised music in different parts of the hotel can lead to a better consumption experience for guests. However, the results of this study showed that 51.4% of participants claimed that music in hotel lobbies should be consistent at different times. This is contrary to Forsey's (2010) research, which thought that playing different music in different periods reflects the cultural characteristics of the hotel so that guests can know more about the hotel culture, thus increasing return customers to create more value and benefits.

In terms of musical preference, the results of this study prove that there are obvious differences in music preferences among different age groups. For example, participants aged 19–29 years prefer pop music compared to people over

Table 3.1. The Impact of Four Musical Variables on Customer Satisfaction.

	n	**Response Rate**	**Penetration rate($n = 50$)**
Tempo	11	27.50%	22.00%
Volume	10	25.00%	20.00%
Genre	12	30.00%	24.00%
Liking	7	17.50%	14.00%
Total	40	100%	80.00%

Goodness of fit test: $\chi^2 = 1.400\ p = 0.706$.

Table 3.2. Chi-Square Test Relationship Between Age and Musical Variables.

		19–29	30–45	46–55	56–65	65+	Total	χ^2	p
				Age-Groups (%)					
15 (A. The Volume is Too High)	0.0	3(75.00)	7(63.64)	9(64.29)	3(42.86)	7(50.00)	29(58.00)	1.872	0.759
	1.0	1(25.00)	4(36.36)	5(35.71)	4(57.14)	7(50.00)	21(42.00)		
Total		4	11	14	7	14	50		
15 (B. Music is Too Fast)	0.0	2(50.00)	3(27.27)	3(21.43)	3(42.86)	3(21.43)	14(28.00)	2.329	0.675
	1.0	2(50.00)	8(72.73)	11(78.57)	4(57.14)	11(78.57)	36(72.00)		
Total		4	11	14	7	14	50		
15 (C. Music Type Does Not Like)	0.0	0(0.00)	7(63.64)	6(42.86)	1(14.29)	9(64.29)	23(46.00)	9.559	0.049
	1.0	4(100.00)	4(36.36)	8(57.14)	6(85.71)	5(35.71)	27(54.00)		
Total		4	11	14	7	14	50		
15 (D. Repetition)	0.0	3(75.00)	4(36.36)	6(42.86)	4(57.14)	4(28.57)	21(42.00)	3.631	0.458
	1.0	1(25.00)	7(63.64)	8(57.14)	3(42.86)	10(71.43)	29(58.00)		
Total		4	11	14	7	14	50		
15 (E. Background Noise)	0.0	2(50.00)	8(72.73)	9(64.29)	6(85.71)	10(71.43)	35(70.00)	1.855	0.762
	1.0	2(50.00)	3(27.27)	5(35.71)	1(14.29)	4(28.57)	15(30.00)		
Total		4	11	14	7	14	50		

$p < 0.05$ $p < 0.01$.

46 years; possibly, this may have been related to the different moods of these two groups' age and also the different purposes of using the lobby as a space. This supports Oakes's (2000) research showing that age differences are important factors in influencing music preferences and thus customer satisfaction. Different age groups showed a 0.05 level of significance compared with other musical variables(Music type does not like) (chi $= 9.559$, $p = 0.049 < 0.05$).

The Findings of the Interviews

All six participants stated in the online interview that 'the background music in the hotel lobby is very important' and that 'a suitable piece of music has a great effect on their satisfaction with their stay'. About half of the participants' most frequent activity in the hotel lobby was chatting with friends, followed by eating and drinking and finally waiting for takeaway. Therefore, most participants indicated that the ambient factors that had the most influence on their experience were temperature, followed by background music.

The musical variables all participants were most concerned with were volume, followed by tempo, type and personal preference. About 70% of male participants prefer high-volume and fast music, while about 80% of female participants like soft music. However, male and female participants generally believe that the volume of the music in the hotel lobby should be low and softer. The hotel should also choose the appropriate type of background music according to its own theme and culture, rather than deliberately cater to the music preferences of a certain age group, and play music familiar to the public. They do highlight the fact that if the ambient is pleasant and background music is suitable, they intend to spend more time in the lobby and most likely to order a cup of tea or coffee or any other beverages while they are working on their laptops and responding to emails or reading news or chatting with friends instead of going to a bar or coffee shop outside the hotel. The following conceptual framework (Fig. 3.1) aimed to show the link between the age and gender of participants in this study their preference towards different types of music and the impact of it on their satisfaction level.

Conclusion

As more and more hotel companies around the world try to build their brand image via offering a unique physical environment, design and atmospheres, an understanding of using space and bringing livelihood to the lobbies becomes a priority for hotel industries. To the authors' knowledge, this study provides a unique angle to enhance our understanding of the relationship of different types of music and their effect on the length of stay in the hotel lobby and on the satisfaction level of customers with regard to their age and gender. This study provides an opportunity for future research on ambient music background to improve our understanding of how hotel lobbies' music background makes customers feel and to what extent these feelings can be linked with customers' length

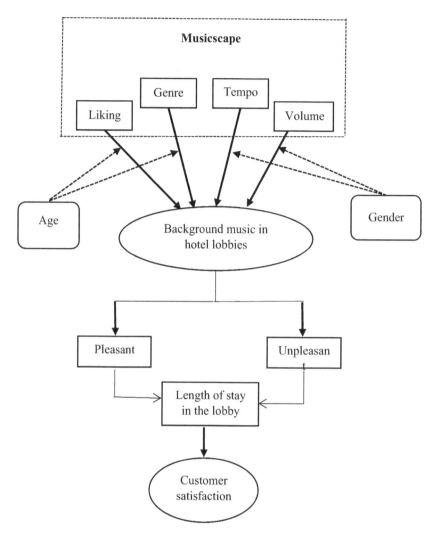

Fig. 3.1.   Conceptual Framework, the Relationship Between
Background Music in Hotel Lobbies and Customer Satisfaction, *Source:*
Authors.

of stay in the lobby and likelihood of purchasing beverage towards enhancing their level of satisfaction.

Although previous studies stated the importance of music background on customer purchasing behaviour, feeling and satisfaction but most of them have investigated in the context of restaurants, shops and supermarkets and limited study looked at hotel lobbies and different preferences of music types in different gender and age groups.

In conclusion, the results of this research confirm that specific musical variables, including tempo, volume, genre and liking, could have different effects on customer satisfaction due to age and gender differences. The hotel lobby should adjust these musical variables according to its own culture and characteristics to meet the requirements of different guests as much as possible so as to improve customer experience and promote the long-term development of the hotel. Meanwhile, different variables could be combined according to the attributes of various music variables to play more effectively so as to improve customer satisfaction through sound marketing.

Theoretical Implications

This study has contributed to the construction of a knowledge system for hotel background music and customer satisfaction research, thereby providing a reference for the service industry literature. Although the literature review shows that music in the service environment can have a great impact on customer behaviour and emotions, there are very limited studies on the effect of background music on customer satisfaction and length of stay in hotel lobbies in previous studies.

Moreover, the results of this study also confirmed that the four musical variables (including musical tempo, volume, genre and liking) have different effects on customer behaviour and emotions. These results are also consistent with previous literature (Bagdare, 2011; Hertzfeld, 2010; Sullivan, 2002). Therefore, the data and information collected in this study are helpful to researchers who are researching the importance and influence of music in hotel lobbies and the length of stay and how to use this space in a better way in hotels.

Managerial Implications

The hotel lobby is particularly important for forming the customer's first impression, so hoteliers attach great importance to the exterior design of the hotel lobby and the creation of the internal environment. Creating a suitable environment based on the target market is crucial to overall customer satisfaction. Therefore, customers' opinions and suggestions are very important. As a result, the background music in the hotel lobby should be adjusted in consideration of different age groups, different genders and different preferences with regard to the hotel targeting position. In addition, the four musical variables will also have a significant impact on the length of time customer spend at the lobby and their satisfaction level. In general, hotels they can use music as an element for their marketing and make their own signature through sound marketing.

This study points out that the background music in the hotel lobby has a positive impact on customer satisfaction and their willingness to spend time in the lobby. The findings make hoteliers recognise the importance of sound marketing in hotels and provide them with valuable insights.

The hotel company can use sound marketing to introduce their own signature music tempo and also use this opportunity to make use of the lobby as a live space to spend time and enhance their revenue by attracting customers to spend more time in the lobby instead of going to a bar or coffee shop outside of the hotel, which leads to enhancing customer satisfaction level. According to the basics of experiential marketing, businesses should focus on creating memorable times for their customers. In today's challenging and competitive environment, customers are both rational and emotional and looking for pleasurable experiences (Schmitt, 2003). Creating direct and valuable connections between brands and their customers is very important in experiential marketing, especially for the millennium, therefore brands try to create a high level of satisfaction by stimulating positive emotion via employing voices or sensory experiences (Lenderman, 2006).

Limitations and Further Research Suggestions

Although the findings provide an insight into the connections between different types of music and different gender and age group preferences and their satisfaction level and length of stay in the lobby, there are still some limitations and unanswered questions that could be addressed in future research. Further research can focus on different parts of the UK hotels and focus only on gender or only on age groups or different market segments based on guests' experience and their characteristics. It would be interesting to see that customers' reaction towards sound marketing in the hotels and not only in the lobby.

However, due to time and manpower constraints, this study only confirms that different musical variables (tempo, volume, genre and liking) can have different effects on customer experience. Therefore, future studies can focus in more detail on exploring the specific effects of changes in each musical variable on customers' emotions and time they are spending in the lobby so as to further explore the relationship between background music and their willingness to spend time in the lobby and their level of satisfaction.

References

Areni, C. S. (2003). Exploring managers' implicit theories of atmospheric music: Comparing academic analysis to industry insight. *Journal of Services Marketing, 17*(2), 161–184.

Ariffin, A. A. M., & Maghzi, A. (2012). A preliminary study on customer expectations of hotel hospitality: Influences of personal and hotel factors. *International Journal of Hospitality Management, 31*, 191–198.

Ariffin, A., Nameghi, E., & Zakaria, N. (2013). The effect of hospitableness and servicescape on guest satisfaction in the hotel industry. *Revue Canadienne Des Sciences de L'administration = Canadian Journal of Administrative Sciences, 30*(2), 127–137. https://doi.org/10.1002/cjas.1246

Beverland, M., Lim, E. A. C., Morrison, M., & Terziovski, M. (2006). In-store music and consumer–brand relationships: Relational transformation following experiences of (mis) fit. *Journal of Business Research, 59*(9), 982–989.

Biswas, D., Lund, K., & Szocs, C. (2019). Sounds like a healthy retail atmospheric strategy: Effects of ambient music and noise on food sales. *Journal of the Academy of Marketing Science, 47*(1), 37.

Bitner, M. J. (1992). Servicescapes: The impact of physical surroundings on customers and employees. *Journal of Marketing, 56*(2), 57–71.

Bowden, C., & Galindo-Gonzalez, S. (2015). Interviewing when you're not face-to-face: The use of email interviews in a phenomenological study. *International Journal of Doctoral Studies, 10*(12), 79–92.

Caldwell, C., & Hibbert, S. A. (2002). The influence of music tempo and musical preference on restaurant patrons' behavior. *Psychology and Marketing, 19*(11), 895–917.

Chang, K. (2000). The impact of perceived physical environments on customers' satisfaction and return intentions. *Journal of Professional Services Marketing, 21*(2), 75–85.

Demoulin, N. (2011). Music congruency in a service setting: The mediating role of emotional and cognitive responses. *Journal of Retailing and Consumer Services, 18*(1), 10–18.

Durst, C. S. (2018). Defining the 2019 hotel lobby. *Lodging Magazine.* https://lodgingmagazine.com/defining-the-2019-hotel-lobby/

Eiseman, L. (2017). *The complete color harmony, pantone edition: Expert color information for professional results.* Rockport Publishers.

Forsey, L. (2010). Sound check-in. *Words & Music, 17*(3), 29. http://search.proquest.com/docview/755054294/

Garlin, F. V., & Owen, K. (2006). Setting the tone with the tune: A meta-analytic review of the effects of background music in retail settings. *Journal of Business Research, 59*(6), 755–764.

Han, H., & Back, K. (2009). Influencing factors on restaurant customers' revisit intention: The roles of emotions and switching barriers. *International Journal of Hospitality Management, 28,* 563–572.

Harrington, R., Ottenbacher, M., & Treuter, A. (2015). The musicscape model: Direct, mediating, and moderating effects in the casual restaurant experience. *International Journal of Hospitality & Tourism Administration, 16*(2), 99–121.

Hertzfeld, E. (2010). Match your music with your culture. (Hotel Operations: MUSIC). *Hotel and Motel Management, 225*(11), 24.

Hunter, P. G., Schellenberg, E. G., & Stalinski, S. M. (2011). Liking and identifying emotionally expressive music: Age and gender differences. *Journal of Experimental Child Psychology, 110*(1), 80–93.

Jacob, C. (2006). Styles of background music and consumption in a bar: An empirical evaluation. *International Journal of Hospitality Management, 25*(4), 716–720.

Jain, R., & Bagdare, S. (2011). Music and consumption experience: A review. *International Journal of Retail & Distribution Management, 39*(4), 289–302.

Jancke, L. (2008). Music, memory and emotion. *Journal of Biology, 7*(21), 1–5.

Kilburn, H. (2018). Spotlight on: Storytelling in the Hotel Lobby. February, 2020. https://hoteldesigns.net

Kim, W. G., & Moon, Y. J. (2009). Customers' cognitive, emotional, and actionable response to the servicescape: A test of the moderating effect of the restaurant type. *International Journal of Hospitality Management, 28*(1), 144–156.

Knoeferle, K., Paus, V., & Vossen, A. (2017). An upbeat crowd: Fast in-store music alleviates negative effects of high social density on customers' spending. *Journal of Retailing*, *93*(4), 541–549.

Lam, L. W., Chan, K. W., Fong, D., & Lo, F. (2011). Does the look matter? The impact of casino servicescape on gaming customer satisfaction, intention to revisit, and desire to stay. *International Journal of Hospitality Management*, *30*(23), 558–567.

Lenderman, M. (2006). *Experience the message: How experiential marketing Is changing the brand world* (1st ed.). Carroll & Graf Publishers. ISBN: 10: 0786718838.

Levy, M., & Weitz, B. A. (2004). *Retailing management* (9th ed.). McGraw-Hill Education. ISBN: 9780078028991, 9781259060663, 007802899X, 1259060667.

Machleit, K. A., & Mantel, S. P. (2001). Emotional response and shopping satisfaction: Moderating effects of shopper attributions. *Journal of Business Research*, *54*(2), 97–106.

Magnini, V. P., & Parker, E. E. (2009). The psychological effects of music: Implications for hotel firms. *Journal of Vacation Marketing*, *15*(1), 53–62.

Manley, B. (2018). Hotel owners focus renovations on public spaces. *Hotel News Now*. https://www.costar.com/article/2010011461/hotel-owners-focus-renovations-on-public-spaces

Marrin, H. (2013). *Hotel Lounging* (Vol. 36). Chatelaine. http://search.proquest.com/docview/1316590209/

Mest, C. (2013). Switching up the sounds. *Hotel Management*, *228*(12), 30. http://search.proquest.com/docview/1448819299/

Michon, R., & Chebat, J. C. (2004). The interaction effect of background music and ambient scent on the perception of service quality. *Journal of Business Research*, *34*(3), 191–196.

Morse, J. M. (2016). *Mixed method design: Principles and procedures* (Vol. 4, p. 194). Routledge. ISBN: 9781598742985.

Nagy, C. (2018). Why the hotel lobby is the perfect antidote to Airbnb? https://skift.com/2018/05/01/why-the-hotel-lobby-is-the-perfect-antidote-to-airbnb/

Nanu, L., Ali, F., Berezina, K., & Cobanoglu, C. (2020). The effect of hotel lobby design on booking intentions: An intergenerational examination. *International Journal of Hospitality Management*, *89*, 102530.

Oakes, S. (2000). The influence of the musicscape within service environments. *Journal of Services Marketing*, *14*(7), 539–556.

Oakes, S., & North, A. (2008). Reviewing congruity effects in the service environment musicscape. *International Journal of Service Industry Management*, *19*(1), 63–82.

Oakes, S., Patterson, A., & Oakes, H. (2013). Shopping soundtracks: Evaluating the musicscape using introspective data. *Arts Marketing: International Journal*, *3*(1), 41–57.

Rogers, D. (2004). bargrooves. *Marketing*, *21*. http://search.proquest.com/docview/214969474/

Rosenbaum, M. S., & Massiah, C. (2011). An expanded servicescape perspective. *Journal of Service Management*, *22*(4), 471–490.

Schmitt, B. (2003). *Customer experience management*. The Free Press.

Schubert, E. (2007). Locus of emotion: The effect of task order and age on emotion perceived and emotion felt in response to music. *Journal of Music Therapy*, *44*(4), 344–368.

Sharma, G. (2017). Pros and cons of different sampling techniques. *International Journal of Applied Research, 3*(7), 749–752.

Shih, Y., Chien, W., & Chiang, H. (2016). Elucidating the relationship between work attention performance and emotions arising from listening to music. *Work: A Journal of Prevention, Assessment & Rehabilitation, 55*(2), 489–494.

Short, E. (2019). Anticipation and Stagnation in the Lobby. In *Mobility and the Hotel in Modern Literature.* Studies in Mobilities, Literature, and Culture. Palgrave Macmillan.

Stroebele, N., & Castro, J. (2006). Listening to music while eating is related to increases in people's food intake and meal duration. *Appetite, 47*(3), 285–289.

Sullivan, M. (2002). The impact of pitch, volume and tempo on the atmospheric effects of music. *International Journal of Retail & Distribution Management, 30*(6), 323–330.

Sweeney, J. C., & Wyber, F. (2002). The role of cognitions and emotions in the music-approach-avoidance behavior relationship. *Journal of Services Marketing, 16*(1), 51–69.

Turley, L. W., & Milliman, R. E. (2000). Atmospheric effects on shopping behavior: A review of the experimental evidence. *Journal of Business Research, 49*(2), 193–211.

Vida, I., Obadia, C., & Kunz, M. (2007). The effect of background music on consumer responses in a high-end supermarket. *International Review of Retail, Distribution and Consumer Research, 17*(5), 469–482.

Wilson, S. (2003a). The effect of music on perceived atmosphere and purchase intentions in a restaurant. *Psychology of Music, 31*(1), 93–112.

Wilson, S. (2003b). The effect of music on perceived atmosphere and purchase intentions in a restaurant. *Psychology of Music, 31*(1), 93–111.

Yalch, R., & Spangenberg, E. (1990). Effects of store music on shopping behaviour. *Journal of Consumer Marketing, 7*(2), 55–65.

Yi, F., & Kang, J. (2019). Effect of background and foreground music on satisfaction, behavior, and emotional responses in public spaces of shopping malls. *Applied Acoustics, 145,* 408–419.

Chapter 4

Hotel Design and Its Impact on the Customer's Booking Decision

Minhan Wang[a], *Saloomeh Tabari*[b] *and Wei Chen*[c]

[a]Surrey Uniiversity, UK
[b]Cardiff University, UK
[c]Sheffield Hallam University, UK

Abstract

Design plays an important role in the hospitality and retail industry. Hotels interior and exterior designs are an important part of hotel operations, and customers are paying attention to them more than ever. The industry is presenting its brand culture through the modern or unique design of its establishments. This chapter is exploring design and its effects on customer satisfaction and the choice of hotel. The chapter attempts to analyse customer psychology and the impact of external architectural style and internal decoration on customer satisfaction and decision-making, followed by investigating the impact of interior design on guest satisfaction. To achieve this, the chapter aimed to answer the following question: how do external and internal design of the hotel influence customer decision-making?

Keywords: Hotel design; internal and external design; architecture; customer choice; customer satisfaction; decision-making

Introduction

Due to increased competitiveness, most research has focused on how hotels can improve their competitiveness to attract guests and achieve higher customer satisfaction. This can be identified as critical reflection, a tool used to improve service and customer experience. This study is on hotel design and customer choice. The purpose of this chapter is to investigate the importance of hotel design and the relationship between customer choice and the design of a hotel. First, we look at the development trend of hotel design and its importance, followed by the

Marketing and Design in the Service Sector, 51–62
Copyright © 2024 by Emerald Publishing Limited
All rights of reproduction in any form reserved
doi:10.1108/978-1-83797-276-020241005

impact of the external environment and design on attracting customers. Finally, the authors will explore the interior decoration and service of the hotel in order to bring unique and regional service to the guests so as to exceed the satisfaction of the guests. Today's hotel is not just a residence, but with the development of society, they now focus extensively on content and form. Hotel design is not limited to decoration and architecture but also includes culture, facilities and services. The design of a hotel seems an effective way to attract a particular group of customers.

Development and Trend for Hotel Design

In the past, hotels were more likely to exclusively provide a place to stay for customers, but now they focus more of their efforts on atmosphere and ambience, therefore, to offer a better experience (Heide et al., 2007). A greater number of people travel around the world as a result of cheaper and more convenient transportation methods, which has led to an increasing number of toe-income families and people who attend a conference want some leisure time apart from work (Huffadine, 2000). However, more challenges are threatening the hotel industry, as well as the planning and design of a hotel. In the 20th century, the hotel focused primarily on the needs of management and resort operations. Despite the emergence of resorts, services and infrastructure were affected by changing customs (Huffadine, 2000). A larger quantity of evidence can prove that customer sentiment is very important to the hospitality sector, and this is largely related to the design of the hotel (Gilmore & Pine II, 2002). Therefore, the hotel will reflect popular taste onto the environment with its distinctive style, rich language, exquisite lighting and unique cultural context.

According to Morandotti & Danio (2009), local culture and environment are affected by tourism, including the dissemination of information and the pursuit of sustainability principles. The sustainable development of hotels includes sustainable design, careful assessment of environmental, cultural and economic resources, effective communication of the nature and principles of the environment, respect and development of local resources and identification of sustainable development models (Morandotti & Danio, 2009).

Architecture and Physical Surroundings

Hotels aim to provide a unique environment for the hotel by enhancing customer experience and providing quality service (Kirillova & Chan, 2018). Mehrabian and Russell (1974) describe environmental psychology as behaviour related to the physical environment. The direct impact on human emotions, and the impact of physical stimulation on various elements, enables hotels to consider the environment carefully. Mehrabian and Russell (1974) also emphasised the importance and necessity of the physical environment. These settings are characterised by what kind of environment the customer is buying and consuming within and what factors the seller controls when designing the sales method, the number of competitors and different strategies for different consumers (Countryman & Jang, 2006). The success of a hotel possesses a certain relationship with the location, so if you want the hotel to operate on the market for a long time, you need to choose a rare location for the hotel. The surrounding environment will affect the criteria for choosing a hotel. If you choose to go to a historical city, the historical atmosphere may be the reason why the hotel chooses its physical location. City-based hotels usually rely upon local cultural construction to attract guests, and local cultural events and visits for guests, including shopping areas, entertainment venues, museums and more (Huffadine, 2000). Ayala (1991) argues that many resorts operate through clever design and management. Guests will choose to remove the hotel in some places, some guests will be willing to go to the resort, but some guests are not interested; guests are ultimately autonomous. The advent of international tourism brought more and more complex challenges, which led to tourism markets creating high expectations. These circumstances forced hotels and resorts to utilise a special method to decorate themselves, which may be inspired by fashionable elements, such as bridges, islands, grottoes, and so on, as a means of variety and to help create the required guest experience. Environmental considerations aim to help guests realise their dreams; it is also a successful marketing tactic, which encourages passengers to pay additional travel costs (Ayala, 1991).

The characteristics of the exterior hotel design have largely influenced the hotel's choice. According to Kirima et al. (2017), about 28% of people can name and point out the impact of hotel design. The hotel's architectural design influenced 3% of the people to choose the hotel, which shows the importance of the hotel design to them; the hotel exterior design has created some value to some extent (Kirima, et al. 2017). Due to the unique design of the hotel, Latham hotel & resort has improved its customer retention rate, which makes it one of the top three best hotels (Siguaw & Enz, 1999). Siguaw and Enz (1999) also illustrate that they are the best hotels because they have established a sense of upscale residence, which is achieved through different curtains and marble floors. The important responsibility of the architect is to consider various facilities in the design process, which must be highly valued by the architect and the surrounding area, such as various styles of restaurants and so forth (Dargahi & Pazhouhanfar, 2014). The relationship between architecture and the environment is the foundation of correct architectural design. In the tourism industry, hotel architecture is like an intermediary between tourists and the environment, creating a kind of cognition by better understanding the needs of customers (Morandotti & Danio, 2009). The environment is not only the centre of society and production but also the competitive advantage of the tourism industry. Tourists' demands are now becoming more flexible, considering a greater amount of non-material territorial characteristics, such as culture, tradition and local characteristics, and taking travel as a method of learning experience (Morandotti & Danio, 2009).

Product and Service Design

Guests are often asked to fill out questionnaires about products and services. Although guests may comment or complain about the design of visual elements, such as lighting angles and other design-related issues. In fact, no new design or improvement has been made since, so product design needs to be part of the marketing mix (West & Purvis, 1992). The customer sees the product with an initial impression, and the customer may consume based on that experience, so product design provides valuable information to help the customer decide on the initial reaction to the product (Bloch, 1995). Product design integrates all the different activities, and consumers ultimately buy and use the product's appearance; therefore, design is a very important factor to consider (Mishra et al., 2015). Improving the product function and design, it can help realise the competitive role, increase differentiation and improve the satisfactory function or style. Design and styling are often regarded as synonymous (West & Purvis, 1992). The core of product development is to create a relationship between design and the surface appearance of the product or environment (Blaich, 1988). There has been a boom in "design hotels" in the UK, where designers have experienced success in using high profile or specific design styles. Under these constraints, the international development of "lifestyle" design will also have to make various changes in order to meet the challenges posed by cultural differences (Ransley & Ingram, 2001). Ransley and Ingram (2001) also showed that most products have a limited product life cycle. Hotels are meeting customer needs and assessing the scale of the hotel, which will affect their net profits. If the scale of the hotel industry is small, most hotel groups extend the write-down period, especially for design-oriented hotels, the look and feel from traditional accommodation properties, which change the dynamics of attracting guests.

For these reasons, the hotel strives to provide the best service environment and emphasises design elements (Baek & Ok, 2017). To a large extent, the service is more of a person's element, or the service as a propaganda theme hotel itself is weak. This is because the service provider and the object are human; they are inevitable. To focus on personalised service and staff training for the hotel is expensive and sometimes even irritates customers (West & Purvis, 1992). Therefore, service is not limited to a face-to-face approach. Some design champions have designed unique emotional experiences to satisfy their guests, including the desire to eliminate adjacent noise problems, isolation with special materials, and, in addition, being able to provide larger comfortable rooms for guests (West & Purvis, 1992). In interpersonal services, the possible response of employees and customers to environmental conditions can be predicted through an effective service environment design, creating an environment for the service (Bitner, 1992). Some several goals and behaviours need to be developed for customers and employees, including their interactions (Bitner, 1992). Researchers and designers try their best to understand real-world experiences from the user's perspective. The core idea of experience design is to put people first and understand the needs and desires of users. This process can discover what is most important to customers and ultimately achieve the best experience, and provide the best service (Lo, 2010).

Customer Psychology

In order to get higher expectations from guests, the hotel needs to be closer to the customer's demand for service design because the higher the score, the more money is spent on the design, so as a high-end hotel analysis of customer behaviour and psychological reactions that is important for the design, the design consultation to set clear goals and plans (West & Purvis, 1992). It has been confirmed by psychologists that the physical environment affects human behaviour; this branch of psychology is called environmental psychology. If the physical environment has an impact on human behaviour, it must be based on the premise of environmental psychology, and it must also have an impact on consumer consumption in the retail industry and tourism industry (Kotler, 1973). Customer satisfaction is related to expectations (Phillips, 2004). Oliver (1997) found that although the service experience was not what guests had originally expected or had received, they were still quite satisfied. Therefore, hoteliers should not use customer satisfaction as a long-term indicator of recommendation intent, but rather as a snapshot of customer experience.

The champions of hotel design realise that the design of the guest room experience itself is a key factor. So, the hotel and the guest room must create an unforgettable experience for the guests through careful design, which is what the guests want (Siguaw & Enz, 1999). Skogland and Siguaw (2004) investigated whether the impact of guest satisfaction on hotels is man-made or hotel atmosphere. The report shows that the hotel's reputation and students are heavily influenced by the hotel environment, that is, the hotel atmosphere and external environment influence customer choice. Face-to-face communication is inevitable when employees are serving guests, and the quality of service provided by the waiter during this process is a direct factor influencing the customer's consumption, purchase and long-term cooperation (Barsky & Labagh, 1992; Bitner et al., 1990; Bolton & Drew, 1992).

Although an increasing number of hotel managers are aware of the needs of guests, emotional and psychological considerations have become very important, but there is still little research on hotel design and guest satisfaction and mood during their stay. Despite a large amount of ongoing research, there is still a limited amount of data regarding emotional design in hotels and a lot of room for research (Lo, 2010).

Methodology

This study adopts a mixed methodology to explore the impact of hotel design on customer selection. The first stage was through a survey questionnaire followed by in-depth interviews to provide clarity on the results of the questionnaires. However, the hotel design is subjective, and the choice of hotel is affected by various factors, such as income, mean of the stay and purpose of the travelling. The self-administered method in the questionnaire is used to propagate through the network (Saunders et al., 2016). The questions mainly focus on the factors such as colour, decoration and appearance. Scoring questions are also designed to investigate whether customers are affected by such factors and the extent of this effect. In this study, subjective questions account for the majority, so a sample size of 85 can greatly reduce the error and minimise survey costs (Brace, 2018). The study involves correlations of sample characteristics, basic behaviours and cognitive attitudes and summary frequency analysis.

Structured interviews consist of a series of pre-determined questions that all interviewees answer in the same order (Connaway & Powell, 2010). According to the results of the questionnaire survey, in addition, six in-depth interviews have been conducted. The interview questions are designed concerning the questions on the questionnaire. To include more age groups, the interview participants include varied and differentiated ages. Due to the impact of the new coronavirus, the interview is conducted in an online format for 20 minutes. First, the interviewer makes an appointment with the participants and then explains the meaning and purpose of the interview, prior to conducting any questioning. The results of the interview method are more subjective, and the survey questions can be adjusted or expanded based on the respondent's feedback.

Findings and Discussion

The chi-square goodness of fit test was used to analyse whether the proportional distribution of each choice in multiple-choice questions was even. It can be seen from Fig. 4.1 that the goodness of fit test presents a significant difference (Chi = 8.586, $p = 0.035 < 0.05$), which means that the selection ratio of each item has a significant difference, and the difference can be compared by response rate or penetration rate. 'Facilities and equipment' and 'All the above' showed significantly higher response rates and penetration rates.

The chi-square goodness of fit test was used to analyse whether the proportional distribution of each choice in multiple-choice questions was even. It can be seen from Fig. 4.2 that the goodness of fit test presents a significance (chi = 55.899, $p = 0.000 < 0.05$), which means that the selection ratio of each item has a significant difference, and the difference can be compared by response rate or

Terms	Response		Penetration (n=50)
	n	Response rate	
Facilities and equipment	25	28.74%	50.00%
Space design	18	20.69%	36.00%
The atmosphere of the hotel	13	14.94%	26.00%
All the above	31	35.63%	62.00%
Summary	87	100%	174.00%
Test of goodness of fit χ^2=8.586 p=0.035			

Fig. 4.1.   The Chi-Square Test of Customer Preference.

Terms	Response		Penetration (*n*=50)
	n	Reponse rate	
Comfort	41	41.41%	82.00%
Taste	24	24.24%	48.00%
Value for money	28	28.28%	56.00%
Status	5	5.05%	10.00%
Other (Please add)	1	1.01%	2.00%
	99	100%	198.00%
Test of goodness of fit	χ^2=55.899 *p*=0.000		

Fig. 4.2.   The Chi-Square Test of Customer Choice.

penetration rate. Specifically, the response rate and penetration rate of Comfort, Taste and Value for money were significantly higher.

Fig. 4.3 shows that using the chi-square test (cross analysis) to study the 'Gender' relationship between the differences in 'Colours', a total of one item. It can be seen from the figure above that there is a difference for the 'Gender' sample and for 'Colours', a total of one item presents a significant ($p < 0.05$) mean for Colours. A total of one item of samples of different Gender presents the travel of the opposite sex, specific recommendations can be combined with brackets percentage difference comparison.

'Gender' revealed a 0.05 level of significance for 'Colours' (chi = 8.499, $p = 0.037 < 0.05$). According to the percentage comparison, the 'Female' sample chose 'Warm Colour' in 88.89%, which was significantly higher than the 'Male' sample in 57.14%. All samples of different genders revealed significant differences in 'Colour' preference.

It can be seen from Fig. 4.4 that the chi-square test (cross analysis) is used to study the differences between 'Gender' and 'Local cultural characteristics'. As can be extracted from the above figure, a total of one item of samples of different genders showed significance to 'Local cultural characteristics' ($p < 0.05$), which means that one item of samples of different genders showed different characteristics. 'Gender' has a 0.05 level of significance to 'Local cultural characteristics' (chi = 8.323, $p = 0.016 < 0.05$). According to the comparison of percentages, the 'Female' category chose 69.44% of 'Yes', which was significantly higher than the

Question	Name	Gender(%)		Total	χ^2	*p*
		Male	Femal			
Colors	Warm color	8(57.14)	32(88.89)	40(80.00)		
	Cool color	1(7.14)	1(2.78)	2(4.00)		
	White and black	1(7.14)	2(5.56)	3(6.00)	8.499	0.037*
	Bright color	4(28.57)	1(2.78)	5(10.00)		
		14	36	50		

* *p*<0.05 ** *p*<0.01

Fig. 4.3.   The Chi-Square Test Between Colours and Gender.

Question	Name	Gender(%)		Total	χ^2 @	p @
		Male	Femal			
Local cultural characteristics	Yes	7(50.00)	25(69.44)	32(64.00)		
	No	3(21.43)	0(0.00)	3(6.00)	8.323	0.016*
	Maybe	4(28.57)	11(30.56)	15(30.00)		
		14	36	50		

* $p<0.05$ ** $p<0.01$

Fig. 4.4.   The Chi-Square Test Between the Local Characteristic and Gender.

	Gender		F @	p @
	Male($n=14$)	Femal($n=36$)		
The decoration of the hotel has an impact on my choice of hotel	3.64±1.08	3.86±0.90	0.530	0.470
The architecture of the hotel has an impact on my choice of hotel	3.50±1.16	3.78±0.90	0.817	0.371
The atmosphere of the hotel has an impact on my choice of hotel	3.71±1.07	4.14±0.83	2.227	0.142
The facility of the hotel has an impact on my choice of hotel	4.14±0.66	4.61±0.60	5.807	0.020*
The space design of the hotel has an impact on my choice of hotel	4.07±0.73	3.86±0.80	0.732	0.396

* $p<0.05$ ** $p<0.01$

Fig. 4.5.   The One-Way Analysis of Variance.

'Male' participants by 50.00%. It can be concluded that all samples of different genders show significant differences in 'Local cultural characteristics'.

'Gender' has an impact on 'The choice of the hotel' at a level of 0.05 ($F = 5.807, p = 0.020$), and specific comparison shows that the average value of 'Male' (4.14) is significantly lower than that of 'Female' (4.61) (Fig. 4.5). It can be evaluated that 'The decoration of The hotel has an impact on my choice of hotel', 'The architecture of The hotel has an impact on my choice of hotel', 'The atmosphere of The hotel has an impact on my choice of hotel', 'The space design of The hotel has an impact on my choice of hotel' are all important yet varied in preference. In addition, 'Gender' samples showed a significant difference in 'The facility of the hotel with an impact on my choice of hotel'.

Interview Summary

International Hotels Should Be Designed according to Local Characteristics or Retain the Overall Corporate Culture and Style?

Standardised and unified design can well shape the corporate image and hotel culture, but sometimes such a design will give people a sense of indifference. Sometimes the design of the hotel is out of step with the local culture and style. On the contrary, large hotels themselves are chain in nature; they have their own unique brand and culture. In other words, when people think of a hotel's decoration style and layout, they think of a large hotel group, so they don't need to redesign the hotel according to local characteristics. In general, the hotel group can retain the overall culture and style. After all, the design of the hotel is not local. Compared with a local B&B or real local hotels, it is difficult to encounter a strong amount of competitiveness. Therefore, it is a good choice to maintain the original culture and style of the hotel. The design and positioning of a large international hotel should depend on its location if it is to be integrated with local characteristics. If the original standardised enterprise design is retained in the urban area and the enterprise standardised design is established in the tourist area, it is more appropriate to properly integrate the local culture and landscape elements.

In Order to Cater to Public Preferences and Aesthetics, What Aspects do Hotel Design Should Pay More Attention to?

Before the design, we should make an in-depth investigation to make sure what the public's preferences and aesthetics are. We can query individuals to see what style of hotel people prefer and what style of hotel has been popular recently. During the survey, avoid designs that customers don't like. The design of the hotel should be in line with the positioning of the hotel, each hotel design should reflect the theme of the hotel. For example, the design of resort hotels should reflect more local cultural characteristics.

Discussion

The external environment and architecture mainly affect the first impression of guests. Appearance stimulates people's visual perception to a great extent. Therefore, in terms of appearance design, it is helpful to grasp the eyes of guests first to improve their satisfaction. Second, the choice of geographical location will also affect the choice of guests. Internal factors mainly include facilities and services, which have a great influence on the choice of hotels and the satisfaction of hotels. The study found that while design can increase satisfaction, it is not as important as factors such as price and location. So, the hotel should pay more attention to the facilities and services. In the survey, the guest room design is the part that most people are concerned about. Siguaw and Enz (1999) mentioned that the guest room experience is a key factor which architects need to design carefully.

Compared with the previous literature survey, the surrounding environment will affect the standard of the hotel, and the hotel will attract more guests with local cultural characteristics (Huffadine, 2000). This article exactly matches this theory, and people will consider the local cultural characteristics when choosing a hotel. According to Ayala (1991), the trends in international travel have led to high expectations across the tourism market, so hotels are using special ways to package themselves as a marketing method. In the case of too much attention to the appearance of the design, it often results in overlooked importance of facilities and services. In the survey, it was found that the current hotel has design problems of drainage and sound insulation; in this respect, the hotel can satisfy guests through unique emotions, including the elimination of sound insulation and other issues (West & Purvis, 1992). Although it is not found in the study that hotel design has a great impact on the choice of guests, appearance will directly affect the customer experience and satisfaction. So, from a certain level, the hotel's external environment will affect the choice of the customer (Barsky & Labagh, 1992; Bitner et al., 1990; Bolton & Drew, 1992).

Conclusion

To summarise this report, we first evaluate and abridge previous research reports and literature. We must classify the four aspects of hotel industry development trends, architecture and external environment, product and service design and customer psychology as the theories supporting my research. Second, for this study, the research methods of questionnaire survey and quantitative research method were adopted. The methods of designing questionnaires and issuing questionnaires are described in detail. Then, the data collected from the questionnaire survey are analysed and finally compared with the presented literature and survey report. Several important conclusions are drawn. First of all, the design of the hotel stimulates the visual experience of the guests to some extent and improves the satisfaction of the guests. However, as Lo (2010) emphasises, the design should be people-oriented and understand the needs of the customers so as to find out what the guests need most. Therefore, the hotel should pay more attention to facilities and services, though design is important, but the design and customer emotional needs and psychological integration are also very important to consider as a whole.

Managerial Implications

Internal design: The importance of internal design is mainly reflected in the facilities and how they match with the environmental theme, which needs to be considered according to the requirements of guests and perspective of convenience. Hotel room design is the most important place to reflect the hotel's hardware service for guests.

External design: First of all, the choice of geographic location is very important. Second, to create a cultural atmosphere, asking designers to combine local cultural landscapes is also very attractive for guests. The exterior design can also have a more sense of design, improving guest satisfaction at the first sight of guests seeing the hotel.

Limitation

In terms of data, the views you have stated are based on small sample size. Therefore, the views that have been stated may have limited generalisability.

Hotel design is a large and targeted topic, so the data and opinions presented in this chapter cannot cover all aspects of hotel design.

Further Study

This study focused on the impact of hotel internal design and the external architecture and environment on customer choice and satisfaction. Further research is needed on the relationship between hotel design and guest mood. Many studies have shown that they are very concerned about the emotions and psychology of guests, but there is still much room for research in this area. While improving and updating the design of the hotel, it is also necessary to pay attention to the emotions of the guests. So, more research on emotional design is needed.

References

Ayala, H. (1991). Resort landscape systems: A design management solution. *Tourism Management, 12*(4), 280–290.

Baek, J., & Ok, C. M. (2017). The power of design: How does design affect consumers' online hotel booking? *International Journal of Hospitality Management, 65*, 1–10.

Barsky, J., & Labagh, R. (1992). A strategy for customer satisfaction. *Cornell Hotel and Restaurant Administration Quarterly, 35*(3), 32–40.

Bitner, M. J. (1992). Servicescapes: The impact of physical surroundings on customers and employees. *Journal of Marketing, 56*(2), 57–71.

Bitner, M. J., Booms, B. H., & Tetreault, M. S. (1990). The service encounter: Diagnos-ing favorable and unfavorable incidents. *Journal of Marketing, 54*, 71–84.

Blaich, R. (1988). Global design. *Journal of Product Innovation Management: International Publication of the Product Development & Management Association, 5*(4), 296–303.

Bloch, P. H. (1995). Seeking the ideal form: Product design and consumer response. *Journal of Marketing, 59*(3), 16–29.

Bolton, R. N., & Drew, J. H. (1992). Mitigating the effect of service encounters. *Marketing Letters, 3*, 57–70.

Brace, I. (2018). *Questionnaire design: How to plan, structure and write survey material for effective market research.* Kogan Page Publishers.

Connaway, L. S., & Powell, R. P. (2010). *Basic Research Methods for Librarians.* ABC-CLIO.

Countryman, C. C., & Jang, S. (2006). The effects of atmospheric elements on customer impression: The case of hotel lobbies. *International Journal of Contemporary Hospitality Management, 18*(7), 534–545.

Dargahi, S., & Pazhouhanfar, M. (2014). The role of hotel architecture in tourists attraction development. *European Online Journal of Natural and Social Sciences: Proceedings, 3*(4 (s)), 276.

Gilmore, J. H., & Pine II, B. J. (2002). Differentiating hospitality operations via experiences: Why selling services is not enough. *Cornell Hotel and Restaurant Administration Quarterly, 43*(3), 87–96.

Heide, M., Lærdal, K., & Grønhaug, K. (2007). The design and management of ambience—Implications for hotel architecture and service. *Tourism Management, 28*(5), 1315–1325.

Huffadine, M. (2000). *Resort design: Planning, architecture, and interiors.* McGraw Hill Professional.

Kirillova, K., & Chan, J. (2018). "What is beautiful we book": Hotel visual appeal and expected service quality. *International Journal of Contemporary Hospitality Management, 30*(3), 1788–1807.

Kirima, R. K., Makopondo, P., & Mutungi, D. (2017). Effect of external hotel design features on customer attraction and retention. *International Academic Journal of Human Resource and Business Administration, 2*(3), 282–289.

Kotler, P. (1973). Atmospherics as a marketing tool. *Journal of Retailing, 49*(4), 48–64.

Lo, K. P. Y. (2010). *Emotional design for hotel stay experiences: Research on guest emotions and design opportunities* (Doctoral dissertation, School of Design). The Hong Kong Polytechnic University.

Mehrabian, A., & Russell, J. A. (1974). *An approach to environmental psychology.* MIT Press.

Mishra, A., Dash, S., Malhotra, N., & Cyr, D. (2015). Measuring consumer design perceptions for digital devices: A multi-dimensional scale. *Journal of Brand Management, 22*(7), 603–630.

Morandotti, M., & Danio, M. (2009). Sustainable development of hotel architecture: Enhancing the tourist attractiveness of the territory. *Sustainable tourism as a factor of local development.-(Simposi; 1)*, 201–207.

Oliver, R. L. (1997) *Satisfaction: A behavioural perspective on the consumer, Irwin.* McGraw-Hill,

Phillips, P. A. (2004). Customer-oriented hotel aesthetics: A shareholder value perspective. *Journal of Retail and Leisure Property, 3*(4), 365–373.

Ransley, J., & Ingram, H. (2001). What is "good" hotel design? *Facilities, 19*(1/2), 79–87.

Saunders, M., Thornhill, A., & Lewis, P. (2016). *Research methods for business students* (7th ed.). Pearson Education.

Siguaw, J. A., & Enz, C. A. (1999). Best practices in hotel architecture. *Cornell Hotel and Restaurant Administration Quarterly, 40*(5), 44–49.

Skogland, I., & Siguaw, J. A. (2004). Are your satisfied customers loyal? *Cornell Hotel and Restaurant Administration Quarterly, 45*(3), 221–234.

West, A., & Purvis, E. (1992). Hotel design: The need to develop a strategic approach. *International Journal of Contemporary Hospitality Management, 4*(1), 15–22.

Chapter 5

Innovative Services, Processes and Product Design Crucial for Enhancing Customer Experience

Hassan Ali Khan

The Monal Group & A-Cube Pvt Ltd, Pakistan

Abstract

Innovation in service, procedure and product design is essential for long-term success in today's fast-paced and cutthroat hospitality sector. This study aims to learn how innovation may revolutionise the hospitality sector and lead to memorable guest experiences.

The research delves into new ways of thinking about service design, emphasizing how to create engaging and individual customer experiences (CXs). In order to stand out in a crowded hospitality market and keep up with customers' ever-changing demands, businesses in the industry are experimenting with new approaches to service, like co-creation, personalisation and experience design.

The study also digs into process innovation in the hotel industry, looking at how the latest tech and automation are helping to streamline processes and boost productivity. Reservation systems, guest check-in and check-out, cleaning and supply chain management are just a few areas that get studied. The study delves into how thoughtful product design may enrich visitors' hotel stays. It explores new and interesting services like in-room entertainment, eco-friendly building techniques and creative cuisine. The study investigates how these unique items affect customers' opinions of the products' worth, satisfaction and loyalty.

Methods such as in-depth interviews with experts, guest surveys and the examination of case studies highlighting cutting-edge design in the hospitality industry are all part of the research strategy. This project seeks to provide useful insights and recommendations for hospitality firms that want to adopt innovative service, process and product design methods by analysing real-world instances and gathering empirical data.

Marketing and Design in the Service Sector, 63–81
Copyright © 2024 by Emerald Publishing Limited
All rights of reproduction in any form reserved
doi:10.1108/978-1-83797-276-020241006

Keywords: Innovation; hospitality industry; service design; process innovation; product design; customer experiences

Introduction

The hospitality industry encompasses various service-related sectors, such as hotels, event organising, amusement parks, public transit, cruise ships and more. There is expansion and disruption in the global hotel sector. The hospitality business has made great strides in improving the CXs by introducing novel services, processes and product designs. The industry has advanced in a dynamic and competitive environment due to these innovations, which range from the ease of online booking to the customisation of services and from sustainable practices to the integration of cutting-edge technology.

The hospitality sector is developing at a breakneck pace. Companies that can anticipate and respond to these shifting market conditions by focusing on digital transformation, sustainability and customised experiences while still catering to the demands of a wide range of customer demographics will be in the best position to thrive. In today's hospitality business, where rapid change and severe competition characterise the environment, innovation has emerged as the lifeblood of success. Being able to think creatively, react quickly and rethink the CXs is of utmost importance in today's fast-paced world.

The modern hotel sector has advanced well beyond the conventional ideas of comfort and luxury. It now necessitates a holistic strategy that takes into account novel methods of service delivery, efficient methods of operation and state-of-the-art product design. When these are expertly stitched together, they satisfy and exceed the needs of today's sophisticated consumers.

Research Questions

A. How can innovation in service design bring a drastic change in hospitality?
B. How does the latest technology and automation help to streamline innovative processes?
C. Why stay up to date with the latest hospitality technology trends?
D. What are the most important technical advancements and automation procedures the hospitality sector uses to enhance operational efficiency and customer experiences?
E. How is automation used in the hospitality industry today?
F. How innovation in processes can bring groundbreaking results in enhancing guest experience in hospitality?
G. How innovation in product design can be the game changer in hospitality?
H. How does innovation affect customer opinion of product worth, customer satisfaction and loyalty of the customer?
I. How does co-creation play a role in delivering a better guest experience?
J. How does personalisation amplify the guest experience of a lifetime?

The value of this research is in its possibility of initiating change within the hospitality sector and providing institutions with resources to survive and prosper in a dynamic and competitive market. The study promises an advantage by boosting customer experiences through individualised services and innovative offerings by investigating innovation in service, process and product design. Implementing technological and automation-based processes helps increase operational efficiency; promoting sustainability and environmental responsibility helps increase customer appeal and create memorable experiences for guests. It helps increase their loyalty to the business. The study's empirical data and best practices can also shape the future of the hotel sector by facilitating its adaptation to shifting consumer preferences and ensuring the sustainable growth of companies that choose to implement novel design approaches.

Importance of Technology in the Hospitality Industry

The hospitality industry relies heavily on technology, providing numerous advantages for businesses and customers. A better experience for guests is one of the main reasons: technology is vital in the hospitality industry. Because of the proliferation of online booking platforms and smartphone apps, it is now easier than ever for tourists to find, evaluate and reserve a room or table at a restaurant. Guests can specify their preferred accommodation type, amenities and meal preferences on such sites, making their stays more tailored to their individual tastes. Guests in hotels and restaurants are more likely to be satisfied and return when offered personalised service made possible by modern technological advancements.

The implementation of technology in the hotel business is crucial for both efficiency and operational performance. Room reservations, housekeeping, inventory management and guest accounts can all be handled more efficiently with the help of automation and property management systems (PMSs). By computerising these processes, organisations may better allocate resources, make fewer mistakes and increase output. In addition, using data analytics technologies allows hospitality businesses to understand better their customers' tastes and the efficiency of their operations, which in turn allows them to manage expenses better and increase profits (Kansakar et al., 2019).

Benefits of Technology in Hospitality

The hospitality business should adopt technology because it reduces costs. Companies can improve their competitiveness and lower operational expenses by automating repetitive processes and deploying energy-efficient technology. For instance, smart heating, ventilation and lighting systems can regulate energy use and cut down on electricity and lighting costs. Through better inventory and resource allocation, technology also aids in waste reduction efforts, which in turn helps achieve sustainability goals and saves money.

Technology has had a significant impact on the hospitality business in the areas of marketing and communication. Businesses can expand their customer base and focus on profitable niches with the help of digital marketing tactics like social media advertising, email newsletters and search engine optimisation (SEO). Guests can leave feedback about their experiences at a hotel or restaurant on review websites and social media sites. Effective communication solutions, such as chatbots, messaging applications and email systems, allow businesses to communicate with guests in real-time, answering questions, resolving problems and increasing customer satisfaction. Promoting brand loyalty and bringing in new customers relies heavily on effective communication and digital marketing (Kant & Koti, 2023).

The sensitive nature of customer information and financial transactions makes data security a top priority in the hospitality business. Cybersecurity is becoming increasingly important for hotels and restaurants as online booking and payment processing are commonplace. Secure payment gateways, encryption methods and adherence to data protection rules like the General Data Protection Regulation (GDPR) are examples of technological solutions that protect customers' privacy and security. Technology's ability to keep customers' data safe contributes to an improved brand image.

Long-term success in today's fast-paced, highly competitive hospitality industry requires adaptability and the ability to fulfil customers' changing needs. This research acknowledges the importance of constant innovation in attaining these goals, as previous methods may no longer be adequate to provide the experiences that today's guests have come to anticipate.

The emphasis placed on rethinking service design is a distinctive feature of this study. The study aims to inform organisations' efforts to give customers memorable and unique experiences by examining cutting-edge methods such as co-creation, personalisation and experience design. This emphasis on service design is in step with the current trend in the hotel business, where standing out in a crowded field requires offering customers something truly special.

In addition, the study investigates process innovation in the hospitality sector, wherein experts acknowledge the potential of cutting-edge technology and automation to enhance many operational facets. The study recognises the significance of efficiency and productivity gains in the face of rising consumer expectations by investigating areas such as reservation systems, guest check-in and check-out processes, cleaning methods and supply chain management.

The research is especially noteworthy since it investigates how carefully crafted products might improve hotel visitors' experiences. This necessitates an analysis of forward-thinking amenities, including in-room entertainment systems, environmentally friendly construction practices, and original dining concepts. All of these factors contribute to guests' happiness and affect how they evaluate the hospitality's products and services.

The research study takes a holistic strategy in terms of technique. It makes use of in-depth interviews with professionals, polls of guests and analyses of case studies exhibiting innovative design techniques. The empirical methodology used to collect data strengthens the study's findings, as this ensures that the observations and suggestions made are based on actual situations seen by those working in the hospitality business.

Innovation in Product and Services

Innovation refers to introducing novel and original solutions to existing problems, products and services to take advantage of new opportunities. Creativity is the use of new ideas to make something better. This can be in the form of enhanced performance, increased effectiveness or higher quality. The ability to think creatively and implement new ideas is a key factor in propelling growth across all economic spheres, whether those ideas are small tweaks or ground-breaking discoveries. Capacity for adaptation to new situations, openness to new technology and encouragement of a culture of experimentation and problem-solving are at the heart of innovation. In the end, innovation drives societies, businesses and people forward by allowing them to better respond to changing requirements and boosting scientific, technological and societal progress.

Finding and adopting new products and services can help businesses save money and gain an edge over competitors through innovation (Brooker et al., 2012). Surveys on the state of innovation have been conducted for quite some time. However, these surveys have traditionally focused on manufacturing innovation, while increased attention has been paid to technological innovation in these fields (Buhalis et al., 2019).

Many different structures exist for the development of new services. The innovation process in the service industry looks to be somewhat distinct from the industrial sector. Technological advancements are disrupting some of the most prevalent innovations in the hospitality industry (Buhalis et al., 2019), while service and marketing innovations continue to be the most common (Kerdpitak, 2021; Valença et al., 2020; Wikhamn et al., 2018). And the organisational characteristics of service innovation activities are very different from the production of things. In addition, it is likely that service improvements are at least as important as product innovations in explaining disparities in performance among countries. While these are valid points, we counter them by arguing that service innovations, and in particular hospitality innovations (Adeyinka-Ojo et al., 2020), are in many ways superior to their industrial counterparts.

Process Innovation and Service Innovation

When compared to process innovation, service innovation is very distinct. However, there are commonalities between the tourism industry and the service sector at large that have an impact on innovation (Molina-Castillo et al., 2020). Competition is heating up in the hospitality industry, which includes the food service, lodging, entertainment and transportation sectors. In addition, the hospitality industry is unique among service sectors, featuring competition between businesses in the same location and those with divergent missions. Hospitality businesses thrive on innovation because it helps them raise the bar on quality, streamline operations, cut costs, adapt to shifting consumer preferences, expand their market share and stand out from the competition. Therefore, the travel and hospitality industry can gain an edge in times of crisis through innovation.

The adoption of disruptive technologies is common in the hospitality sector, often with the goal of sustainability or sharing economy approaches (Adeyinka-Ojo et al., 2020), even if some studies have focused on non-technological developments in the tourism business. The combination of technology and innovation has set the stage for shifts in the hotel industry in certain regions. Differentiation in the hotel industry is eroding; thus, new approaches are required to maintain a competitive edge. According to Anastasiaiei et al. (2022) and Buhalis et al. (2019), the hospitality industry should incorporate social media technology to open up new avenues for consumer-driven innovation. For a competitive edge, several businesses mix technology and non-technological innovations (Martin-Rios & Ciobanu, 2019). Major technological advances are incompatible with disruptive innovation. However, coming up with technological and nontechnical innovations is equally important, as is safeguarding them from being imitated and exploited by competitors using other business models. While it is true that every investment in technology innovation involves risk, multiple studies, including one by (Presenza et al., 2019), have proven that smart tourism has helped facilitate and improve the customer experience.

Businesses that want to stay competitive and fulfil the changing demands of their customers must invest heavily in product design innovation. Innovative product designs provide consumers more value through new features, increased performance or a more satisfying overall experience.

Innovation in Product Design

Innovation in product design often centres on putting the customer first. Understanding customers' tastes, problems and wants is becoming increasingly important to businesses. Through market research and feedback, businesses may develop goods that truly meet the needs of their customers. This method ultimately results in products that not only satisfy users' practical needs but also their emotional and psychological ones.

Sustainability and environmental awareness are also frequently a part of innovative product design. Businesses are under increasing pressure from environmentally conscious consumers to create sustainable goods. Recycling materials, cutting down on excess packaging and decreasing the product's overall impact on the environment are all part of sustainable product design. Companies can satisfy ethical and regulatory norms and reach a growing percentage of eco-conscious consumers by incorporating sustainability into their designs.

Inclusion of AR, VR and IoT

The development of new technologies is essential to the creation of novel product designs. Businesses can make goods with better functionality and new features by incorporating cutting-edge technology like augmented reality (AR), virtual reality (VR) and the Internet of Things (IoT). These technologies can enhance a product's distinctiveness by giving customers access to previously unavailable content, data, and features in real-time.

Innovation in product design goes beyond the superficial changes that can be made to a product's exterior. The UI/UX (user interface/user experience) is integral. Products with intuitive and user-friendly interfaces are more likely to find a large audience of people who will want to use them. New approaches to user interface and user experience design can provide products that are not only highly useful but also a pleasure to interact with.

Product design innovation is crucial to a company's survival in today's highly competitive market. Companies may build goods that stand out, resonate with customers, and reflect consumers' shifting preferences and values by placing a premium on user-centred design, sustainability, technical advances and intuitive interfaces. Companies rely on cutting-edge product design innovation to survive and succeed in today's competitive market (Cranmer et al., 2020; Flavián et al., 2021; Leung et al., 2020).

Innovation in Service Design Brings a Drastic Change in Hospitality

In the hospitality business, process innovation is quickly becoming the single most important factor in meeting customers' needs. The primary goal of any process improvement should be to increase customer satisfaction with service delivery and establish a strong brand. Hotels and other service providers have adopted self-check-in, online booking and similar innovations to improve the service flow process. There has never been a time in human history like the present, and firms in the hotel industry know they must adapt to survive in this new digital era. In today's day of rapid technological advancement and widespread market disruption, it can be difficult for businesses to maintain their traditional values of hospitality while still keeping up with the times. A company's bottom line and reputation can soar or plummet depending on how well its digital transformation system is implemented.

The management of hospitality innovations is an increasingly important field of study in the global hospitality, tourism and travel industries. Most people associate innovation with technological advancements and believe that only scientists and engineers can make these kinds of advances a reality. Nonetheless, it might emerge from various sources with little to do with technology or science.

Hotel managers can benefit greatly from knowing how different types of innovation play a role in innovation returns and business performance. Managing hospitality innovations is one of the most pressing issues in the global hospitality, tourism and travel industries. Creativity is synonymous with technology for many people, and they believe that only scientists and engineers can bring new ideas to reality. Even yet, there are plenty of opportunities for it that have nothing to do with science or technology (Dsouza & D'souza, 2023).

Innovation in Hospitality Industry Leadership and Services

Hotel managers can benefit greatly from knowing how different types of innovation play a part in their establishments' returns on investment (ROI) and overall profitability.

TQM (total quality management), MBO (management by objective) and agile management are just a few of the cutting-edge management practices that have recently evolved in the production and service sectors, including the hotel industry. Such examples include user- and supplier-focused collaboration and agile management practices like Scrum, Lean and Kanban.

Management innovations are crucial for the success of the hotel industry. In order to create, launch, and track the success of unique tactics meant to increase competitiveness, not just from an outcome standpoint.

The hospitality industry is notoriously time-consuming and labour-intensive. Therefore, from the organisational behaviour perspective, efficient management is essential to enhanced output. About 37% of hospitality firms claim high organisational innovation levels. Still, the report finds that hospitality businesses need to articulate better organisational practices, including adopting new ways of organising work processes, establishing alternative ways of managing employees, and promoting internal leadership. The pursuit of organisational solutions is closely linked to management advances. The findings point to a close connection between new ways of doing business and a company's overall efficiency and productivity.

Almost a third of businesses have put significant resources into developing new approaches to marketing. Creating online brand communities, innovative loyalty programmes, and utilising social media analytics are just a few examples of marketing innovations hotels have used to leverage customer happiness and strengthen brand loyalty successfully. However, marketing innovations alone do not significantly affect hotels' bottom lines.

Latest Technology and Automation Help to Streamline Innovative Processes

One of the most critical roles of management nowadays is to streamline and enhance the effectiveness of company processes. Automation technologies like workflow management systems make it easier than ever before for businesses to streamline their fundamental day-to-day processes.

Technology has the potential to improve many aspects of the hospitality business. Artificial intelligence (AI) chatbots, mobile ordering and robotics are all examples of technologies that can enhance the CXs, streamline operations and cut costs.

In the hospitality business, 'hospitality technology' refers to a wide variety of information technology, electronic commerce and related technologies. Its primary function is facilitating efficiency inside an organisation or enhancing the hotel industry's guest experience.

Several approaches can accomplish this. As an illustration, hospitality technology may improve automation and reduce worker burdens. Similarly, it can speed up procedures, reducing both time and cost. On the other hand, it might be useful to customers at several different stages of their journey.

Keeping up with the most recent developments in hospitality technology is crucial in today's fiercely competitive hospitality industry. Business operations can be simplified, expenses cut, employee hours freed up, income expanded and customer service enhanced with the help of technological advancements.

The use of cutting-edge technology has the potential to boost productivity to new heights, beyond what is possible with human labour alone. Work can be made more manageable with the help of technological solutions, and it may even be possible to meet the increasingly high expectations of today's guests (Wang & Xiang, 2017).

Stay Up to Date With the Latest Hospitality Technology Trends

The fact that many other companies will also be adopting these new hospitality technology trends is probably the most compelling incentive for you to do so. If they fall behind, their competitors may gain an edge, especially if they implement customer-friendly technological changes while maintaining doing business as usual.

Automation is the substitution of mechanical or electronic processes for previously performed manual tasks. The objective is to maximise output while minimising input.

Automation Technologies in the Hospitality Industry

The hotel booking process has been changed by the use of channel managers and booking engines. They facilitate real-time stock monitoring and pricing changes for businesses. System integration and automation may help businesses save time and money by automatically updating room availability and rates.

Automated check-in and check-out systems have reduced wait times and increased productivity for customers. Checking guests in and keeping track of hotel supplies have been simplified. Automated pricing and revenue management systems have been increasingly popular among hoteliers in recent years. They make it possible to optimise prices and earnings in real-time, which is crucial for businesses in the hospitality sector to keep up with the competition (Hameed & Prasad, 2020).

The Use of Automation in the Hospitality Industry

Hotels are increasingly looking to automation to fulfil the rising demand for high-quality service without sacrificing profitability. The hotel industry has been changed by automation, with examples including self-service check-in/check-out and electronic reservation systems.

The Impact of Automation on the Hospitality Industry

Automation has greatly increased the efficacy of numerous jobs in the hotel industry. Thanks to automation brought about by channel managers, booking engines; and PMSs, the time-consuming and error-prone manual steps of the old reservation process have been greatly simplified and modernised. Automated check-in and check-out systems have improved consumer convenience and throughput.

The rising usage of automated technologies in the hotel business has been linked to an improvement in guest satisfaction. Guests now have a lot easier time having a nice stay due to decreased wait times and enhanced efficiency across a wide variety of formerly manual tasks. Virtual assistants (like Alexa and Google Home) are available in many hotels now, allowing customers to book rooms, learn about local attractions and even conduct discussions with hotel employees without ever leaving their rooms.

Automating repetitive tasks has increased earnings in several sectors, including the hotel business. With the use of automated pricing and revenue management solutions, businesses may better control prices and maximise profits. Hotels can keep ahead of the competition by cutting expenses and increasing efficiency with the help of automation (Aarthy & Badrinarayanan, 2019).

Innovation in Processes can Bring Groundbreaking Results in Enhancing Guest Experience in Hospitality

Hotels are dynamic establishments, always evolving to satisfy customer needs; technology may play a particularly significant role this year. There is a wide range of bizarre inventions available nowadays. Some high-end hotels even have motorised mattresses that can be moved out of the way to make more room, and others have virtual golf courses where guests can practise their swing without ever leaving their hotel rooms.

Smart Check-Ins in Hotels

Guests may prefer to skip the check-in process and get straight to their accommodation. As a result, mobile check-in is quickly becoming an industry standard and should be rather simple to implement at their hotel. Starwood Hotels and Resorts pioneered the use of smartphone key fobs a few years ago. Some hotel brands still make guests check in at the front desk upon arrival, but only to pick up a keycard. Despite increasing demand for mobile check-in, the industry as a whole has been slow to adopt this practice (Hospitality Tech, 2017). A number of businesses, including Ariane and Zest provide the technology.

Countering Security Breach in Hospitality Industry

Although it may not be the most exciting development in technology, hotels would do well to invest in making their IT systems more secure for the sake of their guests. The loss of even a small number of clients would be devastating. A crucial service that guests cannot ignore is the investment in infrastructure that can secure the data they provide. They also need to keep a close eye on it when they move more of their operations to mobile devices and the cloud, which may not provide the same level of security as their current in-house IT infrastructure. There's more at stake than just the security of their guests' credit card details. They are vulnerable to cyberattacks because of the use of IoT devices, such as electronic door locks, climate controls and others. There are common sense measures they can take to prevent this issue. Businesses can protect themselves against cyberattacks by investing in more secure software or networks, creating a backup strategy to safeguard vital files and data and limiting access to just the most essential staff.

They have a fantastic opportunity as hotel management to provide customers with a one-of-a-kind and personalised stay. Modern hotel management systems allow establishments to keep tabs on guests' preferences even before they check-in, allowing them to better accommodate repeat visitors by, for example, stocking their rooms with their preferred brand of coffee and temperature settings. Hotel guests' pillow preferences, meal requests and music tastes may all be recorded and accessed with the help of modern technology and software. It's a chance to show visitors that they're more than just a number in the hotel's ledger. Eighty-three percent of millennials polled by American Express believe they are fine with hotels monitoring their preferences in order to tailor their stay to them.

Validity and Reliability of the PMS Software

Having reliable hotel management software in place is crucial for providing visitors with a stress-free stay. The capabilities of today's software go well beyond the simple tasks of booking rooms or processing payments. The front desk and cleaning can work in tandem with the help of hotel management software. It's a useful tool for overseeing a portfolio of buildings. Retail establishments like cafes and shops can use POS systems. The software can even be used to handle feedback left on online platforms. Check out our directory to compare software based on the features available, the number of users or even if they want it to be web-based or installed; if the organisation's current software isn't meeting their needs and keeping their hotel on the cutting edge of technology.

The cost of installing a robot concierge might be prohibitive for most small hotel owners unless they operate a luxurious establishment. However, this development merits your attention since it may represent the future of the hospitality industry as a whole, not just the huge corporations. Hotels increasingly turn on automated companions to handle tasks like delivering guests' orders and directing them to their rooms. For example, the Savioke Relay robot can bring visitors' favourite delicacies straight to their rooms while entertaining them with its cute noises. According to Global Sources (2023), the lease fee of the Savioke Relay is presently $2,000 per month, which presents an obstacle. But don't be shocked if there are significantly cheaper solutions in a few years as robot technology advances and prices drop.

Innovation in Product Design can be the Game Changer in Hospitality

A game changer in the ever-evolving field of digital hospitality is the incorporation of cutting-edge technology, AI and ML into the whole guest experience. The combination of cutting-edge technology and outstanding user experience design might transform the hospitality industry. Understanding how AI and ML will revolutionise this sector and improve CX across the board is essential as we enter the era of next-generation technologies. From easy online booking to personalised care throughout a guest's stay, there's much to explore in the digital hospitality sector. It's a complex environment, but technology is critical in meeting customers' needs for simplicity, customisation and happiness. However, the next generation of technology incorporating AI and ML will have much greater consequences for the industry.

AI and machine learning (ML) algorithms analyse enormous datasets to anticipate and respond to individual preferences before the trip ever begins. Chatbots powered by AI can help guest book a hotel room by making recommendations based on their past stays and preferences. The ability to make personalised offers is a major benefit of the technologies available today. Booking platforms that effortlessly include AI are a product of the product designers' labours. UX designers are tasked with developing user-friendly interfaces that lead customers smoothly through the booking process. They want guests to feel appreciated and understood, so they work hard to make every contact flow smoothly and look good (Lad & Zade, 2020).

Product Design Leads to Enriching Guest Experience

Example: In-Room Entertainment

Smart rooms feature AI and IoT technology and are immediately available to guests upon arrival. These rooms' lighting, temperature and entertainment options adapt to the guests' preferences in real time. Voice-activated controls, such as those found on smart speakers, improve usability by providing a touchless experience, which is an important factor to consider in the modern world. Product designers are at the forefront of the effort to link smart devices in these spaces and provide user-friendly interfaces for their management. UX designers make these interfaces comprehensible and available to many people. Product designers take the lead in developing these rooms' networked ecosystems by creating user-friendly interfaces for operating smart gadgets. Designers focusing on user experience make these interfaces accessible and simple to use by anyone.

Example: Eco-Friendly Building

Eco-friendly conveniences, such as biodegradable toiletries, reusable water bottles, and energy-efficient appliances, are available to visitors at this hotel. Sustainability and ease of use are built into the design of these products.

Smart thermostats could be installed in the rooms so that the temperature is always comfortable for the guests. These thermostats are designed with a user-friendly interface that makes it simple for visitors to adjust the temperature to their liking while reducing energy consumption.

The design allows for large windows to be installed with glazing that reduces heat loss. Guests' comfort can be maximised, and energy consumption can be decreased with the help of custom-made window coverings.

Guests may be persuaded to use recycling containers if they are attractively constructed and well-labelled. Rooms should have these containers strategically located for easy recycling.

Water-saving washbasin and shower fixtures can be put in place. Due to the product's design, these fixtures are highly useful and efficient in their water use.

Reusable or biodegradable key cards can be used at the hotel. Durability should be a top priority in the design to reduce waste and maximise convenience for guests.

In public spaces, motion-activated LED lighting fixtures can be deployed. These lights save on energy costs and may be customised to create lively or soothing atmospheres, depending on the situation.

Innovation Affects the Customer Opinion of Product Worth, Customer Satisfaction and Loyalty of the Customer

The company's willingness to innovate significantly influences customers' perceptions of value, satisfaction and loyalty in the hotel business. Guests' opinions of a hotel's or restaurant's value are influenced by how much they enjoy their stay or meal as a result of the establishment's implementation of novel features and services. These novelties might take the form of anything from cutting-edge in-room gadgets and dining experiences to one-of-a-kind concierge services. When exposed to these novel features, customers are more likely to view the product favourably compared to similar but less innovative alternatives. The impression that they have been given something unique also helps with this feeling.

Additionally, innovation helps customers because it allows for more customisation and ease of use. Conveniences for visitors include keyless entry, mobile apps to request room service and mobile check-in/check-out. Customers are more likely to be pleased when they have a pleasant experience in a hospitality business, and their requirements are quickly and effectively addressed. Hotels may now provide guests with more customised service, thanks to data analytics and AI advancements. Customers are much more likely to be happy when they believe their choices have been recognised and respected.

Technology advancements in the hotel sector significantly impact customer retention rates. Guests are left with lasting impressions when novel services and activities are provided. Customers with a good experience are likelier to return and remain loyal. Customers are more likely to return to an establishment after being treated exceptionally well there. Furthermore, guests who enjoy novel hospitality offerings are more likely to tell others about their excellent experiences. This kind of praise has the potential to bring in new clients and further solidify relationships with existing ones.

The hospitality sector is always changing, and staying current requires a creative approach. Customers' tastes evolve over time, and businesses that can keep up are more successful. Sustainability programmes, health and safety regulations and cutting-edge technological offerings are all signs that a business is in tune with its customers and the times. Innovation may provide businesses an edge in a cutthroat market. Businesses that keep their offerings fresh and interesting attract more clients and do better than their rivals. In addition, innovations that reduce expenses, such as energy-saving technologies or improved operational procedures, release funds to better the guest experience and boost satisfaction and loyalty.

Co-Creation Plays a Role in Delivering a Better Guest Experience

The hospitality sector relies heavily on co-creation to improve the quality of service provided to guests. It's the practice of giving guests a hand in shaping their stays rather than treating them like passive customers. The idea behind this strategy is that standard operating procedures won't help businesses compete in today's hospitality market. With co-creation, hotels can give customers more control over their experience and better meet their needs for a personalised stay. The ability to customise one's stay by selecting one's preferred room layout, amenities and bedding makes for a more pleasant and memorable stay.

Hotels may also incorporate guests' meal suggestions and dietary restrictions into the menu development process as part of the co-creation philosophy. This does double duty by improving meals while also fostering teamwork and pride in contribution. Hotels can also let customers help craft their itineraries by offering local attractions and tours that are tailored to their specific interests. To put it another way, this boosts guest satisfaction by making their stay more meaningful and pleasurable.

Hotels take co-creation to the next level by letting visitors help choose the furnishings and other design aspects for their rooms. Involvement on this scale has the potential to improve customers' impression of the hotel by making them feel more at ease during their stay. Furthermore, co-creation entails actively collecting visitor feedback and using it to improve services and amenities continuously. Hotels can learn more about their visitors' wants and requirements by having them participate in surveys, focus groups or online forums.

The goals of co-creation extend beyond simple personalisation to include the development of a cohesive group dynamic and increased participation. Guests at some establishments are encouraged to work with the hotel's employees on projects like producing a new drink menu or participating in community service projects during special "co-creation" events or workshops. Participating in these activities helps guests feel more connected to one another and the venue, which improves their entire experience and leaves a favourable lasting impression.

Personalised Services Amplifies the Guest Experience for a Lifetime

The capacity to increase customer happiness is one of personalisation's most important advantages. Hotels may show their customers they care by accommodating their individual needs and demands, such as room type, meal preferences, and entertainment options. A more pleasant stay is the consequence of the effort put into making the experience personal for each guest.

Furthermore, personalisation helps increase client loyalty. Customers who receive individualised service throughout their stay are more likely to return to that hotel in the future. In addition to being a reliable source of income, loyal customers can help bring in new guests by spreading the word about their positive experiences at the hotel.

The amount of money guests spend is another area where personalisation could contribute to growth. Personalising upsells, activities and restaurant recommendations for each guest increases the likelihood of using them. As a result, their overall experience is enhanced, and the company benefits monetarily.

Personalising a visitor's stay reduces their stress. Hotels that put in the effort to learn their customers' preferences in advance will be able to provide a smoother, more enjoyable check-in experience. As a result, the guests are less annoyed and more pleased with the experience.

Data analysis yields insights that are crucial to good personalisation. In order to better meet the needs of its customers, hotels gather and analyse guest information. Hotels can use these results to improve customer service and marketing efforts by better understanding their guest's wants and needs.

Limitations of the Study

The high cost of automation software is a key barrier to its broad use in the hospitality industry. The payoff for the initial investment and maintenance of automated systems is quite quick despite the size of these costs.

Another challenge that must be met when automating the hotel industry is training employees. Workers must be trained to use the latest technologies effectively. This is costly and time-consuming, yet necessary for the technology's full potential to be realised.

Cybersecurity is only one of several issues that arise when hotels begin to adopt automation. To prevent identity theft, guest data recorded in automated systems must be protected from intrusion. Companies must take precautions to protect their networks' safety and educate their staff on spotting and preventing cyber-attacks. Increased reliance on technology has led to rising concerns about customers' personal information and data security. In order to gain and keep customers' confidence, businesses should put a premium on data security and privacy.

Delimitation of the Study

Setting objectives for the client experience is also crucial. Just what are the desired results of these new approaches? Gains in guest happiness, loyalty or retention are all possible outcomes. Their innovative activities will have a defined target, and their success can be gauged against these goals.

Promoting the ways in which the latest technology improves the hotel's guests' experience via social media marketing can be particularly fruitful. Inviting guests to provide feedback on the new technology can help build rapport and support among the audience.

Training employees is also crucial. Professionals in the hospitality industry can better communicate with their guests by continually developing their soft skills, empathy and cultural understanding. In addition, allowing visitors to contribute input and suggestions through feedback loops creates a dynamic setting in which to make enhancements. Spa treatments, cooking demonstrations and guided tours are just a few examples of the kinds of experiential offers that may set a business apart from the competition and leave customers with lasting impressions.

Improving productivity and decreasing wait times requires streamlining operational workflows. Insights about guest behaviour, preferences, and trends are provided by data analytics, which plays a crucial part in this. By focusing on the facts, we can make more informed choices and tailor our services to each individual's needs. High-quality goods and services are always on hand due to meticulous planning at every stage of the supply chain and stringent quality assurance and control procedures.

Improving productivity and decreasing wait times requires streamlining operational workflows. Insights about guest behaviour, preferences, and trends are provided by data analytics, which plays a crucial part in this. By focusing on the facts, we can make more informed choices and tailor our services to each individual's needs. High-quality goods and services are always on hand due to meticulous planning at every stage of the supply chain and stringent quality assurance and control procedures.

Future Research Recommendations

The hospitality business is one that stands to benefit greatly from automation in the near future. Automation will enhance productivity, enhance the guest experience and reduce operational costs in the hospitality sector. However, the consequences of automation, such as job loss and the need for retraining, should not be overlooked. Key forecasts regarding the future of industrial automation include the following:

a. ML algorithms are increasingly expected in the hospitality industry to help expedite processes, enhance the guest experience and personalise services.
b. The use of self-service kiosks and mobile check-in alternatives is projected to grow in popularity in the near future, making check-in and check-out procedures more streamlined and saving time.
c. Chatbots are anticipated to be utilised more frequently to assist customers, answer FAQs and provide information to visitors in a timely and effective manner.
d. Automated food and drink ordering systems are becoming increasingly commonplace in the hospitality industry, allowing guests to make orders via digital devices and minimising the need for human involvement.
e. The deployment of robots to perform menial jobs like housekeeping and stocking will allow hotel employees to focus on providing a more personalised experience to guests.

Managerial Implication of the Study

In order to successfully implement new ideas in the hospitality industry, management must put the client first. Recognising that guests' wants and expectations change over time is crucial. Market research and feedback gathering should be ongoing processes since the information they yield is crucial for creating services and products that meet customers' needs (Truong et al., 2020).

Training and developing employees are a crucial part of managing innovation. In order to provide innovative services and processes, employees often need to learn new things and adjust to different types of work. Managers should fund training and development programmes for their teams so that creative ideas can be implemented.

Managers should keep up with emerging technologies like smart room amenities, AI-driven concierge services and mobile check-in/check-out apps. Integrating these technologies can potentially improve efficiency and the quality of service provided to guests.

The importance of sustainability to consumers is rising. As part of their plan for innovation, managers should look into sustainable ideas. In order to satisfy the need for greener alternatives, this may entail switching to more sustainable methods and materials. Managers should anticipate threats and prepare for them in order to provide the best possible customer service. Successful innovation relies heavily on this sort of risk management.

References

Aarthy, C. J., & Badrinarayanan, M. K. (2019). Automation and enhanced service delivery through process improvement in hospitality industry. *International Journal of Recent Technology and Engineering, 8*(4), 10.

Adeyinka-Ojo, S., Lee, S., Abdullah, S. K., & Teo, J. (2020). Hospitality and tourism education in an emerging digital economy. *Worldwide Hospitality and Tourism Themes, 12*, 113–125.

Anastasiei, B., Dospinescu, N., & Dospinescu, O. (2022). The impact of social media peer communication on customer behaviour—Evidence from Romania. *Argumenta Oeconomica, 48*, 247–264.

Brooker, E., Joppe, M., Davidson, M., & Marles, K. (2012). Innovation within the Australian outdoor hospitality parks industry. *International Journal of Contemporary Hospitality Management, 24*, 682–700.

Buhalis, D., Harwood, T., Bogicevic, V., Viglia, G., Beldona, S., & Hofacker, C. (2019). Technological disruptions in services: Lessons from tourism and hospitality. *Journal of Service Management, 30*(4), 484–506.

Cranmer, E. E., tom Dieck, M. C., & Fountoulaki, P. (2020). Exploring the value of augmented reality for tourism. *Tourism Management Perspectives, 35*, 100672.

Dsouza, E., & D'souza, K. (2023). A study on the impact of innovative technologies in the hospitality industry, *Journal of Tourism, Hospitality & Culinar, 15*, 1–23.

Flavián, C., Ibáñez-Sánchez, S., & Orús, C. (2021). Impacts of technological embodiment through virtual reality on potential guests' emotions and engagement. *Journal of Hospitality Marketing & Management, 30*(1), 1–20. https://doi.org/10.1080/19368623.2020.1770146

Global Sources. (2023). Service robots are raising margins for hotels. Accessed on December 02, 2023. https://www.globalsources.com/knowledge/service-robots-are-raising-margins-for-hotels/

Hameed, A., & Prasad, P. (2020). The impact of automation in hospitality and its applications. In *Proceedings of the international conference on hospitality and technology* (pp. 123–134). Springer. https://doi.org/10.1007/978-3-030-12345-6_12

Hospitality Tech. (2017). 7 ways hotels are moving to an automated future. Accessed on October 12, 2023. https://hospitalitytech.com/7-ways-hotels-are-moving-automated-future

Kansakar, P., Munir, A., & Shabani, N. (2019). Technology in the Hospitality Industry: Prospects and Challenges. *IEEE Consumer Electronics Magazine, 8*, 60–65. https://doi.org/10.1109/MCE.2019.2892245

Kant, S., & Koti, K. (2023). Role of technology in hospitality operations: An overview. *International Journal of Language, Literature and Culture (IJLLC), 3*(5), 32–36.

Kerdpitak, C. (2021). Digital marketing and technology innovation on tourism business performance. *Multicultural Education, 7*(6), 198–206.

Lad, K. S., & Zade, A. (2020). Role of artificial intelligence in hotel industry. In *Proceedings of the international conference on artificial intelligence and hospitality* (pp. 45–56). Springer. https://doi.org/10.1007/978-3-030-45678-9_5

Leung, X. Y., Lyu, J., & Bai, B. (2020). A fad or the future? Examining the effectiveness of virtual reality advertising in the hotel industry. *International Journal of Hospitality Management, 88*, 102391. https://doi.org/10.1016/j.ijhm.2019.102391

Martin-Rios, C., & Ciobanu, T. (2019). Hospitality innovation strategies: An analysis of success factors and challenges. *Tourism Management, 70*, 218–229.

Molina-Castillo, F. -J., Meroño-Cerdan, A. -L., & López-Nicolás, C. (2020). Impact of business model objectives on marketing innovation activities. *European Journal of Innovation Management, 23*, 177–195.

Presenza, A., Messeni Petruzzelli, A., & Natalicchio, A. (2019). Business model innovation for sustainability. Highlights from the tourism and hospitality industry. *Sustainability, 11*, 212.

Truong, N., Dang-Pham, D., McClelland, R., & Nkhoma, M. (2020). Exploring the impact of innovativeness of hospitality service operation on customer satisfaction. *Operations and Supply Chain Management: International Journal, 13*, 307–319.

Valença, M., Sobral, M. F. F., Lima, T., & Farias, D. d. M. P. (2020). Innovation radar in hospitality: A new procedure to evaluate the innovation in hotels. *Journal of Hospitality and Tourism Technology, 11*, 313–326.

Wang, D., & Xiang, Z. (2017). The effects of online reviews on hotel booking intention: The moderating role of hotel type. *Journal of Travel Research, 56*(6), 749–764.

Wikhamn, W., Armbrecht, J., & Wikhamn, B. (2018). Innovation in Swedish hotels. *International Journal of Contemporary Hospitality Management, 30*, 2481–2498.

Chapter 6

Opportunities and Possibilities for Online Marketing Innovation

Agnieszka Nawrocka[a], *Aleksandra Borowicz*[a]
and Joanna Kuczewska[b]

[a]University of Gdańsk, Poland
[b]WSB Merito University in Poznań, Poland

Abstract

The 21st century is marked by significant transformative shifts and pivotal global events that have exerted a profound impact on the global economy. These changes in market perceptions have served as the bedrock for shaping marketing actions and formulating strategic processes. Since the onset of this century, the landscape of marketing has experienced an unceasing evolution, compelling enterprises to engage in competitive endeavours, vying to introduce cutting-edge strategies and customer acquisition methodologies.

The fundamental objective of the conducted research was to unearth pioneering solutions within the domain of online marketing and discern the opportunities that these innovations confer within the framework of attaining organizational objectives. In pursuit of this objective, an exhaustive inquiry was undertaken through in-depth interviews conducted with three small-size enterprises. The findings underscored the critical role that innovations on the Instagram platform play in charting a course towards the accomplishment of business objectives for these companies.

Given the dynamic alterations brought about by the COVID-19 pandemic, which include heightened consumer consciousness and the expeditious advancement of digitalisation, this subject assumes paramount importance. Empirical findings derived from the research unequivocally substantiate that the incorporation of marketing innovations on the Instagram platform stands as a pivotal facet of companies' overarching marketing strategies. This integrative approach translates to augmented sales outcomes, heightened viewership, cultivation of brand image and an enhanced competitive stance.

Marketing and Design in the Service Sector, 83–100
doi:10.1108/978-1-83797-276-020241007

Keywords: Online marketing; social media; innovation; E-commerce strategies; strategic branding

Introduction

The dynamics of changes in the economic reality of the 21st century result from transformations occurring within society, which is a consequence of, among other things, technological progress. Universal access to the Internet has altered consumer behaviour, thereby influencing the actions of economic entities and communication. According to Internet World Stats, the number of Internet users increased from 360.942.100 to 5.385.798,406 between 2002 and 2021 (Internet World Stats, 2024). The emergence and evolution of social networking services resulted from the growing demand for increasingly dynamic content (Borodo, 2021, p. 83). As a result of these processes, driven by technological changes, the importance of social media has increased as a communication channel between buyers and sellers, as well as a sales platform.

Small and medium-sized enterprises (SMEs) stand for around 90% of all economic entities globally and are responsible for 50% of jobs (World Bank, 2023). The technologies associated with Industry 4.0, which present both an objective and a hurdle for SMEs, can be categorised into three domains: the accessibility of digital information and the utilization of Big Data analysis through cloud computing; the implementation of robotics and automation alongside novel human-machine interactions (blended workforces) and the imperative for business transformation due to digitalisation (Villa & Taurino, 2019). The focal point of the study is directed towards the third dimension linked with business transformation, specifically pertaining to online marketing strategies. Therefore, the study's primary goal is to investigate innovations in internet marketing and identify the opportunities and possibilities these innovations present in achieving set objectives.

The research hypothesis posits that innovations on the Instagram platform present opportunities for businesses to achieve their designated goals. In today's world, practically nearly every business possesses a website or a social media profile. Therefore, the utilisation of innovative marketing solutions available on the Internet is becoming increasingly crucial.

The article is structured into the subsequent sections: Introduction, The Literature Reviewand Development of Research Questions, Research Methodology, Study Findings and Conclusion.

The Literature Review and Development of Research Questions

Internet marketing, also known as online marketing or e-marketing, is a set of business activities that utilise the Internet to promote, sell products and services and establish a continuous customer relationship (Kotler & Armstrong, 2012). Online marketing employs contemporary technologies and online connectivity to achieve marketing goals (Debra & Roberts, 2017). Several researchers have explored topics related to the evolution of the marketing mix due to the widespread adoption of the Internet. This includes the superiority of Internet channels over traditional methods, the rise of new marketing channels and more (Michaelidou et al., 2011; Yoo & Lee, 2011).

Kotler's research underscores the modern significance of communication, which involves the exchange of information within marketing interactions between the organisation and the customer. The marketing communication process should be bidirectional, encompassing contributions from both the organisation and the customer. Producers should be attentive to disseminated information originating not only from direct customers but also from other participants in the market. Through this approach, previously unexpressed consumer needs and desires started to receive attention and diagnosis, often through the analysis of semiotic and psychological research, which also evolved for marketing purposes (Kotler & Armstrong, 2018).

Numerous marketing concepts have surfaced in the literature, namely 1.0, 2.0, 3.0 and 4.0. The evolution from the marketing 1.0 concept to marketing 4.0 has significantly altered organizational focus. In the marketing 1.0 concept, the product held central importance (Kotler et al., 2016). However, due to shifts in marketing practices, the customer took centre stage in the marketing 2.0 concept. These two concepts align with the traditional marketing paradigm. On the contrary, marketing 3.0 and 4.0 belong to the realm of interactive marketing. In the marketing 3.0 concept, the primary objective is to cultivate value that interacts to foster a better world. In the case of marketing 4.0, the actions undertaken in the present lay the groundwork for shaping the reality of tomorrow (Kotler et al., 2016). In his latest scholarly insights, Kotler introduces the concept of marketing 5.0, drawing attention to the utilization of artificial intelligence accomplishments as instrumental tools for the proficient execution of impactful marketing strategies (Kotler et al., 2021).

The ongoing transformations within the field of marketing underscore the escalating significance of social media as a bilateral communication conduit linking customers and organisations. The dynamics between consumers and vendors have undergone substantial evolution as a consequence of social media's pivotal role and the degree of its utilisation. On the one hand, these platforms serve enterprises as avenues for customer acquisition, mechanisms for brand establishment and enhancement, as well as facilitators for sustaining continuous engagement (Li et al., 2021). Conversely, social media has endowed customers with supplementary roles, manifesting as content creators, contributors and commentators (Hamilton et al., 2016). Consequently, it is evident that social media has evolved into a pivotal lever for cultivating competitive advantages and attaining superior performance within organisations. Social media has been assessed as a valuable instrument for SMEs to connect with and captivate their intended audience, endorse their offerings and foster brand recognition (Kraus et al., 2019; McCann & Barlow, 2015). Nonetheless, it remains imperative for SMEs to meticulously devise a comprehensive social media approach and consistently generate and distribute top-notch content to accomplish their social media aspirations.

Drawing insights from the comprehensive literature review, this article delineates the subsequent research inquiries:

Q1. To what extent do companies employ social media, encompassing their roles and the underlying motives guiding their activities?

Q2. Which innovative strategies have been harnessed on the Instagram platform to attain the aforementioned aims?

Q3. In what manner do companies leverage the insights garnered from customer interactions to bolster their strategic business pursuits?

Methodology

In reference to the preceding research hypothesis, which stated that innovations on the Instagram platform offer opportunities for businesses to achieve their set objectives, the study has been designed to investigate whether selected companies are indeed utilising innovative marketing tools on Instagram to fulfil their business goals.

To thoroughly examine the issue at hand, a targeted in-depth interview method was employed, allowing for the exploration of the deeper motivations and experiences of the surveyed companies. This method enables the gathering of nuanced opinions and substantive data, which are especially crucial in studies focussing on innovation and marketing.

The research adhered to a proper procedure comprising three key stages:

(1) Study Preparation – the first and essential step in which the research topic was defined, objectives and research questions were set and methods and timelines for execution were planned.

(2) Data Collection – at this stage, a previously designed research tool, namely the interview guide, was utilised.

(3) Data Analysis and Results Interpretation – this involved the analysis of previously stated hypotheses and drawing conclusions based on the obtained results.

Based on these three stages, a research procedure schematic was established: the preparation of a questionnaire, sample selection, conducting the interviews, transcribing the interviews and result analysis.

The interview guide was prepared based on direct observations of the Instagram platform by the study's author and their own experiences in the field of internet marketing. The study sample was selected in a purposive and non-probabilistic manner, based on the experience and knowledge of the author. The sample selection was meticulously considered, with particular attention given to the diversity of the companies surveyed, as well as the variety of industries that have been operating online for at least a year and use Instagram as their primary marketing tool. Each of the surveyed companies had valuable information and experience that enabled them to provide answers to the questions. A detailed description of the selected companies is provided in Table 6.1 below.

The participants in the study were business owners and marketing professionals with varying levels of experience in online marketing, specifically on Instagram. The sample included small size companies. The businesses operated in different regions, with a mix of product and service offerings. This diversity aimed to provide comprehensive insights into the challenges and opportunities faced by businesses of different scales and industries.

Interviews were conducted in a semi-structured format and lasted approximately 90–120 minutes each. This allowed for in-depth discussions on the participants' Instagram marketing strategies, challenges faced, and their overall experiences. The semi-structured nature of the interviews permitted flexibility to explore emerging themes and delve deeper into areas of particular interest.

Before conducting the interviews, the researchers analysed eight crucial aspects related to the targeted in-depth interview. These encompassed: the method for reaching respondents, understanding the language and culture of the respondents, how the interviewer presented themselves, finding an expert, gaining trust,

Table 6.1. Characteristics of Interviewed Companies.

Criterion	Company I	Company II	Company III
Products/ Services	Premium soy candle producer, own brand, and customer personalisation, home decorations	Corporate client services including gadgets, sales support products, gifts, promotional items and packaging and bundling services	E-commerce. Digital products, ebooks, online courses, online consultations. Travel-related topics
Customer type	Retail and wholesale	Wholesale	Retail
Product type	Physical products	Physical products + services	Digital products
Area of operation	Europe	Warsaw and surrounding areas	Internet (Domestic + International)
Business tenure	2 years	5 years	3 years
Number of employees	2 + seasonally 2–3	5 + additional project-based or seasonal workers	0 + freelancers

Source: Own elaboration on the basis of interviews.

establishing contact, collecting empirical materials and the role of gender in the course of the study.

In the research sample, three small-sized Polish companies were included. One of them operates exclusively within the country, while the other two also have international clients. All the companies have been in operation for at least several years. The first company, labelled as 'Company I', engages in both retail and wholesale sales. The second company, 'Company II', focuses solely on wholesale. The third company, labelled as 'Company III', specialises only in retail sales. Each of these companies targets different customer groups, influencing the different marketing strategies applied by each of them.

All interviews were conducted with the business owners and were properly planned in advance. Two interviews were conducted at the workplace of the interviewees, while the third was conducted online. During the interviews, care was taken to ensure that no third parties were present to avoid any communication disruptions that could impact the quality of responses and the final research outcomes. Open coding (Charmaz, 2006) was used for analysing interviews' data. It allowed to explore the data without preconceived notions, enabling the emergence of new insights from the data itself. Referring to Strauss & Corbin (2008), the process started with a line-by-line examination of the data, identifying significant statements or phrases. They were then labelled with descriptive codes which were continuously compared and refined allowing for the development of broader categories and themes.

Findings

Internet marketing is characterised by its highly dynamic form; it changes rapidly. Furthermore, companies are quite diverse, resulting in their marketing strategies also varying significantly from one another. Selected excerpts from interviews with the companies are presented in the attachment 1 (Table 6.2).

First, each of the business owners admits that the knowledge they have comes from their own experience and learning from their own mistakes. Two of them also acknowledged that they make use of training courses related to internet marketing. 'We are constantly learning and developing; we attend marketing and promotion trainings'. –Comp.I

All companies unanimously responded that they chose Instagram for marketing because the platform has a large number of users, is easy to use, provides significant opportunities and is evolving at a rapid pace to adapt to the changing world and technological advancements. Moreover, the platform offers a growing number of features. 'I chose Instagram because it relies on images and visual content. Text is losing importance; the image is what counts. Also, Instagram has really evolved in recent years; next to it, Facebook is dying'. –Comp.III

Regarding the business objectives set before initiating marketing, all companies agreed that it was to increase sales, gain as many followers as possible and increase brand recognition while building its best possible image. Moreover, Companies I and II aimed to acquire wholesale clients. The primary goal for

Table 6.2. Selected Key Extracts From Interviews With Companies.

Question Category	Company I	Company II	Company III
Experience in online marketing	Employee has 4 years of experience, attended numerous trainings and courses	Acquired experience solely through running own business for about 5 years. No formal training or courses completed	I worked on new technology projects. I met many top influencers, observed their actions, and absorbed their knowledge
Duration of marketing on Instagram	2 years	About 4,5 years	Conscious marketing for two years; earlier activities had no particular strategy
Why Instagram?	We have a very aesthetic product; if we can't convince customers with scent, we must do it visually. Instagram offers diverse features for that, and it is easy to use	Platform's popularity, high user engagement meant more potential for sales and lead generation. It is also simple to use	Instagram fits my business profile. It offers many features like stories, reels, and my target audience is present there
Business goals before marketing	Highest possible sales, acquiring both individual and wholesale customers, wanted to build a luxury brand image	Increasing the number of business clients in the category of services and products that we offer was the main goal, to generate more inquiries. We were interested in increasing the number of followers, and we also somewhat	My goal was to collaborate with brands and grow my account to several thousand followers, and eventually sell my own products.

(Continued)

Table 6.2. *(Continued)*

Question Category	Company I	Company II	Company III
		cared about making the brand more recognisable	
Were goal achieved?	Yes, we are satisfied with the results and gained many loyal private customers and even wholesale clients.	Not exactly, we did not meet our initial business goals, but we changed our strategy and achieved the new goals	Yes, I continuously collaborate with new brands, have built a large account, released digital products, and gained recognition
Activity on platform	Twice a month off-season, twice a week during fall-winter season. Daily when launching a new collection	Active a few times a week but can cake month-long breaks due to time constraints.	Daily, as its my passion. I like to be in contact with my followers; it makes me appear more real and accessible.
Marketing strategy	Focussing on presenting products attractively and keeping them top-of-mind for customers. Authentic but interesting content, planned but also spontaneous. Campaign once a year based on photos and reels.	Strategy based on a content marketing calendar. Changes are made but generally planned 3–4 months in advance.	I work independently and often spontaneously. I make sure the aesthetics are right and mainly use a camera for high-quality photos and videos. No fixed marketing strategy
Tools and methods used	Paid ads, responding to all customer comments, hashtags, barter and paid	Mostly hashtags, transitioned to reels and videos, reduced photo posts. Don't use paid tools or	Sometimes use paid ads, engage the audience through stories and posts. Mainly build organic reach

Table 6.2. (*Continued*)

Question Category	Company I	Company II	Company III
	collaborations with influencers, contests, regularly posting reels and stories	collaborate with influencers	without paid ads. Regularly posting reels and stories, also live transmission occasionally.
Criteria for post themes and formats	Gender, our product is targeted towards women aged 18–60. The colour scheme of our posts is delicate, bright and feminine. We are aiming more at premium clients, which is why we strive to make sure our posts are high-quality in terms of aesthetics and suggest that our product is aimed at people who are at a higher level. We analyse trends in the industry, look at the calendar, and identify all the holidays that could potentially influence interest in candles	We base our content on what is currently seasonal, considering our business clients. Our posts on Instagram are essentially an extension of what we do outside of the platform. For instance, if we send out a newsletter related to seasonality, like Christmas gifts for businesses, we carry out similar activities on Instagram. We post about the gifts we have created, showing what it looked like last year or how we plan for it to look this year	The only criteria are my interests and passions. I sincerely share what interests me and inspire my followers with a love for travel, showing them how I do it. The audience I've built enjoys travel and restaurant reviews, so that's the focus of my profile
Social media trends	The transition from photos to short videos is happening, and we	The trend is leaning towards videos, which is why most of the	Trends change and are irregular. I try to do my own thing and not pay

(*Continued*)

Table 6.2. *(Continued)*

Question Category	Company I	Company II	Company III
	are trying to keep up. Certainly, one of the trends involves ubiquitous perfection; both photos and videos must be of really good quality. Another trend is related to ecological matters. Eco, environmental protection and vegan products encourage us to take care of the planet and the environment. Our products are naturally healthy, eco-friendly, and vegan, and do not contain GMOs, so we don't need to come up with various catchy advertising slogans; we already fit into this trend	content we post on Instagram is related to reels and films – they have a broader reach. We are essentially moving away from captions under photos; no one reads those anymore. When it comes to the category of trends, we are focussing on videos, as Instagram is constantly changing. We are also emphasising quality, because perfectionism is evident when it comes to photos and videos. For some time now, we have been taking product photos and videos with a professional camera, not a phone – all to improve the quality	attention to fleeting 'booms'. I believe that authenticity and creating 'your own trends' is much better than copying others. The 'major' trend I observe is video, which suits me. Text is losing its importance, and it's mostly about visuals, primarily video. I've noticed that sound is very important in videos; it must be clear and without noise.
Challenges and difficulties	Instagram's algorithm is unpredictable and caters more to the platform than the users. Increasing	Difficulties in reaching the audience, with choosing hashtags, and with Instagram's	Instagram often fails technologically. Errors appear, sometimes you simply can't post

Table 6.2. *(Continued)*

Question Category	Company I	Company II	Company III
	competition and growing number of business accounts make it hard to stand out. Hashtag selection	constantly changing algorithm, which really nobody fully understands and also frequent technical errors	stories for the whole day or messages get deleted. Sometimes there are unexplained reach cut-offs. I've also noticed that when I post a link to my online store, the reach of such a story is smaller, which reduces potential sales
Marketing analytics	At the end of the season, the employee presents me with a report, discussing successes and failures. We do this in detail to better plan the strategy for the next year. I also regularly monitor changes in the number of followers and what's happening, using the tools that Instagram itself provides. We compare campaigns to campaigns and one season to another season	We do this quarterly, looking at Instagram results as we begin planning for the next quarter. We summarise the previous quarter and draw conclusions. We mainly focus on the statistics of reels and videos rather than just posts	I use Meta Business for this and do it regularly. As I said, Instagram is my passion; sometimes I can analyse statistics daily, sometimes I do it once a week – but no less frequently.

(Continued)

Table 6.2. *(Continued)*

Question Category	Company I	Company II	Company III
Impact of Improvements	Positive aspects include reels, as well as adding sound, stickers, and a wide range of options for editing stories. There's also the ability to insert a direct link to an online store. Negatively, lately hashtags don't seem to have as much impact on how a post is received by the audience. And then there's Instagram's algorithm, where nobody really knows how it works, and sometimes it seems like the reach of our posts drops for no reason.	Positive is the ability to edit photos/reels directly in the app and the ability to add music. Negative is the algorithm. Theoretically, it is constantly being improved, but in practice, it negatively affects us. Simply put, the reach drops and we don't know what to consider when planning posts or making videos; we can't figure it out	The introduction of reels, which are great for showcasing my travels. The negative impact, I think, is the limitation on the importance of stories; reels have somewhat pushed stories aside. It's a shame because I like to post quick, on-the-spot travel updates that are authentic and unedited
Future upgrades	More advanced analytical tools would help in creating a better marketing plan. The photo and video editing could have more features, so that there wouldn't be a need to use external apps. Also, the	Instagram could think about B2B; perhaps there's an idea for a tool aimed more towards business-to-business. We are waiting for Instagram to introduce something for	Introducing a search engine similar to YouTube's would really make things easier. My profile would rank better, it would be easier to find me; it would be a huge step forward. Personally, I admit

Table 6.2. *(Continued)*

Question Category	Company I	Company II	Company III
	search function could be improved to work more like it does on YouTube or Google	wholesale customers	that I'm really hoping for and looking forward to such modernisation in the app
Future marketing strategy	Our strategy is constantly evolving. Trends, clients, and their needs are constantly changing, and we are changing with them. We plan to maintain the frequency of our posts but focus on creating them in an even more innovative way! We want to create dynamic, engaging posts. We will also start doing live streams and showcasing those unique and standout projects	We will stick with what we have now. We will definitely continue to use Instagram as our portfolio, where we will showcase our projects, take some pride in what we've done for our clients, and post some inspirational content – just as we have been doing so far. We will certainly keep up-to-date with all new features and improvements	I'm constantly striving to improve the content I create, enhance its quality, and refine it further. Besides, I will simply remain true to myself, as it works out best for me, and my audience appreciates it too, which is a huge plus for me. Additionally, I am continually training, so I will definitely adapt my profile to new developments that arise
Current business goal	Maintaining our current position and acquiring an even greater number of clients is our goal. We want to build a larger profile and greater brand recognition,	The primary purpose of our account is to showcase our brand's existence rather than for sales. When I'm preparing an offer for a client, they	I'd like to expand our reach and, most importantly, further develop my online store, as well as secure new collaborations with even larger brands. Now, I'd like to

(Continued)

Table 6.2. *(Continued)*

Question Category	Company I	Company II	Company III
	so that in the future we can also appear in retail chains. And of course, we aim to increase sales through our online store	can check our brand on Instagram. I want them to see that we actually exist, that our account is well-constructed, and that we've had a lot of great projects. Instagram serves as a repository of our projects; it's our portfolio	grow my profile from several thousand followers to tens of thousands and continue to successfully sell my electronic products

Source: Own elaboration based on interviews.

Company III was also to secure paid collaborations with other brands. Two companies spoke optimistically about achieving these goals and are satisfied with the results they obtained. 'I've built a large account; I release my own digital products that are selling better month by month' –Comp.III. However, one company failed to achieve its set goals and changed its strategy after realizing that their target business client is not on Instagram. 'We did not achieve our business objectives, which was initially a surprise, but we quickly changed our strategy and long-term goals. Currently, our goal is not to acquire new clients but merely to build our account to create a portfolio', says Comp.II. It's worth noting that, in this case, the consequence of Instagram marketing isn't direct sales from the platform nor acquiring customers via Instagram. Clients are gained offline, and the social media profile merely confirms its authenticity.

All surveyed companies emphasised that they try to be quite regularly active on the platform. Two of them said that during their peak season (autumn–winter), they are definitely more active, about 2–3 times a week. Off-season activity is reduced but not to zero: 'to appear in the customer's consciousness, so they don't forget about us', says Comp.I. Company III stated that they are available and active daily because it brings them pleasure; the work is their passion. 'I like to be in contact with my followers, thanks to daily activity, and I am realistically and readily available, like a good friend rather than a distant company'.

The marketing strategy in two companies is planned at least a month in advance and is created based on a content marketing calendar that contains detailed information about activities and posts. These companies agree that their goal is to showcase their products and completed projects in the best possible light, and planned posts help maintain harmony and aesthetics on the profile. Company III stands out in this regard, as it acts very spontaneously, without an imposed long-term marketing strategy and campaigns; it creates from day to day and implements ideas that come to mind. 'I create spontaneously; if I decide that my new product will be an interactive map of Madrid, then I go there and post extensive stories and posts from that place to encourage my audience to travel there. It's not a long-term and thoughtout strategy; I simply act from day to day' –Comp.III.

The surveyed companies unanimously stated that they make use of all the latest features available on Instagram, such as business accounts, video formats, ad placements, Instagram Stories and Reels. Reels are particularly praised and are considered by all companies to yield the most significant results, primarily in terms of increasing the number of followers. Additionally, Reels have indirectly impacted sales for two of the surveyed businesses. 'I positively evaluate the option to edit reels directly in the app, insert music, ad effects and GIFs. Instagram is continually expanding the Reels feature. We mainly observe a trend related to videos, which is why most of our content is video-related; they have a much greater reach' –Comp.II.

However, only two out of the three companies have used paid ads and both express negative views about this approach, stating they do not see visible results and do not intend to use such tools in the future. 'I am currently trying to build my reach organically, without paying for ads, so that the number of followers grows on its own'–Comp.III.

All companies confirm they use hashtags and try to align them with the theme of their profile. For example, a company dealing with soy candles uses hashtags related to decor, interiors and elegant style, while a travel-related business uses travel-specific hashtags. All of them appreciate the Stories feature for its extensive editing options, but Business III complained about the recent decline in the importance of Stories compared to Reels.

Another important aspect is influencer marketing. Two of the surveyed companies reported collaborating with influencers: 'We work with influencers both in barter and paid collaborations, and we also organise contests where we give away free products in exchange for increasing the reach of our profile' –Comp.I.

Companies emphasise the importance of authentic engagement with followers. 'We try to respond promptly to all comments and messages, making customers feel a stronger connection with the business', stated Comp.I. Despite continuous updates to the platform, customer feelings remain paramount, echoing the principles of Marketing 4.0, where the consumer is fully aware and values both functional and emotional aspects.

All companies express dissatisfaction with Instagram's algorithm: 'In theory, it's continuously improved and should perform better, but in reality, it negatively impacts us. Our reach is decreasing, and we're not sure what to focus on while planning posts or videos' –Comp.II.

When it comes to improvements, each company suggested the introduction of a Google-like search feature on Instagram, which would allow better profile positioning and direct searches for specific products or services. 'My profile would rank better; it would be easier for people to find me. I'm really looking forward to this innovation' –Comp.III.

Every company confirmed plans to continue marketing on the platform but aims to improve content quality. 'Instagram, trends, customers and their needs are constantly changing, and so are we. We want to create content in an even more innovative way – dynamic and engaging posts', Comp. I. One business expressed an interest in exploring features they haven't tried yet, such as live streaming.

Discussion and Conclusions

Considering the analysis based on fragments of interviews with businesses and relevant literature, it's observable that Instagram, as a rapidly evolving social media platform, offers significant opportunities for companies. This platform enables effective reach to a broad audience through visual content, as well as the creation of authentic dialogue with followers. Companies utilise a diverse range of tools provided by the platform, such as stories and reels, to engage users and build brand recognition. The dynamic nature of Instagram fosters innovative marketing strategies, and constant enhancements like video features and evolving influencer marketing allow for new levels of reach and engagement. The activity of the surveyed companies on the Internet, and especially on Instagram, should be considered innovations at the intersection of procedural and marketing innovation (OECD, Eurostat, 2018).

In the context of the overall opportunities provided by social media, Instagram has become an integral component of modern marketing strategies. This platform opens doors for interactive communication with customers, transforming them into active participants who not only consume content but also create and shape it. Businesses are increasingly aware of the growing influence of public opinion and are thus focussing more on building an authentic image and engaging relationships. At the same time, challenges like changing algorithms and the need for constant innovation require companies to be flexible and adaptable in the fast-evolving social media landscape.

Moreover, Instagram and other social media have opened new opportunities for companies to reach their target audience. With precise targeting tools, companies can more effectively reach interested customers. Content and products are advertised to individuals who may potentially be interested in making a purchase. This approach reduces marketing costs, as advertisements only reach those who are potentially interested.

Instagram is not just a platform for promotion but also for co-creation, image shaping and building deeper relationships with customers. It has become a dynamic arena for interaction between companies and their audiences. Companies are increasingly appreciating the importance of this interaction and engagement from their followers. They expect not just likes and comments from their customers but also constructive feedback that can influence the improvement of offers and product tailoring. Modern marketing is entering an era of interactivity, where customers are seen as active participants in dialogue with companies. There has been a shift from one-way communication to two-way communication, where customers influence the content generated by companies, while simultaneously expecting authenticity and openness from brands. As Instagram and other social media platforms continue to develop their features and tools, the relationships between companies and audiences are likely to become even more symbiotic and valuable for both parties.

However, it's important to note that although customers may act as co-creators of products and organically suggest potential areas for improvement, their opinions and suggestions require skilled interpretation and verification. Not all customer proposals are practical or aligned with the company's long-term strategy. Therefore, the process of integrating customer feedback and creating products relies on a balance between actively listening to market expectations and maintaining brand authenticity and mission. The engagement of customers in co-creating products within the surveyed companies confirms the assertion about the new role of consumers as creators, and the internet-executed marketing strategies enable the alignment with this new stream of activities.

Additionally, Instagram holds immense potential for further development; companies want to be present on this platform, taking advantage of available enhancements. It's even accurate to say that they are eagerly awaiting new features that they can use to attract new customers. Most improvements introduced over recent years have been positively received by small Polish businesses and have directly or indirectly helped them achieve their goals, which mainly focus on increasing follower counts, boosting product and service sales or building brand recognition.

Social media have revolutionised the way businesses conduct their marketing activities. The traditional marketing model has been transformed in favour of a more open, personalised and two-way approach. Instagram is a vital tool in 21st-century marketing, as it offers numerous opportunities for companies to achieve success in a modern digital environment. Moreover, if businesses aim to stand out against competitors, a key element is an innovative marketing strategy that includes all the latest enhancements that social media platforms offer.

References

Borodo, A. (2021). *Ekonomiczne uwarunkowania wykorzystania mediów społecznościowych w handlu elektronicznym.* Uniwersytet Gdański.

Charmaz, K. (2006). *Constructing grounded theory: A practical guide through qualitative analysis.* SAGE.

Debra, Z., & Roberts, M. L. (2017). *Internet marketing: Integrating online & offline strategies* (4th ed.). South-Western Pub.

Hamilton, M., Kaltcheva, V. D., & Rohm, A. J. (2016). Social media and value creation: The role of interaction satisfaction and interaction immersion. *Journal of Interactive Marketing, 36,* 121–133. https://doi.org/10.1016/j.intmar.2016.07.001

Internet World Stats. (2024). World Internet usage and population statistics. 2023 year estimates. https://www.internetworldstats.com/stats.htm. Accessed on January 1, 2024.

Kotler, P., & Armstrong, G. (2012). *Principles of marketing*. Pearson Education Limited.

Kotler, P., & Armstrong, G. (2018). *Principles of marketing* (17th ed.). Pearson.

Kotler, P., Kartajaya, H., & Setiawan, I. (2016). *Marketing 4.0: Moving from traditional to digital*. John Wiley & Sons Inc.

Kotler, P., Kartajaya, H., & Setiawan, I. (2021). *Marketing 5.0. Technology for humanity*. Wiley.

Kraus, S., Gast, J., Schleich, M., Jones, P., & Ritter, M. (2019). Content is King: How SMEs create content for social media marketing under limited resources. *Journal of Macromarketing*, *39*(4), 415–430. https://doi.org/10.1177/0276146719882746

Li, F., Larimo, J., & Leonidou, L. C. (2021). Social media marketing strategy: Definition, conceptualization, taxonomy, validation, and future agenda. *Journal of the Academy of Marketing Science*, *49*(1), 51–70. https://doi.org/10.1007/s11747-020-00733-3

McCann, M., & Barlow, A. (2015). Use and measurement of social media for SMEs. *Journal of Small Business and Enterprise Development*, *22*(2), 273–287. https://doi.org/10.1108/JSBED-08-2012-0096

Michaelidou, N., Siamagka, N. T., & Christodoulides, G. (2011). Usage, barriers and measurement of social media marketing: An exploratory investigation of small and medium B2B brands. *Industrial Marketing Management*, *40*(7), 1153–1159. https://doi.org/10.1016/j.indmarman.2011.09.009

OECD, Eurostat. (2018). *Oslo Manual 2018. Guidelines for collecting, reporting and using data on innovation* (4th ed.). OECD & European Union.

Strauss, A., & Corbin, J. (2008). *Basics of qualitative research: Techniques and procedures for developing grounded theory* (3rd ed.). SAGE.

Villa, A., & Taurino, T. (2019). SME innovation and development in the context of Industry 4.0. *Procedia Manufacturing*, *39*, 1415–1420. https://doi.org/10.1016/j.promfg.2020.01.311

World Bank. (2023). *Small and Medium Enterprises (SMEs) finance*. https://www.worldbank.org/en/topic/smefinance. Accessed on August 28, 2023.

Yoo, W. S., & Lee, E. (2011). Internet channel entry: A strategic analysis of mixed channel structures. *Marketing Science*, *30*(1), 29–41. https://doi.org/10.1287/mksc.1100.0586

Chapter 7

Virtual Design in the Digital Age – Reshaping Hospitality Landscape

Hassan Ali Khan

The Monal Group & A-Cube Pvt Ltd, Pakistan

Abstract

As the hospitality business adapts to the digital age, the importance of using Virtual Design (VD) to create memorable visitor experiences has grown. This study aims to investigate the potential of VD in the hospitality sector, particularly regarding the improvement of guests' overall experiences.

The research study examines how Virtual Reality (VR), Augmented Reality (AR) and other digital technologies are currently used in VD firms. It explores how these simulated architectural features are implemented in other facets of the hospitality experience, like the decor of guest rooms and restaurants and staff responsiveness to guests' needs.

The study also examines VD's potential outcomes and advantages for the hotel industry and its clients. It investigates the potential of VD to help hospitality businesses offer more customised services, boost customer loyalty and gain an edge in the market. VD implementation in the hospitality business may face several obstacles, some of which are discussed in this study.

Methods include both qualitative and quantitative techniques, such as interviews with experts, guest surveys and an examination of the use of VD in specific hotels. This study intends to help the hotel industry benefit from a VD by analysing real-world case studies and gathering empirical data that can be used to draw conclusions and formulate recommendations.

Keywords: Virtual design; hospitality industry; guest experience; virtual reality; augmented reality; technology integration

Marketing and Design in the Service Sector, 101–117
Copyright © 2024 by Emerald Publishing Limited
All rights of reproduction in any form reserved
doi:10.1108/978-1-83797-276-020241008

Introduction

The hospitality sector is essential to national economies in many regions (Martnez-Martínez et al., 2019). Food, drink and housing are the mainstays of the hospitality industry, which can be found in both for-profit and non-profit businesses (Naumov, 2019). Sisson and Adams (2013) state that 'hospitality' refers to the entire sector, including hotels, travel, food and beverage and event organising. In order to succeed, businesses in the hotel industry must rely on public relations and recommendations from satisfied customers. The hotel industry has grown tremendously due to technological advancements and changing consumer preferences. VD has emerged as an integral part of modern hotel management, changing how establishments view guests and operate.

The advent of the digital age has radically altered the hospitality business. A revolutionary change in the hospitality industry is the adoption of CAD software for the development of new hotel designs. Hotels, restaurants and other hospitality organisations have benefited immensely from using CAD software to revamp their interior design and building processes. Both businesses and customers can reap various benefits.

With VD, businesses may experiment with different aesthetics and functionalities without spending a lot of money. Digital modelling allows them to save money on actual prototypes or mockups while still allowing for iterative improvements. This not only aids efficiency and financial savings but also stimulates fresh perspectives on design (Allioui & Mourdi, 2023).

In order to better serve their customers, firms are increasingly turning to VD. Hospitality businesses may learn a lot about their customers through the use of virtual environments and user testing. Using these data, designers can better cater to their intended audience by considering their wants and requirements.

The hospitality industry has seen radical upheaval due to the advent of digital design tools like virtual models. The process of planning and designing commercial spaces has experienced a paradigm shift, becoming more innovative, cost-effective and client-focused. The hospitality industry has also profited from VD since it has made it possible to create interactive virtual tours and tailor guests' experiences to their own preferences. Future hotel construction will be strongly affected by VD due to advancing computer technologies.

The Definition of Virtual Design

The term 'VD' refers to the process of conceptualising and constructing a building's three-dimensional model digitally (Popov et al., 2010). It's a great way to test out concepts before giving them concrete form. VD relies on computer simulations, which help architects and engineers to reduce unnecessary work and costs. Construction, engineering, manufacturing and other industries have all found uses for VD. This innovation has allowed designers to work more quickly and accurately than ever before. The hospitality industry could be profoundly affected by the rising popularity of VD as a disruptive breakthrough. Before starting work on the real thing, hotels can utilise virtual models to try out different designs, layouts and concepts. Because of this breakthrough, hotels have been able to cut prices without compromising on quality.

Designing anything virtually means making a computer model of it. While this technology is not new, it has only lately become practical and cheap for businesses of all sizes. One of the greatest benefits of VD is its adaptability. The capacity to develop 3D models of a hotel's amenities and services could improve the establishment's ability to meet the needs of its visitors. Hotels can use VD to accommodate individual visitors' preferences in terms of room style and facilities.

VD is being used more frequently to give a more immersive experience for guests. VR tours of hotel rooms can get guests excited about their stay and reduce the likelihood that they'll be let down when they arrive. When it comes to saving money and reducing waste, VD is on par with more traditional methods. When hotel owners' experiment with different layouts and designs on digital recreations of their actual buildings and facilities, they can save money on utilities and reduce waste. The hotel's operational costs might be reduced and its impact on the environment could be improved through these measures.

This research aims to analyse the viability of using VD in the hospitality sector to serve visitors better. This study analyses the present condition of digital technologies such as VR, AR and others in VD agencies. This research looks at how hotels and restaurants use architectural simulations to improve guests' experiences in various ways, including in the design of guest rooms and dining establishments and in the speed with which staff members respond to guests' requests.

This study explores the far-reaching effects of VD technologies like VR and AR on the hotel sector. This study explores the dynamic hospitality industry and how technological developments are reshaping guest experiences, streamlining design and prototyping processes, fostering sustainable practises, facilitating workforce development, conferring competitive advantages, augmenting customer engagement strategies and elevating marketing paradigms. Thorough investigation of the study should yield useful information for industry insiders and policymakers alike, allowing for more informed decision-making in the ever-changing digital landscape and helping to keep the hospitality industry flexible, competitive and in step with modern consumer preferences.

Exploring the Potential of Virtual Design (VD) in Hospitality

In the hospitality industry, VD and artificial intelligence (AI)-driven algorithms can work together to improve several processes. With the help of AI, businesses like hotels and restaurants can better plan for the future and distribute their resources in response to customer demand. In addition, it can be used to fuel chatbots and virtual assistants that provide quick support and recommendations to guests.

VD may play an important part in the design of environmentally sustainable houses beyond just the optimisation of lighting and Heating, Ventilation and Air Conditioning (HVAC) system. It paves the way for the use of sustainable resources, such as renewable energy and water-saving technologies, by architects and designers. This is in line with the growing trend of environmentally concerned tourists looking for sustainable lodgings, and it has the added benefit of reducing environmental impact (Chan et al., 2016).

Virtual Design (VD) can help hotel and restaurant companies to comply with local building codes and design standards around the world. Companies can ease their entry into new markets by constructing virtual prototypes to see how well their designs mesh with local cultures and expectations.

Virtual Reality (VR)

The hotel and tourist industries have been among the most enthusiastic adopters of VR technology. The advent of cutting-edge digital technology has transformed customers' use of traditional travel planning methods. Potential visitors can explore their potential locations at their own pace, regardless of location or time of day. Our ability to visualise and organise future travel has been profoundly altered by the advent of VR and other forms of AI. VR allows consumers to experience a lifelike simulation of a product, service or location before making a purchase decision (Tussyadiah et al., 2018).

Amusement parks, museums, hotels and even destination marketing have all seen a rise in the use of VR in recent years. Customers can plan their vacations more strategically after participating in an interactive experience (Wei, 2019). Depending on whether the virtual destination is sufficient to deliver the customer's expected vacation activities, the customer may be prepared to make a booking decision or search for other options that satisfy their upcoming trip needs. The travel and hotel industries could greatly benefit from VR's use as a marketing tool. An example is the virtual tour service offered by the official destination marketing organisation (DMO) for Santa Clara. VR elements and applications published on the destination's website, such as 3D maps, films, audio, 3D graphics and aerial views, make this tour accessible to potential tourists and provide them an immersive, interactive experience of the destination. The question of whether or whether VR satisfies the virtual needs of its users by allowing them to get totally immersed in the location for future trips is an essential one. Developers and industry professionals, however, will need to answer this question.

Due to advancements in technology, consumers now have an easier time interacting with virtual worlds. Using VR support devices (like Google Cardboard) and available VR content (3D maps or contents, web- or mobile-based applications), customers may take virtual tours of cities, hotels, restaurants and other attractions from anywhere in the world (Tussyadiah et al., 2018).

Marketers in the hospitality and tourist industries develop creative strategies to spread the word about a place and encourage more people to travel there (Baker & Cameron, 2008). VR improves hospitality and tourism (Bonetti et al., 2018) by creating a more realistic and interesting virtual setting (Jung et al., 2018).

Role of Robotics as Technology in Hospitality Sector

Robots that provide hotel services have grown increasingly commonplace with the introduction of AI. In order to engage, communicate and provide service to a company's clientele, service robots must be system-based, autonomous and flexible (Wirtz et al., 2018). Distinct from traditional self-service gadgets, service robots allow for unprecedented human–machine interactions in the hospitality industry due to their ability to communicate and engage with humans.

Tuomi et al. (2021) state that service robots can be used for both production and delivery in the hospitality industry. For instance, it has been predicted that by 2020, UV-using disinfection robots would be used in airports and hotels all over the world as part of the service production process to ensure a safe and clean environment (Greg, 2020). The YOTEL Boston was one of the first hotels to install UVD robots. The robots roam the hotel unattended, disinfecting the air of any remaining bacteria or viruses in high-traffic areas and specific guest rooms. The hotel's 'SmartStaySafety' operation, which prioritises the well-being of its guests, relies heavily on the use of UVD robots (Yotel, 2020).

Throughout the service delivery process, service robots help frontline workers by performing mundane duties. Visitor services like greeting, baggage handling, directing and even delivering room service might all be aided by robots. AI and machine learning enable a service robot to respond to and engage with guests, regardless of the customers' native language.

Although robots do enhance operational efficiency, there are valid safety concerns that have been raised. This idea of using robots to replace human workers in the hospitality industry is still in its infancy. It has not been thoroughly explored how they adjust to novel settings. If guests veer off the predetermined course, the service robots might not respond as expected. Therefore, many various types of hospitality firms like restaurants, airlines and theme parks need to carefully assess which service process stage is best suited for service automation and develop unique service recovery procedures in case robots fail to give the intended service.

Service robots are paired with AI-powered web chatbots to provide instantaneous responses to consumer inquiries. Chatbots are a game changer for customer service because they can answer instantaneously to enquiries made through mobile apps, hotel websites or social media all day long. Since the recent pandemic has left the hotel business short staffed, chatbots can be of tremendous assistance.

How Virtual Reality/Augmented Reality Improves Guest Experience

Customers believe that VR simulations are the ideal tool for hospitality businesses to provide a memorable experience. The hospitality industry has seen a rise in the adoption of VR systems in recent years. As the intangibles of the visitor experience continue to gain prominence in the hospitality sector, VR has the potential to revolutionise the booking process. Because of the increased predictability afforded by technology advancements, customers will be more willing to do business with you. The virtual tour video is helpful since it provides viewers with an insider's look at the location. Clicking a mouse or donning a VR headset allows hotel guests to view the room layout and have a virtual tour of the resort from a 360-degree perspective. This paves the way for the hospitality industry to capitalise on the 'try before you buy' marketing principle, as potential guests can get a feel for a property before committing to a reservation (Gursoy et al., 2022).

The goal of AR is to enhance the user's experience of exploring their immediate physical surroundings in real time, as opposed to VR's total immersion in a computer-generated simulated environment (Jung & Tom, 2017). The technology is functional because it overlays digital information on a live video feed of the actual environment, which can be accessed from any mobile device. This proves that AR is a potent tool for enhancing the in-room experiences of hotel customers.

The hotel industry is mostly using AR for fun and ease. One is to provide them with interesting and entertaining things to do while they are there. Best Western is just one hotel chain that has experimented with Disney characters in AR. With the help of a special software on their smartphones, children will have a fantastic time visiting the hotel and seeing themselves in photos with Disney characters at various spots. The use of augmented reality for indoor navigation is becoming increasingly common. According to SenseTime (2021), the IFS Mall in Chengdu, China, is one of the select few commercial structures in the world that employ it. Mini-app 'IFS-ARgo' functions as a mobile version of Google Maps by capturing a real-time image of its users' surroundings through the phone's camera. The scene is then altered by superimposing the instructions and recommendations on top of it. Consumers may easily find stores, lifts and parking spots with the 'IFS-ARgo' microprogram on WeChat.

The VR, AR and MR technologies are contributing greatly to the growth of a new ecosystem in which physical and virtual things are fused across several dimensions (Tümler et al., 2022). Improvements in mobile and embodied technology and the introduction of highly interactive physical-virtual links are reshaping the landscape of consumer experience. Because of this shift, new hybrid types of enjoyment are emerging. However, researchers and experts have not yet established clear boundaries between the various new forms of reality, technology and experiences. The purpose of this research is to improve understanding of these concepts by merging technological (embodiment), psychological (presence) and behavioural (interactivity) perspectives. A new method of categorising technology, the 'EPI Cube', will be introduced due to this amalgamation. The matrix provides a framework for classifying current and future technologies that have the potential to improve and enable client interactions. In addition, these innovations can produce brand-new experiences at every stage of the consumer life cycle.

Many organisations across industries are implementing extended reality technologies to serve their customers better (SmartTek Solutions, 2022). To enhance their guests' dining experiences and, by extension, their health, restaurateurs are increasingly interested in digital technologies. With the advent of VR technology, hotels may expand their horizons in terms of advertising, staff development and guest satisfaction. Especially among those with high elaboration likelihood, VR advertising has been shown to have more initial effects than regular commercials. Nonetheless, there were also indications that viewers of VR advertising had significantly lower buy intentions than viewers of traditional commercials.

The Concept of Metaverse

According to Ball (2021), the Metaverse is an ever-present virtual world where real-world interactions are seamlessly integrated. This concept depends on utilising VR and AR technologies, allowing multimodal interactions with digital environments, objects and people. Because of this, the Metaverse is a collection of social, networked, immersive experiences distributed over persistent multiuser platforms. Through physical things, users can communicate with one another and digital artefacts in real time – a system of interconnected virtual worlds where users' avatars have free reign over their movements. The current generation of the Metaverse consists of social, immersive VR systems compatible with MMOs, open game worlds and AR collaborative settings.

Once hotels begin implementing cutting-edge technological methods, such as the Metaverse's Smart approaches, they will be met with a wide range of responses, worries and inquiries from their visitors.

The effects of a Metaverse hotel's simulated environments, individualised service, active guest participation and post-stay feedback are substantial. It also changes how managers communicate, influences customer relationship management and improves organisational performance, all of which are important in the hotel business. Finally, the technology behind Metaverses presents difficulties in the form of security concerns, technical hurdles, expensive expenditures and unsure user requirements.

In the hospitality industry, the ability to co-create transformative experiences and values between customers and businesses is revolutionised by the use of the Metaverse, which combines the real and virtual worlds in light of the importance of the customer experience and the co-creation of value in the hospitality and tourism industries.

The Metaverse presents exciting new prospects and significant problems for the hotel and tourism industries. The strategic use of the Metaverse by the hospitality and tourist industries will enable the personalisation and co-creation of hybrid virtual and physical experiences for customers before, during and after their trips.

Metaverse Inclusion and Integration With VR

Incorporating the Metaverse and VR into the hospitality sector has the ability to transform visitor experiences and broaden access by removing geographical and cultural barriers and meeting the preferences of a wide range of individuals. However, it must be approached carefully to ensure that everyone can participate and profit from this integration, considering accessibility, privacy and cultural factors.

The hospitality industry is only one of several that have shown keen interest in the Metaverse concept, a collective virtual shared place created by merging technologically improved physical and VR. When combining the Metaverse and VR in the hospitality business to improve accessibility and guest satisfaction, various factors must be considered.

- *VR Hotel Tours:* By using VR, hotels give potential customers a firsthand look at their accommodations, services and even nearby attractions before they book. Those unable to visit the hotel physically can still enjoy the hotel's services through this feature.
- *Virtual Meetings and Events:* Meetings, conferences and other events are held in the Metaverse's digital equivalent of a hotel. This facilitates attendance from all around the world, increasing accessibility for people who cannot physically attend in person owing to a variety of factors.
- *Language and Cultural Inclusivity:* Travelers worldwide can feel more at home due to the Metaverse's ability to host virtual representations of numerous cultural and linguistic aspects. Furthering accessibility for all users is the incorporation of translation tools into VR experiences.
- *Virtual Concierge Services:* VR provides guests with concierge services. This could contain suggestions for Metaverse-based restaurants, shops, attractions and accessibility features.
- *Virtual Training and Onboarding:* Training and new employee orientation are two areas where VR might be useful in the hospitality industry. This ensures that people from a wide range of academic and occupational backgrounds can take advantage of available training materials.
- *Virtual Art and Decor Customisation:* By adjusting the hotel's artwork, lighting, and atmosphere, visitors can create their ideal stay.
- *VR for Relaxation and Wellness:* The use of VR into spa and wellness programmes facilitates the treatment of clients as whole beings. These kinds of software allow for individualised customisation to meet the needs of each user.
- *Metaverse Social Spaces:* Facilitate user interaction and community building by designing virtual gathering spaces in the Metaverse. Better communication between persons of different cultural origins and geographic regions can help spread acceptance and tolerance.
- *Security and Privacy:* Protect the privacy and information of its users by enforcing stringent security measures. This is ground-breaking in creating credibility and guaranteeing acceptance.
- *Feedback and Iteration:* The service's virtual products can be made more appealing to a wider audience and improved based on the feedback of its guests.
- *Accessibility Standards:* To make sure that all users can access and enjoy the offers, it is important to follow accessibility standards and rules for both VR and Metaverse experiences, such as the Web Content Accessibility rules (WCAG).

How VR and Metaverse Combine and Enhance Guest Experience in Hospitality

In: Décor Guest Rooms, Restaurants, Staff Responsiveness to Guest

Combining VR and the Metaverse (a network of interconnected online worlds) allows the hospitality industry to give visitors a more engaging, unique and immersive experience, which boosts the quality of their stay and dining experience. Businesses can differentiate themselves in a crowded marketplace by combining cutting-edge tools with warm hospitality.

According to Aranca (2022), the hospitality business benefits greatly from integrating VR and the Metaverse in areas such as room design, restaurant service and employee responsiveness. Incorporating these technologies into their experience will make it more engaging and unique:

- *Virtual Room Tours:* Before making a reservation, potential guests can use the hotel's virtual tour feature to familiarise themselves with the property and choose a room that best suits their needs in terms of design, layout and facilities. Guests will have a clearer idea of what to anticipate, and the level of transparency will increase.

- *Virtual Room Customisation:* VR allows guests to alter the room's design digitally. They have the freedom to design their ideal space by selecting wall colours, artwork, furnishings and room arrangements. Adding those special touches makes guests feel at home and at ease during their stay.

- *Virtual Restaurant Experiences:* Virtual dining experiences allow customers to virtually visit a restaurant, sample the fare, check out the decor and even watch their food being produced from the comfort of home. This makes the dining experience more exciting by adding interaction and immersion opportunities.

- *Metaverse Social Dining:* The Metaverse can serve as a venue for parties and celebrations, allowing attendees to virtually catch up with loved ones who can't be there in person. These online get-togethers can take place at a specially designed restaurant in the Metaverse.

- *Staff Training and Responsiveness:* VR can be used to train employees by mimicking real-world circumstances to boost responsiveness and service quality. Staff members can improve the visitor experience by learning to anticipate guest needs and respond appropriately.

- *Virtual Concierge Services:* Guests can get immediate answers to questions and suggestions for things to do and see in the area when businesses in the Metaverse adopt AI-driven virtual concierge services. The efficiency and helpfulness of the team will increase as the outcome.

- *Interactive Guest Feedback:* Guests can submit feedback on their stay via VR and Metaverse platforms. Guests can take a more active role in providing this feedback by virtually reliving their experiences and pointing out any problems they encountered.

- *Virtual Events and Activities:* Hotels can serve as venues for Metaverse-based performances, classes and exhibits. Guests' entertainment options are expanded because they can take part from the comfort of their rooms or the company of others in public areas.

- *AR Wayfinding:* AR apps that work with VR and the Metaverse can aid visitors in navigating the hotel and its surroundings by providing them with up-to-the-moment information and guidance.

- *Sustainability and Wellness Virtual Tours:* Hotels can promote their eco-friendly practices and health amenities by providing virtual tours. Guests can learn about green projects or participate in online yoga and meditation programmes to help them lead a more mindful and healthier lifestyle while they're here.

Limitations of the Study

The longevity of the Metaverse is essential to its ability to support many concurrent users and provide uninterrupted services even on low-powered mobile devices. Open-source platforms that encourage communication and cooperation among programmers and subject-matter experts must be constantly improved so that the environment can grow and be used.

Metaverse technologies, including AR, VR, holograms and Head-Mounted Displays (HMDs), need a long-term interface to function. In order to shield young users from potentially harmful sounds in the real world and give them real-time, high-definition visuals, innovative methods are required. Most Metaverse interfaces are visual, with others considering the use of supplementary audio forms or sensors. The demand for comprehensive pre-trained multimodal models to process a wide range of data sources is rising in tandem with the popularity of multimodal learning. This way of learning has produced a rapidly fast way of learning enabling the student to learn quickly in remote areas enabling people to have a better understanding of hospitality and tourism for the people that are deprived of such knowledge.

Non-Player Characters (NPCs) are AI-driven or programmed entities who interact with users in the Metaverse but are not under the control of a human player. These virtual characters are meant to enhance the experience of the user by offering interactive content, helping with tasks, or supporting different areas of the virtual world. Speakers of different languages need a translation service that provides natural expressions through translation so that they can take part in conversations that are regularly conveyed through social networking using both their native language and English. It's obvious that a single Non Player Character (NPC) model without a multi-persona system isn't sufficient to maintain player interest over time.

Metaverse security and privacy concerns are paramount because of the potential for unscrupulous users to track and record users' activities and biometrics in real time. Cybersecurity and privacy issues must be resolved in order to deliver safe and effective services by safeguarding end users and infrastructure from a wide range of vulnerabilities and attacks.

The Metaverse is an online community where many different kinds of personal information are exchanged in real-time, making it difficult to ascertain what safety precautions should be taken. For the virtual world to be safe from cybercrime and attacks, current security protocols and management policies must be modified to fit the unique nature of the Metaverse. Encrypting private information is a good way to lessen the damage that could result from hacking attempts.

Metaverse systems may invade users' privacy because they gather more information about them than traditional ones. Some methods for protecting sensitive data include invisibility, teleportation and many copies of an avatar. The prevalence of several threats in the Metaverse makes it imperative that software be protected against exploitation. Minors could potentially view violent and obscene material, and malicious software could temporarily 'blind' users.

Hardware security is also crucial as hardware (devices) such as HMDs, VR headsets and IoT devices can be utilised to authenticate and control content access. Nonetheless, hostile attackers can exploit security flaws to take over users' or administrators' privileges, remotely manage linked devices, steal data from individual devices, or even get into the management server itself. When participating in the Metaverse platform, all devices should be protected using up-to-date patches and other proven security procedures.

Network security is equally vital since most Metaverse platforms don't encrypt data sent over the network or between Avatars. Network connections in the Metaverse must be encrypted using a safe and efficient cryptography method appropriate to the data and situation to prevent attackers from capturing messages or sensitive information through sniffing or spoofing attempts.

Since the Metaverse is a novel and complicated environment, its security and privacy features will need constant attention from administrators. By adhering to a 'security by design' framework, privacy and security can be built into every step of the service delivery process. Key security properties and privacy concerns must be properly maintained, necessitating cutting-edge protection technologies such as automated, adaptable, encrypted control of data access utilising AI.

Economics and politics centre on the present economic structure that links the Metaverse to the real world, with real-world money flowing into the Metaverse and real-world profits repatriating. The entry of high-end corporations has demonstrated the Metaverse's potential as a revenue model, yet there is substantial asset volatility due to virtual items. Borders or established rules do not constrain political power, and there are no established institutional mechanisms for preserving social standing.

Due to its novelty, complexity and potential utility in a wide range of illegal endeavours, the Metaverse is an especially tempting target for hackers and other harmful actors. Some have even suggested that cyber security is pivotal to the success or failure of the Metaverse.

Complex and potentially insecure design defines the Metaverse as the next step in the internet's evolution. Data and the security environment require architectural security measures, and unsafe design will be a brand-new threat vector in 2021. Complexity is increasing in the Metaverse due to cutting-edge technology, including VR, AR, AI, machine learning and sensors. Cybersecurity threats are amplified by the multifaceted and ever-evolving nature of the technology utilised in the Metaverse for activities as varied as gaming, remote worker cooperation, virtual communities and online commerce.

The foundations of the Metaverse economy are crypto-assets like cryptocurrencies and non-fungible tokens (NFTs). There are many cybersecurity threats to cryptocurrencies and NFTs, from flaws in blockchain platforms to assaults on wallets used to store them, with increasingly severe consequences for users and victims.

The Metaverse's multimodal qualities, such as graphic and 3D design and immersive visual and audio experiences, can amplify the negative effects of undesired and privacy-invasive content on users or victims. Technical repercussions of privacy breaches in the Metaverse are likely to be magnified. Effective security mechanisms in the physical world and the Metaverse must be implemented to reduce the likelihood of these negative outcomes.

Increased reliance on VR headsets for data collection and sharing increases the risk to users in the Metaverse. In order to better target consumers with adverts and persuade them to buy things, companies like Meta are developing high-end VR headsets like Project Cambria, which can reflect a user's facial and eye movements in VR.

More severe effects, such as the theft of cryptoassets or even physical harm to victims, may result from security breaches in the Metaverse compared to the traditional Internet. VR and AR headsets are vulnerable to hacking, which could lead to criminal or violent acts committed by the user.

Regarding privacy and security in the Metaverse, neither organisations nor nations are ready. There aren't enough capable individuals to manage the architecture's complexity and create safe solutions. It is also harder to monitor and detect assaults on these new platforms than it is on traditional ones.

Global policies like the European Union (EU)'s General Data Protection Regulation (GDPR) fall short of what is required to handle privacy concerns in the Metaverse appropriately, demonstrating the lag in data privacy and cybersecurity rules that has accompanied the development of the Metaverse. It is unclear whether or not an avatar's location is subject to the provisions of the GDPR regulating the transfer and processing of data beyond the EU.

Delimitation of the Study

The hospitality sector is extremely sensitive to both external and internal shocks, as evidenced by the recent COVID-19 outbreak and the conflict in Ukraine. Individuals' preferences about lodging and travel may also shift as more people become aware of the impacts of climate change. Concerns about climate change, changing client requirements and preferences, demographic transitions and other external factors have caused an increase in the number of people choosing local travel over foreign travel and in patronising sustainable hospitality businesses. Customers may be more receptive to eco-friendly, time-saving and money-saving hospitality and tourism options as a result of these novel ways of thinking. Examples include bringing meetings, concerts, museum visits and other similar events to customers in the Metaverse. These potential shifts in consumer behaviour emphasise the need for the industry to create accessible technology and widespread user adoption in order to deliver authentic hospitality and tourism experiences in the Metaverse. As both consumers and technologies advance, the increased use of Metaverse applications can boost advertising, customer relationships, communication, customer decision-making and guest satisfaction. Because of this, it's possible that Metaverse experiences may soon become the next big thing in the tourism and hospitality industries.

If the hospitality and tourism industries are going to make money in the Metaverse, they need to provide immersive experiences that people will really pay for. People working in the hospitality and tourist sector need to be creative and innovative to give their consumers memorable and exciting experiences that appeal to all their senses. We use a two-dimensional framework with four quadrants to conceptualise travel and tourism in the Metaverse. The first dimension indicates how interactive the system is, which can be anything from very little to very much. Customers are only minimally involved in low-interactive virtual product and service interactions. Customers may, for instance, perform tasks that don't require their full attention or seek information without paying attention. When clients engage in highly engaging activities like virtual kayaking or first-person shooter games, they are actually interacting with a live virtual world.

Experiences in the Metaverse can be categorised along a second axis describing the hedonic vs instrumental value they provide customers. Users motivated by hedonic values seek pleasurable experiences in the virtual world, whereas those driven by utilitarian values are more interested in finding solutions to practical problems. Metaverse users in search of hedonic experiences can do virtual scuba diving in the Pacific Ocean or Amazonian rainforest. On the other hand, the Metaverse can also cater to more pragmatic wants, such as allowing customers to check out a service before committing to a purchase or reservation.

People can have virtual tours, conferences, meetings and conventions, as well as stay in virtual hotel rooms, prepare virtual meals and fly virtual planes thanks to the Metaverse. To build and manufacture airline services on a unified digital environment in the Metaverse, major travel corporations like Boeing are employing immersive 3D engineering concepts. Customer interest in hotels, restaurants, tourist attractions, flights and other services can be gauged without leaving the house because to these efforts' 'try before you buy' feature. Customers' final decisions to book a service in question may hinge on their ability to first engage with that service in a virtual setting through a Metaverse encounter. If a customer is on the fence about booking, a Metaverse experience can help sway their decision.

There are several ways in which the Metaverse can benefit both service providers and their clients. In addition to providing businesses with valuable marketing and customer interaction opportunities, the Metaverse can help consumers save time and money when organising vacations. In addition, there are almost infinite ways in which the hotel and tourism industries might benefit from virtualisation. People will be able to do things like shop, see exhibits, listen to music and wander through galleries without leaving their computers. Optimistic forecasts are made despite virtual encounters not being expected to replace traditional forms of hospitality and tourism fully. Therefore, many market leaders have started investing in these digital landscapes, and 2022 has the potential to be a breakthrough year for the Metaverse.

Future Research Recommendations

Human–technology interactions have been researched for decades, but technological advancements are altering how people understand their surroundings and engage with businesses and their goods. This study aimed to compile existing information about this marketing phenomenon. We offer our conceptual clarifications and classifications to help scholars and practitioners.

Cybercriminals and other culprits in the Metaverse have both internal and external drives. Interest and enjoyment of an activity are key drivers of intrinsic motivation, while money incentives are an example of an extrinsic motivator. Some hackers target computer systems not for financial gain but for the psychological effect of doing so.

Fears have been voiced that hostile states will resort to novel types of cyberwarfare by attacking each other in the Metaverse. Potential geopolitical ramifications could arise if hostile powers began targeting individuals' biometric data, financial data and other forms of digital assets. Hackers with strong ideological convictions may wage cyberwar against countries they see as enemies out of a sense of duty to their communities and countries.

Hacking VR and AR headsets are only two examples of how the Metaverse's underlying technology can give cyber criminals new avenues for launching cyberattacks. New forms of harmful cyber activity, such as the theft of digital avatars and manipulating people in immersive virtual settings, may be attracted to certain Metaverse technology. As an alternative to cyberbullying, some Internet offenders may resort to abusing avatars in the Metaverse.

More study is needed to determine how the Metaverse can inspire novel cyberattacks and alter the dynamics of existing ones. Consumers have resisted firms' attempts to capture high-velocity data in the non-Metaverse Internet. The Metaverse's potential for harm stems from the fact that it is a multisensory space with extremely intrusive material that could lead to major privacy issues. More research is required to examine how customers in the Metaverse and the real world react to corporations' intrusive data collection practices.

Managerial Implication of the Study

Hotels are changing the way they function and interact with customers as they adopt cutting-edge technologies like VD, Metaverse technology and AI. These technological developments have the potential to provide unprecedented levels of satisfaction to hotel guests. With the help of AI, hotels can sift through mountains of data to provide guests with tailored experiences across the board (from room selection to restaurant suggestions), elevating the quality of their stay and giving them a feeling of specialness and comfort. To take it a step further, hotels are beginning to use Metaverse technology and VD to give potential visitors a first-person look into the rooms and common areas they might be staying in.

The benefits are game-changing from an operational standpoint as well. Chatbots and virtual concierges driven by AI simplify mundane chores, such as check-in, room service and queries, decreasing the need for human assistance. Spaces can be better planned, utilised and maintained, as well as have lower energy and maintenance expenses, with the help of VD. Data security and privacy problems must be carefully considered during the introduction of these technologies, and strong safeguards and adherence to new rules are essential.

Moreover, these developments require a flexible workforce that can adjust to new circumstances. Managers need to put money into training programmes to ease workers into their new collaborative roles with AI technology. Creating harmony between human and AI interactions is crucial to ensure a smooth and pleasurable visitor experience as staff migrate towards more guest-centric positions.

VD, Metaverse technology and AI integration raise issues of cost. It is possible that the long-term benefits of increased productivity, income production and guest happiness will more than compensate for the initial investment in hardware, software and training. Moreover, it is a manager's top priority to keep these systems running smoothly to avoid any disruptions in service.

The hospitality business stands to gain greatly from incorporating AI, Metaverse technologies and VD to serve its customers better. If they want to keep up with the rapidly developing hotel industry and build a positive reputation for their brand, managers will need to master the challenges of data security, employee adaption and cost management while grabbing the benefits given by this cutting-edge technology.

References

Allioui, H., & Mourdi, Y. (2023). Exploring the full potentials of IoT for better financial growth and stability: A comprehensive survey. *Sensors*, *23*(19), 8015. https://doi.org/10.3390/s23198015

Aranca. (2022). *Metaverse in hospitality industry*. https://www.aranca.com/knowledge-library/articles/ip-research/Metaverse-in-hospitality-industry. Accessed on October 20, 2023.

Baker, M. J., & Cameron, E. (2008). Critical success factors in destination marketing. *Tourism and Hospitality Research*, *8*(2), 79–97.

Ball, M. (2021). *Framework for the Metaverse*. https://www.matthewball.vc/all/forwardtotheMetaverseprimer. Accessed on September 18, 2023.

Bonetti, F., Warnaby, G., & Quinn, L. (2018). Augmented reality and virtual reality in physical and online retailing: A review, synthesis and research agenda. In T. Jung & M. Claudia Tom Dieck (Eds.), *Augmented reality and virtual reality* (pp. 119–132). Springer.

Chan, E., Okumus, F., & Chan, W. (2016). The applications of environmental technologies in hotels. *Journal of Hospitality Marketing & Management, 26*.

Greg, P. (2020). What can Marriott, Hilton or Loews teach Macy's and others about COVID customer experience management? *Forbes*. https://www.forbes.com/sites/gregpetro/2020/09/25/what-can-marriott-hilton-or-loews-teach-macys-and-others-about-covid-customer-experience-management/?sh=2d8909ee5847. Accessed on September 04, 2023.

Gursoy, D., Malodia, S., & Dhir, A. (2022). The Metaverse in the hospitality and tourism industry: An overview of current trends and future research directions. *Journal of Hospitality Marketing & Management, 31*(5), 527–534.

Jung, T. H., Lee, H., Chung, N., & tom Dieck, M. C. (2018). Cross-cultural differences in adopting mobile augmented reality at cultural heritage tourism sites. *International Journal of Contemporary Hospitality Management, 30*(3), 1621–1645. https://doi.org/10.1108/IJCHM-02-2017-0084

Jung, T., & Tom, D. M. C. (2017). *Augmented reality and virtual reality: Empowering human, place and business*. Springer.

Martínez-Martínez, A., Cegarra-Navarro, J. G., Garcia-Perez, A., & Wensley, A. (2019). Knowledge agents as drivers of environmental sustainability and business performance in the hospitality sector. *Tourism Management, 70*, 381–389.

Naumov, N. (2019). The impact of robots, artificial intelligence, and service automation on service quality and service experience in hospitality. In *Robots, artificial intelligence, and service automation in travel, tourism and hospitality* (pp. 123–133). Emerald Publishing Limited.

Popov, V., Juocevicius, V., Migilinskas, D., Ustinovicius, L., & Mikalauskas, S. (2010). The use of a virtual building design and construction model for developing an effective project concept in 5D environment. *Automation in Construction, 19*, 357–367.

SenseTime. (2021). SenseTime elevates shopping experience at Chengdu IFS with its SenseMARS AR platform. https://www.sensetime.com/en/news-detail/56225?categoryId=1072&ref=blog.humanode.io. Accessed on August 07, 2023.

Sisson, L. G., & Adams, A. R. (2013). Essential hospitality management competencies: The importance of soft skills. *Journal of Hospitality and Tourism Education, 25*(3), 131–145.

SmartTek Solutions. (2022). Virtual and augmented reality in hospitality industry. https://smarttek.solutions/blog/how-ar-vr-technologies-are-shaping-horeca-industry/. Accessed on October 18, 2023.

Tümler, J., Toprak, A., & Yan, B. (2022). Multi-user multi-platform XR collaboration: System and evaluation. In *Proceedings of the 2022 IEEE International Symposium on mixed and augmented reality*. (ISMAR) (pp. 1–12). IEEE. https://doi.org/10.1109/ISMAR55816.2022.00001

Tuomi, A., Tussyadiah, I. P., & Stienmetz, J. (2021). Applications and implications of service robots in hospitality. *Cornell Hospitality Quarterly, 62*(2), 232–247. https://doi.org/10.1177/1938965520923961

Tussyadiah, I. P., Wang, D., Jung, T. H., & tom Dieck, M. C. (2018). Virtual reality, presence, and attitude change: Empirical evidence from tourism. *Tourism Management, 66*, 140–154.

Wei, W. (2019). Research progress on virtual reality (VR) and augmented reality (AR) in tourism and hospitality. *Journal of Hospitality and Tourism Technology, 10*(4), 539–570.

Wirtz, J., Patterson, P. G., Kunz, W. H., Gruber, T., Lu, V. N., Paluch, S., & Martins, A. (2018). Brave new world: Service robots in the frontline. *Journal of Service Management, 29*(5). https://doi.org/10.1108/JOSM-04-2018-0119

Yotel. (2020). *Yotel Boston X UVD Robots partnership.* https://www.yotel.com/en/press/yotel-boston-x-uvd-robots-partnership. Accessed on August 03, 2023.

Chapter 8

Tourist Experience in Digital Detox Tourism

İsmail Uzut and Serap Özdemir Güzel

Istanbul University-Cerrahpasa, Turkey

Abstract

Digital detox practices seek to encourage tourists to disconnect from their devices and immerse themselves in the destination they are visiting. This may involve activities such as meditation, yoga or simply abstaining from social media and email. The impact of digital detox practices on tourist experiences can vary depending on the individual. While some tourists may find it difficult to disconnect from their devices, others may appreciate the opportunity to fully engage with their surroundings without distractions. Ultimately, digital detox practices have the potential to promote mindfulness and enhance the overall travel experience for those who are willing to try them.

In this section, digital detox defined and different forms are mentioned. The motivation factors of digital detox tourism activities carried out in this context and destinations and businesses for digital detox holidays will be examined. The chapter concluded by analysing the feedback obtained from consumers on TripAdvisor. This chapter provides a valuable contribution to the present digital detox tourism, which is in the market as a new touristic product by offering a comprehensive literature review. In addition, the chapter examines the review of comments made by tourists on TripAdvisor about digital detox tourism. The chapter further offers recommendations to tourism businesses on how to enhance their services in this domain. As a result, this section is expected to make a valuable contribution to both the academic literature and the tourism industry, specifically in the area of digital detox tourism.

Keywords: Digital detox tourism; Tripadvisor; tourist experience; digital-free tourism; unplugged tourism

Marketing and Design in the Service Sector, 119–136

Copyright © 2024 by Emerald Publishing Limited

All rights of reproduction in any form reserved

doi:10.1108/978-1-83797-276-020241009

Introduction

The advancement of information and communication technologies has led to the formation of a broad user base. This number has reached approximately 5.3 billion people worldwide (www.itu.int, n.d.). While digital technology offers numerous benefits, it's essential to strike a balance between its use (Duncan, 2004). The development of digital technology has also introduced a new phenomenon known as digital detox. This concept has been growing in recent years (Li et al., 2018). The emergence of this concept is driven by the negative impacts of digitalisation on human health and the tendency to disconnect from real-life experiences (Pawlowska-Leywand & Mataga, 2020). Over time, users have come to realise that they are trapped in a digital captivity, leading to a desire to disconnect from this digital enslavement for a certain period (Smith & Puczkó, 2015). Digital detoxes provide a reset button, allowing individuals to return to their digital lives with a refreshed perspective and healthier habits. As the role of technology continues to evolve in our lives, digital detox becomes an important tool for maintaining well-being and fostering a healthy relationship with technology.

Digital detox tourism involves holidays where there is reduced use of electronic devices and the internet (Li et al., 2018). In this type of tourism, tourists select destinations and accommodations that offer opportunities for unplugging and disconnecting from digital devices and technologies during their trip. These tourists actively seek environments that promote relaxation and limit digital distractions, enabling them to engage with the destination more authentically and mindfully. Consequently, excessive technology use during vacations impacts the tourist experience, as tourists rely on their mobile devices to connect with work and social life, manage their itineraries and fill their free time (Ferraro et al., 2006).

This chapter examines the emerging phenomenon of digital detox tourism. Elaboration on the topic starts with the definition, characteristic features, motivational factors and activities of digital detox tourism. Comments provided by consumers on lodging establishments offering services related to digital detox tourism on platforms such as TripAdvisor have been analysed in the context of consumer experience.

Digital Detox

The concept of digital detox has emerged as a result of the harmful effects brought about by the development of information and communication technologies. The term was first used in 2012 (Radtke et al., 2022, p. 192). Digital detox is described as 'conscious, voluntary, temporary and specific to the place and time of non-use' (Jiang & Balaji, 2022, p. 456). Furthermore, the social media aspect of digital detox is also relevant. In this context, digital detox 'can be defined as a periodic disconnection from social or online media or strategies to reduce digital media involvement' (Syvertsen & Enli, 2020, p. 1269). Digital detox can range from an hour to several weeks in duration (Syvertsen & Enli, 2020).

In conclusion, when defining digital detox, certain points are highlighted. These include (Syvertsen & Enli, 2020)

- a period disconnection from IT;
- a period of disconnection from social media;
- reduction of digital devices.

The purpose of a digital detox is to alleviate the negative effects of excessive digital usage, such as stress, anxiety, sleep disturbances and decreased productivity (Lee et al., 2014). It allows individuals to take a break from the constant digital stimuli and reconnect with the real world, promoting overall well-being and mental health.

Digital detox, which is based on staying away from digital stimuli for a certain period of time, has various types. These include temporary disconnection, setting boundaries, limiting social media usage and deleting apps and accounts, engaging in offline activities, participating in retreats or workshops, using digital detox apps, choosing tech-free accommodations and digital free-zones at home.

- *Temporary Disconnection:* Digital detox often involves taking a short break from using digital devices and platforms. This could be a few hours, a day, a weekend or even an extended vacation period. During this time, individuals consciously avoid checking emails, social media and other digital platforms to reduce screen time.
- *Limiting Social Media Usage and Deleting Apps and Accounts:* Digital detox may include reducing the time spent on social media platforms or taking a complete break from them for a set period. Digital detox can involve uninstalling or temporarily deactivating certain apps or social media accounts to minimise distractions and reduce the urge to check notifications constantly.
- *Engaging in Offline Activities:* To disconnect from the digital world, individuals engage in activities that don't require digital devices. This can include reading physical books, practicing hobbies, spending time in nature or having face-to-face conversations.
- *Participating in Retreats or Workshops:* Some people can immerse themselves in a technology-free environment and participate in activities focused on mindfulness and well-being.
- *Choosing Tech-free Accommodations:* Digital detox tourists may select accommodations that specifically promote unplugging or remote destinations with limited internet access.
- *Digital-Free Zones at Home:* Establishing specific areas within the home as 'digital-free zones' can encourage family members to interact without the distraction of devices.
- *Setting Boundaries:* Some people may designate certain hours of the day as 'tech-free' or choose not to use digital devices during meals, social gatherings or before bedtime.

Digital Detox Tourism

Digital detox tourism, also referred to as digital detox holiday, unplugged tourism, disconnected tourism or digital-free tourism/holiday/travel, involves tourists visiting destinations where temporary disconnection or controlled digital technology usage is in accordance with their preferences (Altınay-Özdemir & Goktas, 2021; Jiang & Balaji, 2022; Li et al., 2018). According to Stäheli and Stoltenberg (2022, p. 3), it is a temporary abstinence from digital media. Syvertsen (2022, p. 195) defines offline tourism as 'intensifying the experience of taking a break, realising what tourists perceive to be the true nature of outdoor life, heightening the sense of adventure and self-reliance'. Digital detox holidays is 'a tourism form in which individuals who want to get away from ICTs due to social, physical, or mental effects are voluntarily and consciously engaged in activities such as outdoor, experiential, well-being, and health activities in places (e.g., digital detox hotels, campsites, rural areas, small towns, or woodlands) that have none limited connectivity, and remain unconnected during their holiday except for calling home' (Altınay-Özdemir & Goktas, 2021, p. 23). In other words, digital detox tourism refers to a specific form of travel where individuals purposefully seek destinations and experiences that encourage them to disconnect from digital devices and technology (Li et al., 2018). Travel agencies also offer three basic digital detox packages in this context, namely (Hoving, 2017, p. 4)

(1) Detox packages that make the tourist responsible for not bringing digital devices to the destination;
(2) Digital detox packages for businesses and destinations that do not offer digital devices but provide ICT connectivity;
(3) Packages for destinations that are either far from ICT connections or lack connection.

The primary goal of digital detox tourism is to allow travelers to take a break from constant connectivity, reduce digital distractions and focus on genuine experiences, mindfulness and well-being during their trip. The characteristics of digital detox tourism can be listed as follows:

* *Technology-Free Zones:* Digital detox tourism often involves staying at accommodations or resorts that provide designated technology-free zones. These areas may have limited or no internet access and discourage the use of digital devices, promoting a tech-free environment.
* *Mindfulness and Well-being Activities:* Digital detox tourism packages often include activities focused on mindfulness, relaxation and well-being. These may include yoga sessions, meditation classes, spa treatments or nature walks; all aimed at promoting mental and physical rejuvenation.
* *Engagement with Nature:* Destinations for digital detox tourism are frequently located in natural and serene settings, such as remote forests, beaches, mountains or eco-lodges. This allows travelers to reconnect with nature and enjoy outdoor activities without digital distractions.

- *Offline Experiences:* Travelers are encouraged to participate in offline experiences and activities that don't require the use of digital devices. This can include immersive cultural experiences, cooking classes, art workshops and other hands-on engagements.
- *Unplugged Social Interactions:* Digital detox tourism promotes face-to-face interactions and encourages travelers to connect with each other and the local community without relying on digital communication.
- *Tech-Free Travel Itineraries:* Itineraries for digital detox tourism are designed to minimise digital reliance. Travelers may receive physical maps, guides and printed materials instead of digital ones.
- *Promotion of Mindful Photography:* While digital detox encourages less reliance on smartphones, some travel experiences may promote mindful photography, where travelers use cameras to capture memories instead of constantly being behind screens.
- *Encouragement of Unplugged Reflection:* Digital detox tourism encourages travelers to take time for personal reflection, journaling and contemplation without the distraction of digital devices.
- *Flexible and Customisable Packages:* Digital detox tourism providers often offer flexible packages, allowing travellers to tailor their experiences to match their desired level of disconnection and preferred activities.

The Motivation Factors of Digital Detox Tourism

The motivations behind digital detox tourism can vary among individuals, but some common motivational factors in the literature are as follows (Floros et al., 2021; Jiang & Balaji, 2022, p. 459):

- *Novelty:* For some, digital detox tourism might simply be a unique and intriguing experience, a way to break away from the usual travel routines and try something different.
- *Stress Reduction/Technostress:* Many people feel overwhelmed by the constant influx of information and connectivity that digital devices bring. Digital detox tourists seek to escape the pressures of their fast-paced and technology-driven lives.
- *Reconnecting with Nature:* By reducing their reliance on digital devices, they can fully immerse themselves in the beauty of nature and the culture of the destination.
- *Well-being and Health:* Unplugging from technology can lead to reduced stress and anxiety, improved sleep quality and enhanced mental clarity. Digital detox tourism offers a chance to take a break from the digital world and focus on self-care.
- *Mindfulness and Presence:* Disconnecting from technology allows travellers to be more present in the moment and engage fully with their surroundings, enhancing their travel experiences.

- *Relaxation:* Digital detox will bring tourists tranquillity and peace, thereby helping them refresh their body and mind.
- *Self-Expression:* It allows tourists to truly be him or herself towards their personal lifestyles (e.g. peaceful, simple and authentic) and values (e.g. work–life balance and family bonds).
- *Social Bonding:* Digital detox tourists have the opportunity to connect more deeply with the people they travel with and the locals they meet.
- *Escapism:* Tourists can get away from the negativities created by information and communication technologies and temporarily escape from problems.

Digital Detox Tourism Activities

Tourists who embark on their journeys for diverse motivations often demonstrate a proclivity to partake in specific forms of tourism or engage in various activities encompassed within the realm of that specific tourism category at their chosen destination. For example, visitors who immerse themselves in culinary tourism exhibit an inclination towards pursuits such as exploring vineyards, participating in tasting sessions, engaging in food and beverage-centric festivals like Oktoberfest and enrolling in culinary workshops. This inclination is frequently driven by their personal preferences or the array of opportunities presented by the destination. Drawing upon this premise and the explications furnished in the preceding sections, this discussion will expound upon the array of activities undertaken by tourists who elect to participate in digital detox tourism during the course of their travels. Additionally, the sources constituting the supply of digital tourism will be elucidated.

In the literature survey focused on digital detox activities and supply sources, Topsakal and Dinç (2022) have classified businesses into three categories based on the degree of intensity characterising digital detox pursuits during travel: those offering soft, high and comprehensive detox services. Within the framework of this investigation, it has been discerned that preeminent among the activities provided across 33 diverse establishments in 22 countries are cycling tours, hiking and nature walks. Altınay-Özdemir and Goktas (2021, p. 24), in contrast, have systematically analysed the engagement of tourists motivated by digital detox in a tripartite structure: outdoor activities and sports, well-being endeavours and experiential activities centred on health. In addition, Egger et al. (2020, p. 5) have drawn conclusions, drawing from qualitative research encompassing participants from various nations, suggesting that tourists, during the phase of digital detox, incline towards outdoor activities, diverse sporting endeavours or engagement in cultural activities.

Through an exhaustive review of scholarly contributions, Dickinson et al. (2016) deduced that tourists undertaking camping vacations, either voluntarily or under obligatory circumstances (in locales deprived of internet or telephonic connectivity), tend to gravitate towards outdoor undertakings. Li et al. (2018, p. 328) have categorised these undertakings as spanning outdoor sports, skill enhancement, wellness and retreat programs, collective or team-oriented games, as well as experiences imbued with spiritual and cultural dimensions. Moreover, insights gleaned from investigations conducted by academicians including Fan et al. (2019), Pathak (2016), Sunar et al. (2018), Hoving (2017), Emek (2014), Pawłowska-Legwand and Matoga (2020), Gençoğlu (2019), Stäheli and Stoltenberg (2022), and Schwarzenegger and Lohmeier (2021) were meticulously reviewed and methodically categorised, culminating in the formulation of the Table 8.1 presented hereunder.

Table 8.1. Activities Preferred by Tourists to Participate in Digital Detox Tourism.

Activity Type	Content
Outdoor activities	Camping, Zip-line canopy, High ropes obstacle courses, Skylight/sunrise/sunset watching (e.g., northern lights), Star-gazing, Wildlife watching, Husky/reindeer sledding, Sled ride, Donkey riding, Camel riding, Fly fishing, Fishing, Bird watching, Swimming with dolphins
Sport activities	*Outdoor Sports* Hiking, Walking, Cycling, Rock climbing, adventure trekking, Horseback riding, Mountain climbing, Golf, Desert golf, Desert surfing, Tennis , Soccer, Trap and skeet shooting, Waterfall climbing, Snowshoeing expeditions, Tramping, Extreme sports *Water Sports* Sea kayaking, Kayaking, Snorkeling, Rafting, Scuba diving, Sailing, Canoeing, Swimming, Sailing, Water ski, Kite surfing, Deep water running, Cross-country skiing, Rowing *Indoor or Outdoor Sports* Fitness classes, Gym, Stretching, Tai-Chi, Rock wall, Dodgeball
Games	Scavenger hunting, Board games, Fireside sing-alongs, Capturing the flag, Talent shows, Team games, Location based games
Skill Development activities	Yard work, Farm chores, Design Work, Tie dye, Working farms, Harvesting, Tree planting, Crafting workshops, Thematic workshops
Tours	Visiting city landmarks, Sightseeing, Safari, City tours, Participating events and festivals Listening to folklore, Archaeological exploration, Visiting

(Continued)

Table 8.1. *(Continued)*

Activity Type	Content
	museums and heritage sites, Boat excursions, Visiting religious holy lands, temples and monasteries, Tropical tours, Forest tour, ATV tour, Hunting tour, Waterfall tour, Wildlife tour.
Health	Wellness, Spa, Massage, Body treatment, Healthy eating, Organic facials, Detoxifying scrubs, Hot spring bath, Finnish sauna, Mindful tea, Medical care and therapy, Group therapy
Well-being activities	Raga Therapy, Silent Walking Meditation, Group therapy session, Yoga, Qi gong, Doing pujas/prayers, Silent walking meditation, Zen-like activities, Silent meal
Art/Artistic activities	Art classes, Painting, Watercolour classes, Glass mosaic workshops, Pond studies, Drawing, Poetry sessions
Gastronomy	Gourmet meals, Organic fresh farm meals, Nutritional cooking, Cooking, Food or wine testing, Preparing local dishes, Healthy eating
Others	Shopping, Writing (book, poem etc.), Book reading, Taking picture, Communicate with local people, Seminar with monks or nuns, Ability to join monks or nuns in the work, Pilgrimage, Fasting

Source: Created by the authors.

It can be argued that the diversity of recreational activities available for engagement or contemplation during leisure time by participants in digital detox tourism, as presented in Table 8.1, stands as a substantial allure. In this context, it can be posited that two distinct categories of resources are put forth: those intrinsic to the destination and those established by investors. Through these resources, a spectrum of activities accessible to tourists is delineated across 10 categories, including 'Outdoor activities, Sport activities, Games, Skill development activities, Tours, Health, Wellbeing activities, Art/Artistic activities, Gastronomy and Other'.

Furthermore, it can be asserted that within the lodgings or locales of choice for tourists, some of the previously mentioned activities are frequently made available simultaneously, housed within the same establishment. In conjunction with the aforementioned activities, an exploration of the lodgings or destinations frequently favoured by participants in digital detox tourism and the pertinent details would prove advantageous. In this context, the subject matter is expounded upon in the ensuing section.

Case Studies of Digital Detox Tourism at the Hospitality Sector

Within the context of digital detox, numerous hotels are capable of offering tailored digital detox packages despite possessing a full array of digital amenities. However, in specific destinations, it can be asserted that tourists are compelled to undertake digital detox as a result of limitations in infrastructure or facilities. To exemplify, the Westin Dublin, an international hotel chain located in the digitally well-equipped city of Dublin, provides visitors the voluntary option to choose digital detox packages (Sissons, 2014). Conversely, in certain rural areas, such as the Skiary region in Scotland, amenities such as electricity, mobile phone connectivity and internet access are either sparse or entirely absent (often influenced by the operational preferences of the establishment). Therefore, a more accurate approach involves conducting assessments at the facility level rather than limiting the analysis to specific destinations within the domain of digital detox tourism. In this context, the fundamental characteristics of digital detox practices in facilities located in different countries are outlined below. (Greyfield Inn, n.d.a, n.d.b; Golden Door, n.d.a, n.d.b; Hariharalaya Yoga and Meditation Retreat Center, n.d.a, n.d.b; Mumbo Island, n.d.; Skiary, n.d.; Sivanda Bahamas, n.d.; SHA Wellness, n.d.; Veda5, n.d.a; Three Camel Lodge, n.d.a, n.d.b; Tripadvisor, n.d.a, n.d.b; Turtle Island, n.d.; Wills, 2011);

• Due to their geographical locations, certain lodging establishments are situated in regions entirely devoid of modern technology. Nevertheless, some accommodation facilities also have limited phone signal or Wi-Fi access owing to similar factors.
• Some lodging establishments do not offer guests planned or mandatory access to electricity, television, mobile phone signals and Internet connectivity in their rooms. However, in these types of accommodations, traditional practices such as using stoves for cooking and heating are employed. Furthermore, unique experiences are provided through amenities like Rayburn-heated hot water, Tilley lamplight during evenings and a cosy ambiance illuminated by paraffin lamps, tea lights and a hearth kindled with driftwood.
• Throughout travels, diverse approaches concerning the utilization of technology are evident within lodging establishments. For instance, certain enterprises mandate guests to securely store all digital devices in a safe during the check-in process. Conversely, another category of establishments grants permission exclusively for the use of e-book readers, such as Kindles, for reading purposes. It can be asserted that the former group enforces stringent regulations pertaining to digital detox, while the latter group embraces more flexible guidelines. These guidelines permit activities such as sending emails,

composing SMS messages, utilising electronic devices during specified hours of the day or indulging in music listening with headphones solely within the confines of the designated rooms.

- In establishments that implement digital detox, an extensive array of activities is curated for guests to engage in during their leisure time. These activities encompass yoga, pranayama (breathwork), seated meditation, swimming, rock climbing, reading, healing practices, cinematic experiences, a dojo, ice baths, participation in arts and music, involvement in games, guided hikes, leisurely walks, indoor rowing, water fitness exercises, swimming, Tabata training, rejuvenating spa experiences, diverse massage therapies, comprehensive body and skin care programs, guided bee tours, butterfly walks, cooking schools, astrology sessions and various other offerings.

Methodology and Results

Within the scope of the research, the objective was to scrutinise the tourist evaluations pertaining to enterprises, as described above, engaged in activities or offering packages encompassing digital detoxification. The ultimate goal was to decipher and expound upon the narratives encapsulating tourists' experiences with digital detox, as gleaned from the conducted analyses. To accomplish this, qualitative research methodologies were deliberated for implementation. In the purview of this study, the feedback of patrons who availed themselves of lodging services from 10 distinct enterprises, each of which was investigated and established to provide digital detox regimens or packages, was procured through the medium of the www.tripadvisor.com platform. Evidently, a multitude of reviews in diverse languages were identified. However, to ensure the fidelity of the ensuing analytical process, exclusivity was granted solely to those reviews composed in the English language. Table 8.2 serves as the repository for the entities constituting the focal units of analysis, proffering intricate insights into the multifaceted spectrum of commentaries engendered in response to the services of these identified enterprises.

Upon scrutiny of the TripAdvisor reviews pertaining to the establishments presented in Table 8.2, a total of 4,621 reviews were identified, of which 4,359 were composed in the English language. Notably, the English-language reviews encompassing these enterprises were sourced from the www.tripadvisor.com domain during the temporal span from 1 August 2023 to 21 August 2023. These specific reviews were methodically conducted utilising the content analysis approach, a qualitative research methodology. The selection of content analysis as the chosen methodology is underscored by its inherent aim to elucidate the conceptual underpinnings capable of expounding upon the assimilated data or commentaries, while further illuminating the intricate interrelationships inherent within these conceptual domains (Yıldırım & Şimşek, 2016, p. 242).

Table 8.2. Descriptive Profile of Analysis Unit.

The Companies	Country	Total No of Reviews	Total No of English Reviews
1.	Scotland	23	23
2.	Mongolia	145	135
3.	Fiji	536	528
4.	Cambodia	1,395	1,299
5.	USA	344	344
6.	USA	32	32
7.	India	740	760
8.	Bahamas	882	902
9.	Spain	330	164
10.	Malawi	194	172
Total Number of Reviews	–	**4,621**	**4,359**

Source: Created by the authors.

In conjunction with the methodology employed in this study, the data obtained underwent primary analysis utilising thematic and sub-codes. This analytical process drew insights from scholarly contributions by Pearce and Gretzel (2012), Li et al. (2018), Floros et al. (2021), Egger et al. (2020), Jiang and Balaji (2022), Topsakal and Dinç (2022), Altınay-Özdemir and Goktas (2021), Dickinson et al. (2016), Li et al. (2018), Fan et al. (2019), Pathak (2016), Sunar et al. (2018), Hoving (2017), Emek (2014), Pawłowska-Legwand and Matoga (2020), Gençoğlu (2019), Stäheli and Stoltenberg (2022) and Schwarzenegger and Lohmeier (2021), among other esteemed academics, whose works were meticulously scrutinised and evaluated. Concurrently, the authors of this research undertook a comprehensive literature review and, based on the assimilated comments, delineated the themes and corresponding codes. In the subsequent phase of analysis, the researchers harnessed the MAXQDA 2020 software, a widely employed tool in qualitative research endeavours.

In the realm of qualitative research, one of the most prominent challenges encountered is ensuring reliability. To address this concern, an inter-coder consensus procedure was meticulously adhered to. Within this scope, all codifications were independently executed by two designated authors. Subsequently, the resulting two analysis files underwent a process of inter-coder consensus utilising the MAXQDA 2020 software. Through the meticulous execution of this protocol, the foundational reliability of the study was firmly established. Following the systematic coding of comments that had their reliability firmly established, a comprehensive total of five distinct thematic dimensions were discerned. A visual representation containing pertinent insights into these thematic dimensions is thoughtfully presented in Fig. 8.1.

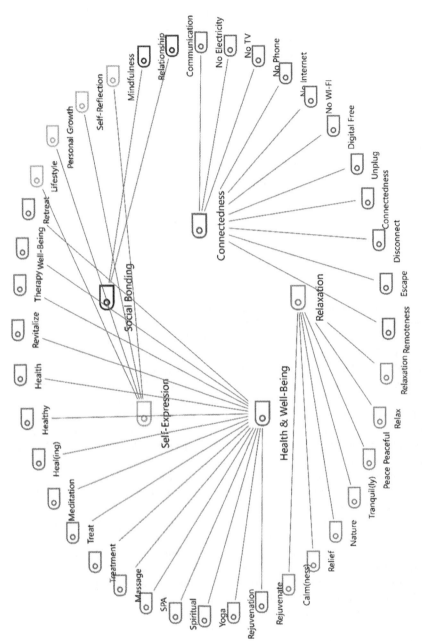

Fig. 8.1.   Information on Theme and Sub-codes. *Source:* Created by the authors.

As a result of the conducted codifications, a comprehensive set of five distinct themes emerged: 'Connectedness', 'Relaxation', 'Health & Well-Being', 'Self-Expression', and 'Social Bonding'. Beneath the umbrella of these over-arching themes, a total of 40 sub-codes were meticulously delineated. For the sake of enhancing thematic clarity and coherence, a coherent colour-matching scheme was thoughtfully employed, wherein themes and their corresponding sub-codes were thoughtfully colour-coded in tandem. Upon the meticulous determination of these themes and sub-codes, an intricate word cloud visual-isation was curated, encapsulating the sentiments contained within the 4,359 comments associated with the 10 surveyed establishments. In its essence, a word cloud functions as a visual instrument that encapsulates recurrent words within the corpus of examined data, documents or comments, prioritising these words based on their relative frequency or repetition count. This visualisation tech-nique is marked by the prominence of words, proportionally scaling their font sizes to mirror their recurrence frequencies.

It is important to note that, in order for the generated word cloud to convey substantive meaning, certain linguistic elements were strategically omitted from the word cloud generation process. These include conjunctions, prepositions, articles, non-contributory words and numerical values. The resultant word cloud, elegantly depicted in Fig. 8.2, stands as a testament to this meticulous process, capturing the essence of the study's findings.

Fig. 8.2.   Word Cloud of Comments by Users Participating in Digital Detox Tourism. *Source:* Created by the authors.

Upon examining Fig. 8.2, it becomes apparent that in the reviews of the 10 establishments offering digital detox activities or packages, tourists frequently employ words such as yoga, place, food, amazing and experience. Within this context, it can be confidently posited that the words manifested in the word cloud are aligned with the themes and sub-codes that have been established through the analysis. It is pertinent to note that these words, as encapsulated within the word cloud, are remarkably congruent with the overarching theme of 'Health & Well-Being'. Notably, this theme encompasses concepts that wield both physiological and psychological influence over health, epitomised by terms like yoga, meditation and wholesome nourishment. Correspondingly, words such as comfortable, nature, great and wonderful seamlessly resonate with the thematic essence of 'Relaxation'.

When contextualised within the thematic framework of 'Self-Expression', a distinct array of lexicon emerges, including words such as yourself, special, feel and private, all of which distinctly evoke the notion of self-exploration and individuality. Meanwhile, the thematic realm of 'Social Bonding' is intricately woven into the narrative, evident in words such as staff, family, friendly and people, signalling a sense of communal connection and interpersonal warmth. In contrast, an intriguing observation unveils itself as words associated with the 'Connectedness' theme are relatively inconspicuous. This phenomenon can be attributed to the compositional structure of numerous terms within the 'Connectedness' theme, such as no phone, no internet, no Wi-Fi, and digital free, which inherently consist of two-word constructs. Consequently, the limited representation of words tethered to the 'Connectedness' theme within the word cloud can be ascribed to the focus on single-word terminology during the cloud's formulation.

Following the development of themes and codes, as well as the evaluations related to the word cloud, an analysis of correlations among the themes was undertaken. In this context, a code co-occurrence model was constructed to investigate the presence and intensity of relationships among the established themes. The ensuing model, designed to scrutinise the interrelationships between themes, has been visually presented in Fig. 8.3 for reference.

Upon examining the code co-occurrence model, it becomes evident that correlations exist among all themes; however, the intensity of these relationships varies. Within this context, the most pronounced relationship is observed between the 'Relaxation' and 'Connectedness' themes. It should be noted that despite comparatively lower perceived relationships among other themes in comparison to the 'Relaxation-Connectedness' association, it is justifiable to assert that these relationships still maintain a significant degree in terms of the px value. Moreover, it is quite common to anticipate that visitors, when seeking 'Connectedness', will distance themselves from the demands of daily life to experience a more serene and tranquil interval. However, it's worth noting that expecting such a transition is more feasible. On the other hand, the weakest relationship is identified between the 'Self-Expression' theme and the others. Nevertheless, considering that visitors driven by the motive of self-expression often adopt activities like yoga as an inherent lifestyle choice, optimise their time through meditative practices, liberate themselves from dependencies such as smoking, establish structured sleep and dietary routines for personal development, it is plausible to posit that profound

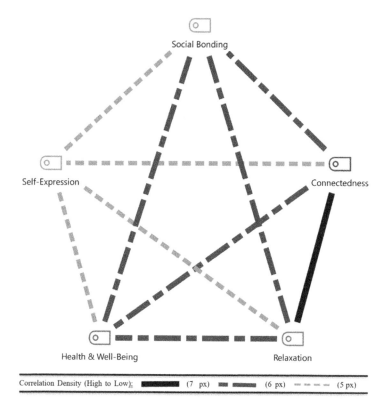

Fig. 8.3.   Code Co-occurrence Model. *Source:* Created by the authors.

self-reflection, an endeavour seldom feasible within the realm of daily routines, can be actualised through interventions such as digital detox, the provision of serene environments and avenues for self-enhancement.

Conclusion

This section addresses the emerging phenomenon of digital detox tourism in recent years. In this context, the concept of digital detox, digital detox tourism, its characteristics, motivational factors and activities are expounded upon. To examine tourist experiences from the perspective of digital detox tourism, comments on 10 digital detox tourism establishments on TripAdvisor have been scrutinised.

In accordance with the findings of the study, thematic dimensions pertinent to digital detox tourism have manifested as 'Connectedness', 'Relaxation', 'Health & Well-Being', 'Self-Expression' and 'Social Bonding'. When constructing a word cloud based on the comments, prominent keywords include yoga, place, food, amazing and experience. These keywords align with the experiential focus and health philosophy of digital detox tourism. Another research outcome indicates correlations among the five themes. The strongest correlation is observed between 'Relaxation' and 'Connectedness', while the weakest correlation appears between 'Self-Expression' and other themes.

In conclusion, tourists in the context of digital detox tourism pay heed to specific key aspects in their chosen destinations and establishments. First and foremost, it's imperative to recognise that this tourist profile embodies a conscientious consumer. The desire to temporarily escape the adverse effects of digitisation and the aspiration to engage with the real world take precedence. This enables tourists to attain a unique experience through engagement with the real world.

For businesses providing services in the domain of digital detox tourism, it is advisable to pay heed to fundamental considerations. Packages offered to tourists should meticulously evaluate the extent to which individuals will disconnect from technology. Within the scope of detox, businesses should concentrate on factors that are fundamental motivators for individuals, such as novelty, technostress, well-being and health, relaxation, social bonding and self-expression. It is crucial not to lose sight of the fact that tourists are seeking respite from information technology.

References

Altınay-Özdemir, M., & Goktas, L. S. (2021). Research trends on digital detox holidays: A bibliometric analysis, 2012–2020. *Tourism & Management Studies*, *17*(3), 21–35. https://doi.org/10.18089/tms.2021.170302

Dickinson, J. E., Hibbert, J. F., & Filimonau, V. (2016). Mobile technology and the tourist experience: (Dis) connection at the campsite. *Tourism Management*, *57*, 193–201.

Duncan, M. (2004). Autoethnography: Critical appreciation of an emerging Art. *International Journal of Qualitative Methods*, *3*(4), 28–39. https://doi.org/10.1177/160940690400300403

Egger, I., Lei, S. I., & Wassler, P. (2020). Digital free tourism – An exploratory study of tourist motivations. *Tourism Management*, *79*, 104098. https://doi.org/10.1016/j.tourman.2020.104098

Emek, M. (2014, August). Digital detox for the holidays: Are we addicted? In C. Kerdpitak, A. Benabdelhafid, K. Keuer, & G. Nartea (Eds.), *Proceedings of European Academic Conference on Business Tourism & Apply Sciences in Europe & America 2014 International Conference on Tourism Transport & Technology ICTTT 2014* (pp. 1–3). The Brunel University.

Fan, D. X., Buhalis, D., & Lin, B. (2019). A tourist typology of online and face-to-face social contact: Destination immersion and tourism encapsulation/decapsulation. *Annals of Tourism Research*, *78*, 102757. https://doi.org/10.1016/j.annals.2019.102757

Ferraro, G., Caci, B., D'amico, A., & Blasi, M. D. (2006). Internet addiction disorder: An Italian study. *CyberPsychology and Behavior*, *10*(2), 170–175.

Floros, C., Cai, W., McKenna, B., & Ajeeb, D. (2021). Imagine being off-the-grid: Millennials' perceptions of digital-free travel. *Journal of Sustainable Tourism*, *29*(5), 751–766. https://doi.org/10.1080/09669582.2019.1675676

Gençoğlu, F. (2019). Lüks Turizmde Dijital Detoks Dönemi. https://www.aa.com.tr/tr/sirkethaberleri/turizm/luks-turizmde-dijitaldetoks-donemi/651915. Accessed on August 1, 2023.

Golden Door. (n.d.a). https://goldendoor.com/pre-arrival-faqs/. Accessed on August 28, 2023.

Golden Door. (n.d.b). https://goldendoor.com/the-experience/. Accessed on August 28, 2023.

Greyfield Inn. (n.d.a). About. https://greyfieldinn.com/about/the-inn/. Accessed on August 28, 2023.

Greyfield Inn. (n.d.b). About. https://greyfieldinn.com/activities/. Accessed on August 28, 2023.

Hariharalaya Yoga and Meditation Retreat Center. (n.d.a). https://hariharalaya.com/faq/#digital. Accessed on August 28, 2023.

Hariharalaya Yoga and Meditation Retreat Center. (n.d.b). https://hariharalaya.com/facilities/. Accessed on August 28, 2023.

Hoving, K. (2017). *Digital detox tourism: Why disconnect?* Umea Universitet, Department of Geography and Economic History Master's Programme in Tourism Master Thesis. https://www.diva-portal.org/smash/get/diva2:1119076/FULLTEXT01.pdf

Jiang, Y., & Balaji, M. S. (2022). Getting unwired: What drives travellers to take a digital detox holiday? *Tourism Recreation Research*, *47*(5–6), 453–469. https://doi.org/10.1080/02508281.2021.1889801

Lee, Y. K., Chang, C. T., Lin, Y., & Cheng, Z. H. (2014). The dark side of smartphone usage: Psychological traits, compulsive behavior and technostress. *Computers in Human Behavior*, *31*, 373–383. https://doi.org/10.1016/j.chb.2013.10.047

Li, J., Pearce, P. L., & Low, D. (2018). Media representation of digital-free tourism: A critical discourse analysis. *Tourism Management*, *69*, 317–329.

Mumbo Island. (n.d.). https://mumboisland.com. Accessed on August 28, 2023.

Pathak, D. N. K. (2016). Digital detox in India. *International Journal of Research in Humanities & Soc. Sciences*, *4*(8), 60–67.

Pawłowska-Legwand, A., & Matoga, Ł. (2020). Disconnect from the digital world to reconnect with the real life: an analysis of the potential for development of unplugged tourism on the example of Poland. *Tourism Planning & Development*, 1–24. https://doi.org/10.1080/21568316.2020.1842487

Pearce, P. L., & Gretzel, U. (2012). Tourism in technology dead zones: Documenting experiential dimensions. *International Journal of Tourism Sciences*, *12*(2), 1–20. https://doi.org/10.1080/15980634.2012.11434656

Radtke, T., Apel, T., Schenkel, K., Keller, J., & Von Lindern, E. (2022). Digital detox: An effective solution in the smartphone era? A systematic literature review. *Mobile Media & Communication*, *10*(2), 190–215.

Schwarzenegger, C., & Lohmeier, C. (2021). Creating opportunities for temporary disconnection: How tourism professionals provide alternatives to being permanently online. *Convergence*, *27*(6), 1631–1647.

SHA Wellness. (n.d.). https://shawellness.com. Accessed on August 28, 2023.

Sissons, J. (2014). https://www.bbc.com/worklife/article/20140821-time-for-a-digital-detox

Sivanda Bahamas. (n.d.). https://sivanandabahamas.org. Accessed on August 28, 2023.

Skiary. (n.d.). https://www.skiary.com/. Accessed on August 28, 2023.

Smith, M., & Puczkó, L. (2015). More than a special interest: Defining and determining the demand for health tourism. *Tourism Recreation Research, 40*(2), 205–219. https://doi.org/10.1080/02508281.2015.1045364

Stäheli, U., & Stoltenberg, L. (2022). Digital detox tourism: Practices of analogization. *New Media & Society.* https://doi.org/10.1177/14614448211072808

Sunar, H., Gökçe, F., & Cihangir, I. S. (2018). A new approach to tourism: Digital restoration. In *Innovation and global issues in social sciences III* (pp. 326–338). (Patara Antique City Parliament Building), April 26-29, Antalya.

Syvertsen, T. (2022). Framing digital disconnection: Problem definitions, values, and actions among digital detox organisers. *Convergence: The International Journal of Research into New Media Technologies, 29.* https://doi.org/10.1177/135485 65221122910

Syvertsen, T., & Enli, G. (2020). Digital detox: Media resistance and the promise of authenticity. *Convergence, 26*(5-6), 1269–1283. https://doi.org/10.1177/ 1354856519847325

Three Camel Lodge. (n.d.a). Our story. www.threecamellodge.com/our-story/. Accessed on August 28, 2023.

Three Camel Lodge. (n.d.b). *Activities.* https://www.threecamellodge.com/activities/. Accessed on August 28, 2023.

Topsakal, Y., & Dinç, A. (2022). Çevrimdışı Tatil: Dijital Detoks İçin Ekoturizm. *Journal of Tourism Intelligence and Smartness, 5*(1), 1–10.

Tripadvisor. (n.d.a). *Three Camel Lodge Review.* https://www.tripadvisor.com/Hotel_ Review-g6998668-d606052-Reviews-Three_Camel_Lodge-Gobi_Gurvansaikhan_ National_Park.html. Accessed on August 28, 2023.

Tripadvisor (n.d.b). Accessed on August 28, 2023. https://www.tripadvisor.com

Turtle Island. (n.d.). Experiences. https://www.turtlefiji.com/experiences/. Accessed on August 28, 2023.

Veda5. (n.d.). https://www.vedafive.com. Accessed on August 28, 2023.

Wills, D. (2011). https://www.theguardian.com/travel/2011/apr/27/scotland-guesthouse-skiary-loch-hourn

Yıldırım, A., & Şimşek, H. (2016). *Sosyal bilimlerde nitel araştırma yöntemleri.* Seçkin.

www.itu.int. (n.d.). https://www.itu.int/en/ITU-D/Statistics/Pages/stat/default.aspx. Accessed on August 25, 2023.

Chapter 9

Customer Experience Design in Sportswear Retail Stores

Sardar Mohammadi[a], *Abed Mahmoudian*[a]
and Manuel Alonso Dos Santos[b]

[a]University of Kurdistan, Iran
[b]University of Granda, Spain

Abstract

Currently, attention to customer experience management is one of the most important management approaches in the business field. Focussing on improving customer experience and having a customer experience management strategy is one of the actions that service providers can take to improve their marketing performance by providing superior experiences to customers. The nature of customer experience is very important for the retail industry, especially for sportswear stores, because sports products are mostly experience-oriented and can be classified as a general experience. Despite the importance of consumption experience in consumer behaviour studies, the design of sports customer experiences has received less attention from researchers. Therefore, this chapter seeks to answer the question of what aspects of creating and developing customer experience in sportswear retail stores are. To answer this question, this chapter attempts to identify the areas of creating customer experiences in sports stores by using the views of sports marketing experts through qualitative research and using content analysis techniques. The findings indicate that sports stores try to provide the best experience for their customers by considering six aspects of human resources and employees, products, interior design, exterior space, technology and interaction and communication in their strategic marketing plans and investing in creating and developing these aspects. They create a distinct experience for customers and provide a basis for purchasing, satisfaction, loyalty and other positive marketing consequences for customers.

Marketing and Design in the Service Sector, 137–152
Copyright © 2024 by Emerald Publishing Limited
All rights of reproduction in any form reserved
doi:10.1108/978-1-83797-276-020241010

Keywords: Sportswear stores; sportswear; sustomer experience; sports marketing; sports industry; sports business

Introduction

Companies are moving away from traditional marketing features and benefits towards creating experiences for their customers (Eskiler & Safak, 2022). Consumer experience has introduced a new approach to marketing and has shifted the focus of marketers towards the importance of creating a valid, honest, attractive and memorable experience for the consumer (Chang et al., 2020). Consumer experience was first discussed and conceptualised in the articles of Holbrook and Hirschman (1982) and is recognized as a prominent approach for marketing researchers and specialists (Eriksson et al., 2018). Some studies show that providing a superior customer experience is one of the ways to achieve successful marketing results and competitive advantages (Gao et al., 2020).

Klaus and Maklan (2013) define customer experience as the cognitive and emotional evaluation resulting from direct and indirect interactions between the customer and the organisation. Customers want to be engaged in effective purchasing (cognition) and, on the other hand, seek to enjoy the experience (emotion). This concept includes all customer interactions with the company, including before, during and after purchase or consumption. Some findings consider the concept of customer experience as a multidimensional structure from the customer's perspective (Kuppelwieser & Klaus, 2020) and define the structure of customer experience by focussing on the cognitive, emotional, behavioural, sensory and social responses of the customer to the company's suggestions throughout the customer's shopping journey (Lemon & Verhoef, 2016). Customer experience creates perceptions that are stored in the customer's memory and a positive customer experience leads to satisfaction, trust, repeat visits, repeat purchases and customer loyalty (McLean, 2017). Currently, attention to customer experience management is one of the most important management approaches in the business field. Focussing on improving customer experience and having a customer experience management strategy is one of the actions that service providers can take to improve their marketing performance by providing superior experiences to customers. This process, from before the selection, purchase and use of services to the process of purchasing services and the stages after using services, affects customers and improves satisfaction, ultimately leading to increased profitability for the company (Mansoor et al., 2020).

A large volume of studies conducted on the design, staging and management of customer experiences in various sectors in recent years shows the importance and complexity of customer experiences and the considerations that still need attention (Happ et al., 2020). Businesses operate in an increasingly competitive world, and customer expectations for a complete and satisfying experience are increasing. No longer is competition just about product quality, service quality or price, and companies have begun to focus on the overall customer experience. Therefore, a better understanding of how to create and manage customer experiences over time is very important (Ta et al., 2022). Sports equipment managers can create a real experience in their physical stores by investing in specialised, enthusiastic and technological personnel to create a real experience in the store of the product and sports training. While sports equipment retailers acknowledge the importance of providing a memorable shopping experience for customers by creating a memorable environment and placing multiple touch-points in stores, management researchers have paid little attention to sports stores. This study examines ways in which sports retail managers can effectively design their stores in experiential conditions (Bonfanti & Yfantidou, 2021).

Customer experience is an important and relatively new concept for service businesses to gain a sustainable competitive advantage. Although the literature on customer experience is expanding, there is a gap in customer experience in the sports field (Eskiler & Safak, 2022). Sports researchers, retailers and service management have paid less attention to customer experience in sports stores. Some studies have focused on the physical and digital environment and the atmosphere of sports stores, especially music. Some studies have examined sports purchasing behaviour by proposing a scale to measure sports customer experience and identifying relationships with other elements such as overall satisfaction and intention to repurchase the brand. Other studies have considered the role of flagship brand stores in promoting a more enjoyable brand experience and attracting consumers who are looking for a combination of entertainment and shopping. Given that customer experience in sports stores is based on service management and retail models, research on this topic in the sports field is in its early stages, and scientific knowledge, both theoretical and practical, is limited and scattered (Bonfanti & Yfantidou, 2021). Therefore, the present study was conducted with the aim of designing customer experience in sports apparel retail stores.

Theoretical Framework

Customer experience

Customer experience is a key part of the consumption experience, and its goal is for consumers to actively express their psychological and behavioural reactions to buying and experiencing different emotions. Experience is considered a specific event that occurs in response to the five senses of the consumer and is usually obtained through direct or virtual participation in the event (Bonfanti & Yfantidou, 2021). Experience is considered a psychological state that is felt by the consumer, and its characteristics include that it is not created on its own and depends on the type of event that the consumer faces. It has a complex, evolutionary and ascending structure, is unique and somewhat irreproducible and takes shape in different stages of the purchasing cycle, such as before, during and after purchasing (Rather, 2020).

Customer experience in the store can be defined as 'a multidimensional structure focussing on the cognitive, emotional, behavioural, sensory and social responses of the customer to a company's proposals throughout the customer's shopping journey' (Lemon & Verhoef, 2016, p. 316). To create a memorable experience in the store, retailers essentially use the sales environment with intervention in four dimensions in the DAST model (Design–Environment–Social–Acceptance): (a) design elements, which include the functional and aesthetic aspects of the store, such as layout, design and furniture. (b) Environmental factors, which are based on individual consumer senses (such as vision, sound, smell and touch) and background conditions (such as light, music, smell, temperature, lighting, sounds and entertainment). (c) Social features, namely interaction with people present in the environment (such as store employees and other customers) and (d) Acceptance, which refers to the ability of customers to test the product/service, such as tasting a food sample, trying on clothes, or using equivalent digital technologies through augmented or virtual reality, to discover products. Retailers create customer experience through several store features that they can control, such as pricing, assortment, product display, sales staff, knowledge provision, product testing, layout, and store space and many factors beyond their control, such as consumer motivation to visit the store, their mood and available time for shopping, the sense of entertainment and socialising in the store (Roggeveen et al., 2020).

Customer Experience in Sports Retail

Given that customer experience in a store has multiple touchpoints resulting from the interaction between the consumer and the retailer, technology and digitisation, especially interactive technology, play a key role in facilitating store experience management (Mohammadi & Dickson, 2021; Siregar & Kent, 2019). By creating an attractive environment that makes the customer experience memorable and enjoyable, this is particularly true in the field of sports retail, as studies have shown that sports consumption involves experiences based on interaction between individual consumers and the sports environment, which are mediated physically, technologically and digitally (Funk et al., 2012).

The assumption that sports has unique characteristics can lead to the fact that customer experience in sports is different from customer experience in other areas (Happ et al., 2020). Additionally, sports centres offer a range of services (García-Fernández et al., 2022a, 2022b; Siani et al., 2022). Customers (members) see the quality of their output (technical quality) and their interaction with service providers and other customers as part of their experience. Therefore, new technologies help sports centres improve their service performance and effectively understand and manage their customers' desires before, during and after purchase, as well as improve their understanding of competition (García-Fernández et al., 2022a, 2022b; Siani et al., 2022).

Bustamante and Rubio (2017) conceptualised and validated a comprehensive scale for measuring customer experience in stores, taking into account the characteristics of customer experience. Previous studies have examined customer experience and customer experience in sports through different lenses. Researchers who measure customer experience have mainly focused on the value–experience relationship and its impact on satisfaction and loyalty, while researchers who measure customer experience in sports have focused primarily on sports events and participation (Hwang & Lee, 2018). Therefore, there is still a shortage of research on measuring customer experience, especially customer experience in stores, in sports settings and analysing the retail-customer perspective instead of the spectator or participant perspective, which has been extensively studied (Happ et al., 2020). The most relevant studies conducted are described below; Happ et al. (2020) stated in a study entitled 'Insights into Customer Experience in Sports Retail Stores' that customer experience in stores has a significant impact on customers' satisfaction with sports retail and the likelihood of recommending the store to friends, which in turn is significantly influenced by customers' satisfaction with retail. Additionally, social responses to actors involved in service encounters, such as interactions with employees, play an important role in customer experience in stores. Therefore, sports customers strive not only for inherent performance benefits in interacting with customers and employees but also for social benefits. Furthermore, Bonfanti and Yfantidou (2021) stated the importance of comprehensive design dimensions, sensory elements of the environment, social relationships, testability and sharing of real experience in designing a memorable shopping experience in sports stores.

Customer experience in the field of sports has been the subject of scattered research. However, two main gaps remain: first, studies have focused on sports events and/or participants and have ignored customers of sports retailers and their experience. Second, there is a lack of repeated studies from other fields developed to fit the sports context (Funk, 2017; Ghasemi Siani et al., 2021). Ultimately, the assumption that sports has unique features can lead to the fact that customer experience in sports retail stores is different from that of other industries (Happ et al., 2020). Therefore, the present study aims to answer the question of what are the capacities of sports retail stores to create a desirable customer experience.

Methodology

Research Context – Sports Sportswear Retail Stores in Iran

In recent years, conditions in the country have led to a decrease in people's tendency to buy; inflation, unstable exchange rates and unprecedented sanctions have increased costs in various industries. These ups and downs and economic crises have made many retailers, especially sports stores, vulnerable and made it very difficult to adapt to these challenging economic conditions. In 1391–1392, the growth of the tendency to consume was 35%, meaning that every year they would buy more than 35% compared to the previous year. Currently, with the conditions that have arisen, this has reversed; in 1393, the growth of people's consumption has reached below 15%, and it is estimated that this downward trend will reach below 10%, which is a serious problem for the retail industry (Izadi et al., 2023).

Therefore, with the conditions that have arisen, not only attracting customers but also retaining them has become a challenge for retailers, especially sports stores; the main challenge for sports stores is to some extent to manage the downward trend of their consumers' tendency. It seems that managing the customer experience can somewhat slow down this downward trend. Sport stores can increase the likelihood of their customers' repurchase by designing distinct multisensory experiences or keep it at an acceptable level (Dos-Santos et al., 2023).

Participants and Procedure

Given the lack of comprehensive research on customer experience design in sports and recreational facilities, a qualitative research method was deemed appropriate for this study. McCracken (1988) argues that 'when questions for which data are sought are likely to cause difficulty and greater inaccuracy for respondents, a wider and more flexible network provided by appropriate qualitative techniques is suitable' (p. 17). Additionally, since qualitative research methods emphasise understanding the meanings of participants and provide a broader picture of the research field (Creswell & Creswell, 2017), they are particularly suitable for providing a complete understanding of experience design in the sports field.

Since the experience of participants is the criterion for their expertise in the relevant field in qualitative research, the largest and most famous marketing managers of sportswear retail stores across the country were selected as the statistical population and suitable for interviews. After preparing a list of these centres and their marketing managers, coordination was made to conduct interviews and due to the long geographical distance, all interviews were conducted online via the WhatsApp social network and video calls. The interviews were in-depth, and each interview lasted about an hour (50–70 minutes), and each participant introduced themselves as an expert in marketing for the desired stores. The extensive interviews allowed us to experience the world from the perspective of experience experts (McCracken, 1988). We continued to collect data until we reached theoretical saturation, and no other participants mentioned a new aspect or feature for customer experience design. This was achieved through interviews with eight individuals. Initially, participants were invited to describe their job and responsibilities in detail at the relevant store. Then, to achieve the research goal, questions such as their plans and strategies for attracting customers to their store, their methods of communicating and interacting with customers, their strategies for creating a desirable experience for customers, their methods for creating new experiences for customers, their plans for the future of customers and so on were asked. All interviews were transcribed word for word for further analysis. Table 9.1 shows the list of interviewees and their primary demographic characteristics.

Data Analysis

The content analysis technique was used to analyse the data from the interviews. First, the data were manually coded according to the instructions of Rossman and

Table 9.1. Demographic Characteristics of the Interviewees.

Participant	Age	Gender	Education	Job
P1	40	Female	Masters	Marketer and public relations manager
P2	44	Man	P.H.D	Marketer and sales manager
P3	31	Female	Masters	Marketer
P4	28	Man	Masters	Marketer and content manager
P5	32	Man	P.H.D	Page marketer and administrator
P6	29	Female	Masters	Marketer and sales manager
P7	42	Man	P.H.D	Internal marketer and manager
P8	53	Man	P.H.D	Marketer and store manager

Source: Authors.

Rallis (2011), and then the codes were registered in the NVivo qualitative data analysis software. The interview text was reviewed several times to fully understand the aspects of customer experience creation in the interview. This stage was interpretive analysis (Creswell & Creswell, 2017) because understanding the statements of participants was the main interest of the researchers. After that, phrases (single words or small sets of words) were categorised into larger coding concepts based on semantic units. In the next stage, these codes were classified according to the research question. Then, the obtained concepts were related to more abstract codes. In this stage, the codes explicitly showed the content of each category. To provide titles and names for the codes, titles were selected that represented each category. Since the qualitative research process is nonlinear, the coding process was repeated until stable codes that defined concepts, sub-themes and themes were obtained. To evaluate the reliability of coding, three stages were performed. First, the coding process was repeated with five interview texts 30 days after the initial coding. The test–retest reliability of the coding process by the researcher in two time intervals was easily above the necessary thresholds (83%) (Gwet, 2014). Second, following the recommendations of Creswell and Creswell (2017), official and professional qualitative data analysis software (NVivo) was used for coding and tracking codes. Finally, the proposed approach of Scott (1955) was used to evaluate the reliability of coding. To achieve this goal, 10% of the interview text was provided to another researcher for coding categories, subcategories and indices according to the guidelines developed by the primary coder (Creswell & Creswell, 2017). The percentage of agreement between the two coders was 78%, which was higher than the recommended threshold of 70% to indicate high reliability (Scott, 1955).

Results

The aim of this study was to design customer experience in sports retail stores using the case of Enghelab Sports and Recreational Complex. The findings showed that the aspects of sports customer experience include 11 main aspects and 82 general concepts (see Fig. 9.1 and Table 9.2).

Discussion and Conclusion

Sporting goods stores are no longer just retail locations where customers purchase sports products. They have become social and entertainment spaces where exercise and sports are encouraged through the equipment and spaces provided by the store. The ability to spend enjoyable moments in sporting goods stores shows that managers must not only design the store with spaces dedicated to the community but also provide the ability to share experiences through social media. Essentially, purchasing from a place that makes customers feel good facilitates life and creates a sense of curiosity, not only attracting followers but also encouraging them to share photos. In this way, a community of brand and store enthusiasts who feel like part of the shopping experience is created (Bonfanti et al., 2020).

Customer experience in offline retail stores has been studied, but there is still a need for further research in various areas to develop comprehensive knowledge

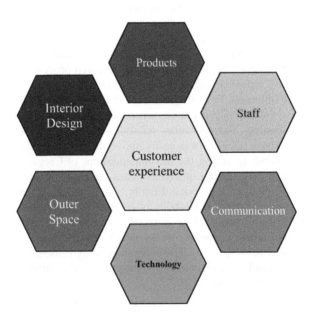

Figure 9.1.   Customer Experience Model in Sportswear Retail Stores
Source: Authors.

Table 9.2. Customer Experience Coding in Sports Stores.

Sub Themes	Components
Staff	Sports style
	Uniform sports clothing
	Color of sports clothing
	Young employees
	Male and female employees
	Physical attractiveness
	Fitness
	Sexual attractiveness
	Social interaction
	High public relations
	High knowledge of products
	Tone of voice
	Effective consultation and guidance to customers
	Presentation of employees' experiences to customers
Products	Classification and differentiation of products
	Color and design variety
	Inclusion of product information
	Price variety
	Diverse and appropriate timing for providing services day and night
	Size variety
	Quality variety
	Appropriate and attractive arrangement
	Variety of promotional methods (types of discounts, types of advertising, etc.)
	Chic packaging
	Gift and prize giving
	Online services
	Continuous customer needs assessment
	After-sales services
	Continuous innovation in product sales and service delivery
	Providing diverse products and services based on gender and different ages

(Continued)

Table 9.2. *(Continued)*

Sub Themes	Components
	Customization of products
	Attractiveness and innovation in the style of presenting products
	Providing accessories for products
Interior design	Appropriate lighting
	Open space
	Crowded store
	Music distribution (volume, type of music, etc.)
	Pleasant scent (pleasantness, stimulation, and intensity)
	Colorful and vibrant
	Attractiveness and seductiveness
	Exciting environment
	Color combination inside the store
	Appropriate air conditioning
	Temperature
	Cleanliness
	Proper arrangement of corridors and their size
	Fast stores
	Physical and psychological security of sports spaces
	Amazing interior architecture
	Creating a pleasant environment for shopping
Outer space	Designing showcases
	Showcase color
	Showcase structure
	Showcase lighting
	Showcase arrangement
	Store color scheme
	Amazing exterior architecture
Information technology	Variety of payment methods
	Using technology to test products
	Using technology to present and display products
	Using technology to present and display product information

Table 9.2. *(Continued)*

Sub Themes	Components
Communication and interaction	Continuous innovation in product sales and delivery
	Producing content based on customer purchases
	Producing content based on customer feedback
	Continuous customer surveys using various offline and online methods
	Increasing feedback collection methods from customers
	Desirable behavior and speech of employees in physical and virtual spaces
	Understanding customer needs and characteristics
	Desirable communication and interaction
	Creating and providing opportunities for more customer interaction with each other
	Providing previous customer feedback to new customers
	Establishing and maintaining continuous communication with customers
	Managing the website and social media pages to provide and sell products
	Creating a friendly and intimate feeling among customers
	Providing 24-hour response and service

Source: Authors.

about customer experience. In addition, repeating customer experience research in sports in other countries leads to the generalisation of results and the creation of an even stronger theory (Happ et al., 2020). Given that customer experience in sports has been studied in fitness centres and sporting goods retail stores, and this concept has been overlooked in sporting goods retail stores, this study was conducted to identify the potential of sporting goods retail stores to create a distinct customer experience. The findings indicate that managers of sporting goods retail stores can provide a desirable customer experience by investing in 75 aspects that consist of a total of six components: human resources, products, interior design, exterior space, technology and interactions and communications.

Thus, the first step in designing customer experience in sporting goods retail stores that should be of interest to store managers, entrepreneurs in this field, internal managers, and marketing managers of sporting goods stores is the component of human resources or the store employees. In this regard, Happ et al.

(2020) supported that the support provided by educated employees in the store can increase social interaction with customers. Schwarz and Hunter (2008) investigated that sports retail is not a 'normal' retail business. Sporting goods store employees must be highly educated and reputable in their field. Therefore, the use of sports-oriented and athletic employees and salespeople with a sports style and physique can facilitate or shape part of the cognitive, interactive, sensory and even aesthetic experience of sporting goods store customers. Additionally, sports customers should be attracted to in-store cognitive stimuli designed to create a good mood or feelings of excitement. Therefore, the use of employees and salespeople with attractive physical features and sex appeal can facilitate or shape part of the emotional and even affective experience of sporting goods store customers.

In the second step towards creating a desirable customer experience, sporting goods retail store a pleasant experience in the store that reflects their understanding of sports shopping, so they can tell their friends about a particular retail store and recommend it (Happ et al., 2020). Additionally, attention to real testability and sharing of experience is important: sporting goods store managers can invest in creating live experiences in the store from products before customers purchase them through store design and technology (Bonfanti et al., 2020). For this purpose, they can shape part of the cognitive experience of their customers by offering and displaying a variety of products with different designs, colours and prices for people of different genders and ages.

Furthermore, sporting goods store managers can provide a beautiful and sensory customer experience by designing interesting and attractive interior decoration, even based on sports themes. The store interior should meet the cognitive information needs of sports customers. With the rapid development of new digital channels, retailers must support cognitive in-store stimuli with online tools such as augmented reality to take advantage of them in-store. Customers can immerse themselves in a video that shows the technical features and various applications of the product, along with emotional content that affects the shopping experience in the retail store. Additionally, digital mirrors can make clothing sales easier and more enjoyable (Happ et al., 2020). Moreover, the combination of colour schemes, lighting, product classification and arrangement, fast store environment, the use of themes and sports spaces, increased customer engagement methods and opportunities for creativity and curiosity can create a pleasant experience based on aesthetics and sensory aspects for sporting goods store customers.

In continuation, managers of sports stores should pay special attention to the design of the exterior of the store in addition to the interior design, and by creating an attractive architectural design, they can differentiate their store from others and attract customers' attention. Research shows that stores with strong cognitive, sensory and emotional effects create an experiential purchase. It is worth mentioning that some sports equipment retailers create experiential architecture and interior design that reflect the world of sports as much as possible so that the interactive elements of the store can create an amazing and memorable experience for customers (Siregar & Kent, 2019). To achieve an attractive and amazing design, the colour scheme and lighting of the exterior of the store and the arrangement of its showcases should be on the agenda of the store manager and marketer. Because the exterior and showcases of the store are the first point of contact between the customer and the store and therefore have special importance.

The fifth step in creating a desirable experience for customers in sports apparel retail stores is the use of technology in the store environment. Bonfanti et al. (2020) believe that new technologies help retailers improve service performance and effectively understand and manage their customers' needs and desires before, during and after purchase. Sports retailers are operating in a changing environment where customers' needs for information are constantly changing, and existing technologies combine traditional and online channels in all stages of their smart shopping. This aspect suggests that the physical store is very important to customers and will always be so. Therefore, the competitive advantage of sports retailers depends on their ability to develop a store that meets the needs and expectations of their customers. The physical and digital worlds are no longer separate, and customers consider the shopping experience as a whole (Bonfanti et al., 2020). Wearable technology is becoming increasingly popular among sports franchises, impacting coaching choices, players' safety and performance. These gadgets can be built into sporting clothing, affixed to an individual's body, or placed straight in sports goods. In-game technology and tracking for specific sports technology have found their way through every sporting activity. The use of technology in sports equipment design has affected equipment design at all levels, from low-level recreational activities to high-level competitive sports. The application of technology to sports equipment is not universal and is unevenly applied. However, technology is proving to be a great ally for retailers, and there are solutions for every type of retailer and product.

Therefore, managers and marketers of sports stores should invest heavily in using technology to create and develop customer experience. The use of technology for product testing by customers, presenting and displaying products and even their information in written or video format can be the basis for creating another part of the overall customer experience in the purchasing process.

Finally, attention to the communication and interaction of the store with the customer is the last step in creating the customer experience. O'Donnell et al. (2016) described sports customers as 'market culture' who want to interact with other customers or employees. Support and expertise of store employees are very important (Lichtle & Plichon, 2014). In our field, this means that sports customers want to interact with employees, talk to other customers and make a memorable product decision in the store (Happ et al., 2020). In terms of social relationships, even in sports stores, customer shopping experiences can be influenced physically, emotionally and cognitively by interactions with store personnel (employees and other customers), as management studies often argue. Exactly, the ability of employees to listen, express empathy with customers: Sports retail staff understand, interpret and respond to customer needs and expectations by creating active trust (Bonfanti et al., 2020). Therefore, managers and marketers of sports clothing stores can increase desirable interaction and communication between the store and customers by investing in areas such as customer surveys using different offline and online methods, creating and providing opportunities for more customer interaction with each other, establishing and maintaining continuous communication with customers, providing previous customer feedback to new customers, producing content based on customer purchases and feedback, and so on, to ultimately benefit from the positive consequences of marketing.

Also, identifying and prioritising the key characteristics of sports store sellers from the point of view of sportswear buyers can be an interesting and practical issue for rational researchers in this field. In addition, the combination of different methodologies such as structural equations and qualitative fuzzy approach can be useful to identify complex compositions in the behaviour of sportswear buyers. Because the results of such research bring valuable data and better insight to sports store managers. Also, more researchers' focus on conducting experimental research such as neuromarketing, Eye Tracking, brainwave analysis of buyers, etc. can create a huge revolution in the behaviour of sports consumers. Finally, the research focus on observing the seller–buyer relationship and analysing the influence and power of the seller and buyer can shed new light on this research field.

References

Bonfanti, A., Canestrino, R., Castellani, P., & Vigolo, V. (2020). The in-store shopping experience: A systematic literature review. *Handbook of research on retailing techniques for optimal consumer engagement and experiences*, 110–141. https://doi.org/10.4018/978-1-7998-1412-2.ch006

Bonfanti, A., & Yfantidou, G. (2021). Designing a memorable in-store customer shopping experience: Practical evidence from sports equipment retailers. *International Journal of Retail & Distribution Management*, 49(9), 1295–1311. https://doi.org/10.1108/IJRDM-09-2020-0361

Bustamente, J. C., & Rubio, N. (2017). Measuring customer experience in physical retail environments. *Journal of Service Management*, 28(5), 884–913. https://doi.org/10.1108/JOSM-06-2016-0142

Chang, W. J., Liao, S. H., Chung, Y. C., & Chen, H. P. (2020). Service quality, experiential value and repurchase intention for medical cosmetology clinic: Moderating effect of Generation. *Total Quality Management and Business Excellence*, 31(9), 1077–1097. https://doi.org/10.1080/14783363.2018.1463156

Creswell, J. W., & Creswell, J. D. (2017). *Research design: Qualitative, quantitative, and mixed methods approaches*. Sage publications.

Dos-Santos, M. A., Alguacil, M., Pérez-Campos, C., & Velasco-Vizcaíno, F. (2023). How to improve sports fans' attitudes toward the sponsor through brand management? A PLS and QCA approach. *Physical Culture and Sport. Studies and Research*. 100(1), 61–74.

Eriksson, M., Bäckström, I., Ingelsson, P., & Åslund, A. (2018). Measuring customer value in commercial experiences. *Total Quality Management and Business Excellence*, 29(5), 618–632. https://doi.org/10.1080/14783363.2016.1224084

Eskiler, E., & Safak, F. (2022). Effect of customer experience quality on loyalty in fitness services. *Physical Culture and Sport*, 94(1), 21–34. https://doi.org/10.2478/pcssr-2022-0003

Funk, D. (2017). Introducing a Sport Experience Design (SX) framework for sport consumer behaviour research. *Sport Management Review, 20*(20), 145–158. https://doi.org/10.1016/j.smr.2016.11.006

Funk, D. C., Beaton, A., & Alexandris, K. (2012). Sport consumer motivation: Autonomy and control orientations that regulate fan behaviors. *Sport Management Review, 15*(3), 355–367. https://doi.org/10.1016/j.smr.2011.11.001

Gao, L., Melero-Polo, I., & Sese, F. J. (2020). Customer equity drivers, customer experience quality, and customer profitability in banking services: The moderating role of social influence. *Journal of Service Research, 23*(2), 174–193. https://doi.org/10.1177/1094670519856119

García-Fernández, J., Valcarce-Torrente, M., Gálvez-Ruiz, P., & Mohammadi, S. (2022). The challenges of digital transformation in the fitness industry in the world. In *The digital transformation of the fitness sector: A global perspective* (pp. 1–3). Emerald Publishing Limited. https://doi.org/10.1108/978-1-80117-860-020221001

García-Fernández, J., Valcarce-Torrente, M., Mohammadi, S., & Gálvez-Ruiz, P. (Eds.). (2022). *The digital transformation of the fitness sector: A global perspective.* Emerald Publishing Limited. https://doi.org/10.1108/978-1-80117-860-020221024

Ghasemi Siani, M., Mohammadi, S., Soltan Hosseini, M., & Dickson, G. (2021). Comparing young adult responses to rational and emotional sports product advertisements: The moderating role of product type and gender. *International Journal of Sports Marketing & Sponsorship, 22*(4), 798–815. https://doi.org/10.1108/IJSMS-04-2020-0045

Gwet, K. L. (2014). *Handbook of inter-rater reliability: The definitive guide to measuring the extent of agreement among raters.* Advanced Analytics, LLC.

Happ, E., Scholl-Grissemann, U., Peters, M., & Schnitzer, M. (2020). Insights into customer experience in sports retail stores. *International Journal of Sports Marketing & Sponsorship, 22*(2), 312–329. https://doi.org/10.1108/IJSMS-12-2019-0137

Holbrook, M. B., & Hirschman, E. C. (1982). The experiential aspects of consumption: Consumer fantasies, feelings and fun. *Journal of Consumer Research, 9*(2), 132–140. https://doi.org/10.1086/208906

Hwang, J., & Lee, K.-W. (2018). The antecedents and consequences of golf tournament spectators' memorable brand experiences. *Journal of Destination Marketing & Management, 9*, 1–11. https://doi.org/10.1016/j.jdmm.2017.09.001

Izadi, B., Rouzfarakh, A., & Mahmoudian, A. (2023). Investigating the mediating role of functional and emotional value in relation to consumer experience and consumers' intention to repurchase (Case Study: Consumers of sports shops in Yasuj). *Consumer Behavior Studies Journal, 9*(4), 44–68. https://doi.org/10.34785/J018.2022.015

Klaus, P., & Maklan, S. (2013). Towards a better measure of customer experience. *International Journal of Market Research, 55*(2), 227–246. https://doi.org/10.2501/IJMR-2013-021

Kuppelwieser, V. G., & Klaus, P. (2020). Measuring customer experience quality: The EXQ scale revisited. *Journal of Business Research, 126*, 624–633. https://doi.org/10.1016/j.jbusres.2020.01.042

Lemon, K. N., & Verhoef, P. C. (2016). Understanding customer experience throughout the customer journey. *Journal of Marketing, 80*(6), 69–96. https://doi.org/10.1509/jm.15.0420

Lichtle, M.-C., & Plichon, V. (2014). Emotions experienced in retail outlets: A proposed measurement scale. *Recherche et Applications en Marketing, 29*(1), 3–24. https://doi.org/10.1177/2051570714524880

Mansoor, M., Awan, T. M., & Alobidyeen, B. (2020). Structure and measurement of customer experience management. *International Journal of Business and Administrative Studies, 6*(4), 171–182. https://dx.doi.org/10.20469/ijbas.6.10001-4

McCracken, G. D. (1988). *The long interview.* Sage.

McLean, G. J. (2017). Investigating the online customer experience–a B2B perspective. *Marketing Intelligence & Planning, 35*(5), 657–672. https://doi.org/10.1108/MIP-12-2016-0222

Mohammadi, S., & Dickson, G. (2021). Online shopping for sporting goods: The role of flow, e-satisfaction, and e-loyalty. *Global Business Review.* https://doi.org/10.1177/09721509211019516

O'Donnell, K. A., Strebel, J., & Mortimer, G. (2016). The thrill of victory: Women and sport shopping. *Journal of Retailing and Consumer Services, 28*, 240–251. https://doi.org/10.1016/j.jretconser.2015.10.005

Rather, R. A. (2020). Customer experience and engagement in tourism destinations: The experiential marketing perspective. *Journal of Travel & Tourism Marketing, 37*(1), 15–32. https://doi.org/10.1080/10548408.2019.1686101

Roggeveen, A. L., Grewal, D., & Schweiger, E. B. (2020). The DAST framework for retail atmospherics: The impact of in- and out-of-store retail journey touchpoints on the customer experience. *Journal of Retailing, 96*(1), 128–137. https://doi.org/10.1016/j.jretai.2019.11.002

Rossman, G. B., & Rallis, S. F. (2011). *Learning in the field: An introduction to qualitative research.* Sage.

Schwarz, E. C., & Hunter, J. D. (2008). *Advanced theory and practice in sport marketing.* Butterworth Heinemann.

Scott, W. A. (1955). Reliability of content analysis: The case of nominal scale coding. *Public Opinion Quarterly*, 321–325.

Siani, M. G., Mohammadi, S., & Veisi, K. (2022). Digital Transformation in Iranian Fitness Centres. In J. García-Fernández, M. Valcarce-Torrente, S. Mohammadi, & P. Gálvez-Ruiz (Eds.), *The digital transformation of the fitness sector: A global perspective* (pp. 159–164). Emerald Publishing Limited. https://doi.org/10.1108/978-1-80117-860-020221021

Siregar, Y., & Kent, A. (2019). Consumer experience of interactive technology in fashion stores. *International Journal of Retail & Distribution Management, 47*(12), 1318–1335. https://doi.org/10.1108/IJRDM-09-2018-0189

Ta, A. H., Aarikka-Stenroos, L., & Litovuo, L. (2022). Customer experience in circular economy: Experiential dimensions among consumers of reused and recycled clothes. *Sustainability, 14*(1), 509. https://doi.org/10.3390/su14010509

Chapter 10

Applying the Strategic Model of Customer Experience in the Field of Sports: The Customer Experience Model in Sports and Recreation Complexes

Sardar Mohammadi[a], Abed Mahmoudian[a] and Mike Rayner[b]

[a]University of Kurdistan, Iran
[b]University of Portsmouth, UK

Abstract

Although the needs and desires of customers are different, obtaining positive and negative experiences is an inevitable consequence of consuming products and services purchased by the consumer. The nature of these experiences is very important for the retail industry and in particular sports stores, as the intangible experience includes the main essence of the products and services provided by businesses; in other words, sports products are mostly experience-oriented and can be classified as an overall experience. Despite the importance of the consumer experience as a dominant and effective paradigm in consumer behaviour, the design of sports customer experience has received less attention from researchers. Therefore, the present study seeks to answer the question of what aspects of creating and developing the customer experience in sports and recreational complexes are. To answer this question, this chapter attempts to identify the areas of creating customer experiences in sports and recreational environments by examining the case of the Enghelab sports and recreational club (in Tehran, Iran) using qualitative research methods and interviewing experts in this field and using the content analysis technique. The findings indicate that cognitive, functional, comprehensive, human, physical, functional, aesthetic, sensory, social, emotional and communal components are the most important components of creating and enhancing customer experience in sports and entertainment complexes.

Marketing and Design in the Service Sector, 153–173
Copyright © 2024 by Emerald Publishing Limited
All rights of reproduction in any form reserved
doi:10.1108/978-1-83797-276-020241011

Therefore, the owners, managers and marketing unit of these collections should invest in the creation and development of these components in the design of their strategic marketing plans in order to provide a memorable experience for the customer during their journey and finally be able to benefit from the subsequent positive consequences such as customer satisfaction, word-of-mouth advertising, loyalty and return intention.

Keywords: Customer experience; recreational sports complexes; ports industry; sports marketing; sports customers; sports organisations

Introduction

On the one hand, the emergence of postmodern philosophy and, subsequently, postmodern consumer culture, has been accompanied by the expansion of experience-based approaches to consumption. The postmodern consumer culture does not consider consumers as a logical element that regulates their purchasing behaviour based on rational processing but rather as emotional and irrational human beings whose behavioural responses are influenced by symbolic meanings, aesthetic criteria and sensory experiences (Skandalis et al., 2019). In contrast, in the pre-postmodernist (traditional) view, brand management and consumer behaviour are focused on physical and functional aspects to attract the consumer's attention through tangible and visible aspects of the brand (such as price and quality). Based on the dominance of this hedonistic postmodernist view, the consumer experience has become one of the vital survival strategies for many companies. Therefore, marketing managers have confirmed the importance of providing unique experiences instead of relying solely on selling products and services to create distinctive value for the consumer (Mohammadi & Ghobadi, 2022; Wiedmann et al., 2018). On the other hand, the changing needs of consumers in the competitive conditions of the modern era have forced companies to use new strategies to differentiate themselves from their competitors and gain a competitive advantage. Therefore, in the experience economy, theorists and marketing practitioners are searching for unique and entertaining experiences to establish a connection with the customer and differentiate themselves (Izadi et al., 2023). Because the consumer experience is a growing philosophy of marketing that is very effective in guiding consumer behaviour (Le et al., 2019). The emergence and expansion of the idea of the consumer experience was first discussed in articles and conceptualised as an important element in understanding consumer behaviour through a comprehensive consumption experience and is recognized as a prominent approach for marketing researchers and experts (Eriksson et al., 2018). The consumer experience has introduced a new trend in marketing and has shifted the focus of marketers to the importance of the process of creating a credible, honest, attractive and memorable experience for the consumer (Izadi et al., 2023).

Experience has a complex, evolutionary and unique structure that is somewhat irreproducible and takes shape in various stages of the purchasing cycle, such as pre-purchase, during purchase, and post-purchase (Alkilani et al., 2013), covering extensive networks of actors, stakeholders, consumers, managers and small-scale retailers (Jaakkola et al., 2015). In recent years, designing customer experience has become a priority for managers and marketers, and it is a relatively new concept in marketing that has emerged with the aim of creating a unique, enjoyable and memorable experience. In recent decades, it has attracted a lot of attention from researchers and experts. In summary, the customer experience is a new concept in marketing that has received a lot of attention in both theoretical research and practice because what people are really after is not the product but satisfying experiences (Izadi et al., 2023). The assumption that sports have unique characteristics can lead to the fact that the customer experience in sports is different from the customer experience in other areas (Happ et al., 2020). Additionally, sports centres offer dense services (García-Fernández et al., 2022a, 2022b; Siani et al., 2022). Customers (members) see the quality of their output (technical quality) and their interaction quality with service providers and other customers as part of their experience. In fact, experiences are not generally the same in different service areas. In particular, consumer behaviour for the sports field should also consider behaviours that drive members in an enjoyable and emotional way, not entirely logical models (Cetin & Dincer, 2014). Additionally, sports managers can create a real experience of their product and exercise by investing in expert, enthusiastic and technological personnel and their physical environment (Bonfanti & Yfantidou, 2021).

A substantial body of research conducted in recent years underscores the importance and complexity of customer experience design, segmentation and management across various sectors. Within the framework of strategic marketing management, many companies have embraced the concept of customer experience management and have incorporated it into their mission statements (Bonfanti & Yfantidou, 2021). However, limited attention has been given to customer experience in the realm of sports. Furthermore, despite the considerable attention that customer experience has received in recent years, creating and managing experiences remains one of the most significant challenges for the sports industry, much like other service industries (Cetin & Dincer, 2014; Walls et al., 2011). It can be argued that more research is needed for consumer experience, given the rapid advancements and competition in the sports industry (García-Fernandez et al., 2020). Bonfanti and Yfantidou (2021) also argue that researchers in sports, retail and service management have paid relatively less attention to the topic of customer experience in the context of sports. Considering that customer experience in sports is based on service management and retailing studies and models, the research conducted in this area is still in its nascent stages, and the scholarly knowledge, both in theoretical and practical terms, is limited and scattered. Moreover, Gammelsæter (2020) has called for research on customer experience in various domains. Furthermore, customer experience is a crucial and relatively new concept for service businesses seeking sustainable competitive advantage. While the literature on customer experience is expanding, there remains a gap in the context of customer experience within sports organisations (Eskiler & Safak, 2022). In the past decade, several large sports and recreational centres have been designed and established in Iran with the aim of creating and managing the customer experience. These facilities offer a diverse range of services in various sports disciplines, including tennis, golf, cycling, walking tracks, indoor and outdoor skating rinks, fitness clubs, children's sports and gymnastics clubs, natural and artificial football fields, shooting clubs, billiards clubs, skating, fantasy sports, bowling, massage, hydrotherapy, family sports centres and more. Alongside pioneering a new trend in the field of sports and recreational services, these businesses have achieved significant success and gained considerable popularity. Therefore, this research aims to design a model for creating the customer experience in multi-user sports and recreational complexes.

Theoretical Framework

Customer Experience: Definition, Management and Significance

Experience is regarded as a specific event that occurs in response to the stimulation of the consumer's five senses and is typically derived from direct or virtual participation in the event (Rather, 2020). This concept encompasses all customer interactions with a company, including pre-purchase, during-purchase and post-purchase stages. Theoretically, researchers have defined the structure of the customer experience by focussing on cognitive, emotional, behavioural, sensory and social responses of the customer to the company's offerings throughout the customer's journey (Lemon & Verhoef, 2016). In other words, customer experience is a broad concept that encompasses the dimensions of both customers and organisations and includes customer experiences during interactions with products, systems and services throughout the customer's journey. These experiences are related to cognitive, emotional, sensory, social and physical customer responses (Bascur & Rusu, 2020).

De Keyser et al. (2015) believe that the customer experience has three fundamental principles. The first fundamental principle is its interactive nature, meaning that the customer experience always arises from interactions between a customer and one or more market actors through various intermediaries, both human (e.g. employees) and non-human (e.g. collection technologies). The second fundamental principle asserts the specific uniqueness of each customer experience. The third fundamental principle relates to the multi-dimensional nature of the customer experience. This experience-centric marketing perspective encourages suppliers and service providers to create unique experiences for consumers because research shows that consumers are not only seeking to purchase products and services but are profoundly influenced by the experience of buying. Therefore, through a comprehensive and multi-sensory experience, it is possible to intensify consumer emotions, increase the value of consumer perception and consequently influence the final purchasing decisions (Wiedmann et al., 2018).

Currently, customer experience management is one of the most important managerial approaches in the business domain. Focussing on improving customer experience and implementing a customer experience management strategy is an action that service-providing companies can take to enhance their marketing performance. This process, from before selection, purchase and usage of services to the post-purchase stages, influences customers, enhances satisfaction and ultimately contributes to the company's profitability (Mansoor et al., 2020). Customer experience management, as a strategy, centres around the customer's needs and leads to a win-win situation between the organisation and the customer, aiming to shift customers from satisfaction to loyalty and advocacy. It extends beyond customer relationship management, encompassing a broad perspective on how a company and its products can engage with a customer's life (Ceesay, 2020). Ferraresi and Schmitt (2018) argue that customer experience management provides an opportunity to differentiate the offering, increase customer loyalty, boost positive word-of-mouth promotion, promote sales, reduce price sensitivity and enhance positive reputation. Organisations typically seek to manage the customer experience by depicting it as a customer journey, which includes numerous touchpoints and direct and indirect interactions between the customer and the organisation (McColl-Kennedy et al., 2019). At each distinct touchpoint, customers provide cognitive, emotional, behavioural, sensory and social responses in their interactions with the organisation, resulting in a static (or discrete) customer experience (Kranzbühler et al., 2018). In recent years, organisations have shifted their focus from managing individual touchpoints during the customer journey towards managing the entire customer journey (Homburg et al., 2017). This shift is because Kuppelwieser and Klaus (2020) believe that the concept of customer experience has a multi-dimensional structure from the customer's perspective, and customers perceive the experience as an overall evaluation. Consequently, customer experience management aims to create and provide a dynamic, cumulative or holistic customer experience before, during and after purchasing or using services through various channels and touchpoints (Holmlund et al., 2020).

Customer experience creates perceptual insights stored in the customer's memory, and positive customer experiences lead to satisfaction, trust, repeat visits, repurchasing and customer loyalty (McLean, 2017). The increasing relevance of the customer experience domain stems from the growing complexity in channels, interactions, choices and customer journeys, prompting companies to respond to these challenges by intensifying their comprehensive efforts (Kuppelwieser & Klaus, 2020). Companies are shifting from traditional marketing focussing on features and benefits towards creating experiences for their customers. Today, experiences are the cornerstone of the exchange process. Creating a superior customer experience and ensuring its sustainability appear to be primary objectives for service-oriented companies, such as sports centres (Eskiler & Safak, 2022). Scholars and experts concur that customer experience, with its ability to create happy customers and increase company revenue, is a prerequisite for a successful business (Lipkin & Heinonen, 2022). Furthermore, successful customer experiences are crucial for companies, necessitating a strategic approach to achieve these goals (Ta et al., 2022). Theoretical consensus exists that customer experiences are key priorities for companies (Pardo-Jaramillo et al., 2020). On the other hand, the increasing competitive market, coupled with digitalisation, compels companies to place the customer at the centre of their decision-making and to deliver better customer experiences (Cain, 2022).

Customer Experience in the Field of Sports; Formation, Differentiation, Scientific Gap and Importance

To create a memorable customer experience, retailers fundamentally use the DAST (Design–Atmosphere–Social–Test) model by intervening in four dimensions in the sales environment: (a) Design elements, which include the practical and aesthetic aspects of the store, such as layout, design and furnishings. (b) Environmental factors, based on individual consumer senses (such as visual, auditory, olfactory and tactile) and background conditions (such as light, music, scent, temperature, lighting/contrast, sounds, advanced zoom features and entertainment aspects). (c) Social features, which involve interactions with individuals present in the environment (such as store employees and other customers). (d) Testability, which refers to customers' ability to experiment with a product/service, such as tasting a food sample, trying on clothes or using digital equivalent technologies through augmented or virtual reality to explore products (Roggeveen et al., 2020). Retailers create the customer experience through several controllable store characteristics, such as pricing, product display, sales personnel, knowledge provision, product trials, layout and store ambiance, as well as multiple factors beyond their control, such as consumers' motivation to visit the store, their mood and the time available for shopping, the sense of enjoyment and socialising, all of which collectively shape the customer experience in the store (Terblanche, 2018).

Holbrook and Hirschman (1982) generally express that consumption should be perceived as an experience encompassing a continuous flow of various customer fantasies, emotions, enjoyments and perceptions. In this context, customer experience includes various entertainment activities, sensory pleasures, dreams, aesthetic enjoyments and emotional responses. Similarly, sports offer cognitive and emotional benefits, such as enhancing life experiences, promoting entertainment, empowering self-awareness and recharging life energy. In this case, the benefits derived from mental sports and personal experiences (Bueno et al., 2019). In other words, the services of sports centres, as an action, endeavour or performance, are an experience (Eskiler & Altunisik, 2019). In this regard, the customer experience of sports centres can be evaluated as enjoyable, interesting and unforgettable activities and moments. Sports centre services, like other services, have tangible, inseparable, perishable and heterogeneous characteristics that cannot be owned, and members pay for not only the main product (sports centre membership) but also for 'irreplaceable' experiences in the sports environment because fitness services are enjoyable (Eskiler & Safak, 2022).

Sports possesses distinct and unique characteristics that make it a unique commercial entity (Gammelsæter, 2020). Given the features sports offers, it's natural that (1) sports products, (2) customers of sports goods and (3) the sports customer experience exhibit distinctive qualities. Researchers and sports managers emphasise the inherent features of sports products, linking them to result uncertainty, supply and demand fluctuations, intangibility, the paradoxical nature of sports, reliance on product development, customer knowledge and the way sports are consumed (Shilbury et al., 2014). Funk (2017) introduced the framework for sports experience design, consisting of three interconnected elements: (1) the sports context, where a sports customer moves through an experience and interacts with touchpoints, (2) the sports user with cognitive processes, psychological needs and individual characteristics and (3) the sports organisation that produces the sports experience to achieve organisational goals (Happ et al., 2020). Unlike a classic hedonistic shopper, for whom the shopping process is guided by amusement, self-indulgence and impulsiveness, a sports shopper is task-oriented, ego-focused and socially validated. Thus, they can be attributed with highly focused, duty-bound and rational characteristics (Gammelsæter, 2020). In that sense, shopping is not inherently a recreational activity; it's a form of sport (O'Donnell et al., 2016). Increasing the overall customer experience is one of the most critical issues among product manufacturers and retail stores (Yoshida et al., 2013). Furthermore, Kwak et al. (2011) confirmed that sports provide a unique opportunity for individuals to explore emotional performance. Without a doubt, strong emotional responses, such as suspense, excitement, for spectators, and also for participants in the sports consumption experience, play a fundamental role.

A review of studies in the field of customer experience in sports is as follows: Bonfanti and Yfantidou (2021) in their research titled 'Designing a Memorable Customer Shopping Experience in Sports Equipment Stores: Practical Evidence from Sports Retailers' (p. 1295), highlight the comprehensive design dimensions, sensory environmental elements, social relationships, testability and the sharing of real shopping experience in designing a memorable shopping experience in sports stores. They believe that the role of sports stores in the field of sports is shifting from a sales space to an interactive, pervasive, engaging and enjoyable place. Additionally, Happ et al. (2020) in their research titled 'Insights into Customer Experience in Sports Retail Stores' state that customer experiences in sports retail stores significantly impact customer satisfaction with sports retail and the likelihood of recommending the store to friends, which, in turn, is significantly influenced by customer satisfaction with the retail store. Moreover, social responses to players involved in service encounters, such as interactions with employees, play a crucial role in the customer experience in the store. On this basis, sports customers strive not only for intrinsic performance benefits in interacting with customers and employees but also for social benefits. Finally, Eskiler and Safak (2022) in their research titled 'The Effect of Customer Experience Quality on Loyalty in Fitness Services' (p. 21), report that service outcome quality, customer–employee interaction quality and customer–customer interaction quality affect the quality of the customer experience, which, in turn, affects customer loyalty.

A vast body of research conducted in recent years on the design, staging, and management of customer experiences across various sectors highlights the importance and complexity of customer experiences and the considerations that still need attention (Homburg et al., 2017). Lemon and Verhoef (2016) stressed the need for further scientific research in various domains to develop comprehensive knowledge about customer experience, its formation, effectiveness and implementation. Gammelsæter (2020) also called for research in customer experience in various areas. Furthermore, while literature on customer experience is expanding, there is a gap in understanding the antecedents and consequences of customer experience in the sports context, and this is especially true for the realm of sports retail (Eskiler & Safak, 2022). Studies show that providing a superior customer experience is one of the ways to achieve successful marketing outcomes and competitive advantages (Gao et al., 2020). Previous studies in the sports field have examined customer experience and sports experiences through various lenses. Researchers measuring customer experience have primarily focused on the value–experience relationship and its impact on satisfaction and loyalty, whereas those measuring customer experience in sports have primarily emphasised sports events and sports participation. Therefore, there is still a shortage of research on measuring customer experience – especially customer experience in sports retail settings – as opposed to a spectator or participant perspective, which has been extensively studied. Research in the field of sports customer experience has been conducted sporadically. However, two main gaps remain. First, studies have predominantly focused on sports events or participants in sports, neglecting sports retail customers and their experiences. Second, there is a lack of repeated studies from other fields adapted to the sports context (Happ et al., 2020). Lastly, researchers in sports management, retail and service management have paid limited attention to sports retail stores. Some studies have concentrated on the physical and digital store environment and store atmosphere, especially music (Bonfanti & Yfantidou, 2021). Additionally, some studies have examined sports purchasing behaviour while offering a scale to measure sports customer experience and identifying relationships with other elements such as overall satisfaction and brand repurchase intention (Mortimer et al., 2018). What's crucial to note is that previous studies have predominantly focused on specialised sports segments like events, fitness centres and sports retailers that offer more specialised services. What matters is the growing trend in establishing and expanding the architecture of recreational sports complexes in recent decades, providing diverse opportunities for customers to acquire exciting and thrilling experiences that have been largely overlooked by researchers.

Methodology

Research Context – Iran and the Establishment of Sports-Recreational Complexes (Enghelab Sports Complex)

In Asia, customer experience is increasingly seen as essential for future business growth (Tivasuradej & Pham, 2019). Studies also indicate that marketers in the Asia-Pacific (APAC) region prioritise customer experience innovation over marketing communications and campaigns. Today, innovation in customer experience sets a brand apart, providing a clear competitive advantage and prompting more companies to invest in it (Tivasuradej & Pham, 2019). Over the past decade, businesses in the field of sports and recreation centres in Iran have been pursuing the establishment and design of multi-purpose sports facilities. The architecture of these facilities is designed to offer a wide range of sports and recreational services to people of various ages and interests. Enghelab Sports Complex in Tehran is one of the most popular destinations for leisure and sports activities. People of different age groups visit this club every day to engage in sports and recreation in its extensive and suitable environment. The club, situated on a vast land, offers facilities for various sports disciplines. Enghelab Sports Complex is not limited to sports facilities; it also includes several office buildings, restaurants and cafes. Individuals, whether alone or in groups, can engage in sports and spend quality time in this complex. The covered and open sports facilities at Enghelab Sports Complex enable participation in a wide range of sports and activities. Furthermore, the club offers cafes and restaurants where you can engage in sports and recreation with your companions.

The golf club at Enghelab Sports Complex is one of the country's standard golf clubs and is the only one with a standard grass field. The club also has a popular jogging path that attracts many people for outdoor walks. This beautiful path is adorned with tall and lush trees, making walking on it even more delightful. The tennis courts at Enghelab Sports Complex are the largest in the Middle East and meet high standards. Approximately, 30 tennis courts are located side by side, allowing spectators to watch up to four matches simultaneously. In addition to men's and women's sports clubs, there is also a club dedicated exclusively to women. It encompasses three sections: aerobics, bodybuilding and health and beauty. The health and beauty section offers services such as therapeutic massages, hair treatments, skin care and hydrotherapy. For children, there are sections for gymnastics, a children's park and an art section. Enghelab Sports Complex has several swimming pools, including indoor and outdoor pools, as well as seasonal pools. These pools offer therapeutic services such as therapeutic massage and amenities such as cafes and restaurants. The club's bowling alley is one of its most attractive features. Moreover, Enghelab Sports Complex boasts a football field with both artificial and natural grass surfaces. The artificial grass field is suitable for football training for individuals above the age of five. The club also has a shooting club that offers services for both men and women over six years of age. The family section in the club is always appealing to families and includes four halls with necessary facilities for volleyball, basketball and futsal. Additionally, the exciting sections of the club include a rock climbing section, a caravanserai, a conference hall, a cinema and a food court.

Participants and Procedure

As McCracken (1988) stated, 'When questions for which data are sought are likely to be difficult and less accurate for respondents, the broader and more flexible network offered by qualitative techniques is appropriate' (p. 17). Since qualitative research methods emphasise understanding participants' meanings and provide a broader picture of the research context (Creswell & Creswell, 2017), they are particularly suitable for gaining a comprehensive understanding of customer experience design. Given the lack of comprehensive research on customer experience design in sports-recreational complexes, a qualitative research method was chosen for this study. Because participants' lived experiences are the criterion for their expertise in the field under study, members of the board of directors, public relations team, media team and marketing team of Enghelab Sports Complex were selected for suitable interviews. Each interview lasted approximately one hour (40–75 minutes), and each participant introduced themselves as an employee of this sports-recreational complex. Extensive interviews allow us to experience the world from the experts' perspective (McCracken, 1988). We continued data collection until we reached theoretical saturation, meaning that additional participants did not introduce new aspects or features for customer experience design. This saturation point was reached after interviewing nine participants. Initially, participants were invited to describe their roles and positions in the complex in detail. Subsequently, to achieve the research objectives, questions such as the participants' plans and strategies for attracting customers in their respective departments, their methods of communicating and interacting with customers, the strategies in their departments for creating a desirable customer experience, the methods they use to create new customer experiences and their future plans for customers were posed. All interviews were transcribed verbatim for further analysis. Table 10.1 lists the interviewees and their demographic characteristics.

Data Analysis

The thematic analysis technique was employed to analyse the interview data. Initially, the data were manually coded following the guidelines of Rossman and Rallis (2011). These codes were then recorded in the NVivo qualitative data analysis software. The text of the interviews was reviewed several times to fully grasp the aspects of creating customer experience discussed during the interviews. This stage was inductive analysis (Creswell & Creswell, 2017) because understanding participants' statements was the primary focus of the researchers. Next, phrases (single words or small groups of words) were categorised into larger conceptual codes based on their semantic units. These codes were further categorised according to the research questions. Subsequently, the obtained concepts were associated with more abstract codes. In this stage, the codes explicitly represented the content of each category. Titles and names for the codes were chosen to reflect each category. Since the qualitative research process is non-linear, the coding process was repeated until stable codes were achieved, defining concepts, sub-themes and themes. To assess the reliability of the coding process, three steps were taken. First, the coding process was repeated with five interview transcripts

Table 10.1. Demographic Characteristics of the Interviewees.

Participant	Age	Gender	Education	Job
P1	44	Man	Masters	Content production expert
P2	51	Female	Masters	Director of Public Relations
P3	35	Man	P.H.D	Board of Directors
P4	50	Man	Masters	Instagram page admin
P5	33	Female	P.H.D	Public affairs expert
P6	30	Man	P.H.D	Admissions Manager
P7	42	Female	Masters	Places expert
P8	46	Man	Masters	Recovery Manager
P9	34	Man	Masters	Board of Directors

30 days after the initial coding. The reliability test/retest of the coding process by the researcher within two time intervals was 81%, comfortably exceeding the necessary thresholds (Gwet, 2014). Second, following the recommendations of Creswell and Creswell (2017), professional qualitative data analysis software (NVivo) was used for coding and tracking codes. Finally, Scott's (1955) recommended approach was used to assess the reliability of coding. To achieve this, 10% of the interview text with operational definitions was provided to another researcher for coding. An independent coder categorised the main codes, sub-codes and indicators according to the guidelines developed by the initial coder (Creswell & Creswell, 2017). The agreement percentage between the two coders was 80%, exceeding the recommended threshold of 70% to demonstrate high reliability (Scott, 1955).

Results

The aim of this chapter was to design the customer experience in the field of sports using the case of the Revolutionary Sports and Recreation Complex in Tehran. The findings indicated that the customer experience design in sports encompasses 11 main aspects and 82 general concepts (see Fig. 10.1 and Table 10.2).

Discussion and Conclusion

Rather (2020) considers the intention to purchase as a function of customer experience and believes that if businesses are seeking repeat purchase intent and subsequent customer loyalty, they have no choice but to develop positive experiences for them. Studies indicate that the point of sale has evolved. Sports and recreation centres are not merely places for exercise and shopping; they are designed as places for immersion and socialisation in the world of sports on emotional, physical and intellectual levels. Sports and recreation centres have the opportunity to create an experience-centric journey for customers in various aspects of interaction, entertainment, education and joy, among others. Since customers of sports and recreation centres engage not only for goods and services but also for the experience of participation, they prefer centres that can attract, engage and entertain them socially. As a result, sports and recreation centres emphasise the importance of investing in attractive architecture, exciting spaces and up-to-date technology to create and develop the customer experience. In this regard, the present study aimed to design a customer experience model in sports and recreation centres. The findings indicate that the best strategy for sports and entertainment centres to create and develop customer experience is to pay special attention to 11 customer experience components, including cognitive, functional, comprehensive, human, physical, functional, aesthetic, sensory, social, emotional and sharing components. This ultimately results in positive marketing outcomes, including satisfaction, loyalty, and repeat intent.

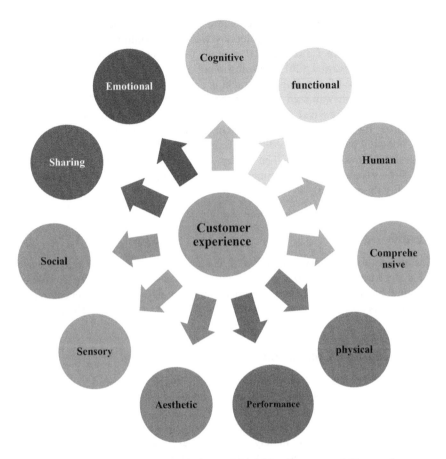

Fig. 10.1.   Customer Experience Model in Sports and Recreation
Complexes. *Source:* Authors.

Theoretical Applications

Customer experience in the field of sports is a relatively new area of research that
has recently garnered the attention of management and sports marketing
researchers, with limited research in this domain thus far. Previous researchers
have explored customer experience in areas such as sports events and sports
participation, retailing of sports equipment (Bonfanti & Yfantidou, 2021),
customer experience in sports retail stores (Happ et al., 2020) and the quality of
customer experience in fitness centres (Eskiler & Safak, 2022). In the present
study, we focused on customer experience in sports and recreation centres. We
responded to the requests of previous researchers to expand the concept of
customer experience into new domains and fields (Lemon & Verhoef, 2016),

Table 10.2. Customer Experience Coding for Sports and Recreational Complexes.

Sub-theme	Concepts
Functional	Diversity and Suitable Quality of Services and Products
	High Safety of Products and Assurance of Service Quality
	Physical and Psychological Security of Sports Spaces
	Standardisation of Products
	Diverse and Appropriate Pricing of Products and Services
	Diverse and Suitable Design of Products
	Continuous Innovation in Product Sales, Service Delivery, and Decorative Design, etc.
	Varied and Appropriate Scheduling for Providing Services Day and Night
	Offering Diverse Products and Services Based on Gender and Age Groups
	Differentiation and Grading in the Provision of Services and Products to Customers
Comprehensive	Family-friendly sports spaces
	Presence of traditional, fantasy, and electronic sports
	Simultaneity and adjacency of sports and recreational spaces
Human	Offering diverse services and products
	Providing diverse facilities
	Online services
	Continuous customer needs assessment
	After-sales services
	Customer profiling
	Creating diverse channels for customer feedback
	Continuous improvement of staff technical knowledge
	Respecting customer opinions and implementing them
Physical	Store layout
	Astonishing interior architecture
	Product and service categorisation and filtering
	Public product testing area
	Product testing space
	Digitalisation of sports spaces
	Digitalisation of sports services

(Continued)

Table 10.2. *(Continued)*

Sub-theme	Concepts
Emotional	Creating excitement in customers
	Creating satisfaction in customers
	Increasing hope in customers
	Creating an enjoyable environment for sports and recreation
Cognitive	Effective consultation and guidance
	Providing experiences to customers
	Offering knowledge and information to customers
	Customer education in sports, products, and services
	Fostering curiosity and stimulating customer creativity
Functional	Providing instant and specialised services
	Diversity and ease in payment methods
	Adherence to customer-seller agreements
	Speed of service operation
	Ease of use of products and services
	Quick stores
	Providing the best choices for customers
	Providing technical specifications of products
	Product customisation
	Various sales and delivery methods
Aesthetic	Appealing visual design
Beauty	Open layout and decoration
	Stylish attire and appearance of staff
	Colour schemes
	Presentation style
	Accessories
	Lighting
	Attractive product presentation style
	Enhancing the attractiveness and diversity of service and product promotion methods
Sensory	Pleasing music
	Daily cleanliness
	Scenting the space
	Illuminated signage
	Creating a calming environment

Table 10.2. *(Continued)*

Sub-theme	Concepts
	Creating an enchanting green space in the facility
	Stylish attire and coverage for facility staff
	Appropriate temperature and ventilation
Social	Direct communication with customers
	Desirable staff behaviour and speech
	Understanding customer needs and characteristics
	Effective communication and interaction
	Creating and offering opportunities for increased customer interaction
	Sharing previous customer feedback with new customers
	Creating a space for understanding the social context of customers
	Continuous training in modern communication and interaction methods for employees
	Presence and meetings with celebrities, athletes, and artists in the facility
	Establishing and maintaining continuous customer relationships
Sharing	Opportunities for experimental participation in various sports
	Specialised sports product testing
	Opportunities for product testing and trials
	Utilising offline and online technology for product testing
	Providing feedback from previous customers to new customers
	Providing coupons for customers to participate in other sections
	Producing engaging and customer-focused content

Source: Authors.

including Gammelsæter (2020) and the antecedents and consequences of customer experience in the sports context (Eskiler & Safak, 2022).

This research introduced a new insight into the elements and important aspects of creating and developing customer experience in the field of sports, particularly in sports and recreation centres. It made a theoretical contribution by shedding light on aspects of customer experience that had previously been overlooked in the scholarly literature. We provided a comprehensive list of significant aspects involved in designing, creating, shaping and developing customer experience in sports. This research, in response to the demands of previous researchers in this field and considering their research limitations, established a general framework for the concept of customer experience in the sports domain. Our findings comprise a list of customer experience design aspects, which consist of 11 main dimensions described by 82 specific concepts articulated by study participants. This study bridges a gap in the customer experience literature in sports, contributes to ongoing scholarly discussions and serves as a foundation for new, engaging and practical studies within the sports industry.

Practical Applications

Sport retailers recognise the importance of providing a memorable shopping experience for customers by creating a memorable environment and placing multiple touchpoints within their stores. They aim to make the customer's shopping journey experiential by creating special and memorable store environments, utilising elements of ambiance, and incorporating various touchpoints in the stores such as smartphones, monitors and digital video walls related to sports (Bonfanti & Yfantidou, 2021). In recent years, the trend of establishing sports and recreation centres has increased. The convergence of diverse sports disciplines alongside recreational opportunities has created a diverse range of experiences for customers in these centres. The present study identified 11 aspects for creating and developing customer experiences in the sports domain.

Our findings provide a cohesive perspective on the factors shaping customer experiences in sports and recreation centres. Managers and owners of sports facilities need to design their venues and spaces in a way that caters to various recreational activities alongside sports disciplines, offering diverse experiences for individuals of different genders and age groups. The current study is relevant to sports managers and marketers and provides a unified perspective for creating customer experiences in sports and recreation centres. The proposed model assists managers in monitoring and evaluating their performance in creating and developing customer experiences over time. Additionally, it demonstrates a precise structure through which managers can efficiently deliver the customer experience process, enhance customer perception of quality and achieve these objectives with minimal time and cost.

Sports and recreational centres should incorporate the identified aspects into their sports marketing strategies and create the conditions for implementing these aspects. The future of their business and competitive position in the market depends on creating these experiences for customers. Managers of these sports facilities should also recognise the key role of social media in exchanging sports experiences because through customer feedback, they can become aware of their mistakes and shortcomings and, based on this feedback, refine their service delivery and enhancements. Furthermore, retailers can also educate their customers about sports by changing their approach through information displayed on screens and the competence of store staff. Customers can learn about one or more aspects related to the sports they engage in and their desire for improvement in their games. Or, for those who do not know but are interested in learning to play, this can be an opportunity. Ultimately, sports and recreation centres create conditions for customers to enjoy a social activity and ensure that their shopping experience and presence are shared with others, which is based on customer relationships and active participation. Considering that customer experience has multiple touchpoints resulting from interactions between consumers and retailers, technology and digitisation, especially interactive technology, play a crucial role in facilitating customer experience management. This is particularly true in the context of sports retail, as discussed in consumer behaviour studies in sports (Funk, 2017), which indicates that sports consumption involves individual experiences mediated by the physical, technological and digital sports environment. In fact, new technologies assist sports and recreational centres in improving service performance (García-Fernández et al., 2022a, 2022b; Siani et al., 2022) and enable them to effectively understand and manage customer desires before, during and after purchase. They also enhance their understanding of competition and operational cost reduction, providing customers with positive experiences such as 24/7 access to comprehensive experiences and continuously updated information about sports and recreational centres. Smart facilities enrich customer experiences and consequently increase competitiveness in the market.

Furthermore, managers and owners of sports and recreational facilities should be aware that many positive customer experiences involve recreational areas such as cinemas, libraries, cafes and restaurants within these facilities. In other words, the intersection of sports and recreational experiences has facilitated the attraction, retention, satisfaction and loyalty of customers and consequently, the platform for their success. Customers find themselves in an environment during their journey that includes various and engaging experiential touchpoints. On the other hand, managers and owners of recreational areas should also understand the importance of establishing sports sections within their facilities. Alongside recreational areas, by activating spaces and sports disciplines, they can introduce new experiences to their customers. Ultimately, by increasing the perceived quality of the customer experience, they can achieve customer satisfaction and loyalty.

In conclusion, managers and owners of sports and recreational facilities must have a comprehensive understanding and awareness of the concept, conditions, antecedents and aspects of the customer experience. They should tailor their marketing strategies and short-term plans to be experience-focused. They need to consider customer experience management and the enhancement of perceived quality across all aspects of sports and recreation through continuous innovation in architecture, design, products, services, aesthetics and technology. Striving to create memorable and holistic experiences in both sports and recreational aspects is the key to the success of customer experience management and, consequently, the success of their businesses.

References

Alkilani, K., Ling, K. C., & Abzakh, A. A. (2013). The impact of experiential marketing and customer satisfaction on customer commitment in the world of social networks. *Asian Social Science, 9*(1), 262. https://doi.org/10.5539/ass.v9n1p262

Bascur, C., & Rusu, C. (2020). Customer experience in retail: A systematic literature review. *Applied Sciences, 10*(21), 7644. https://doi.org/10.3390/app10217644

Bonfanti, A., & Yfantidou, G. (2021). Designing a memorable in-store customer shopping experience: Practical evidence from sports equipment retailers. *International Journal of Retail & Distribution Management, 49*(9), 1295–1311. https://doi.org/10.1108/IJRDM-09-2020-0361

Bueno, E. V., Weber, T. B. B., Bomfim, E. L., & Kato, H. T. (2019). Measuring customer experience in service: A systematic review. *Service Industries Journal, 39*(11–12), 779–798. https://doi.org/10.1080/02642069.2018.1561873

Cain, P. M. (2022). Modelling short-and long-term marketing effects in the consumer purchase journey. *International Journal of Research in Marketing, 39*(1), 96–116. https://doi.org/10.1016/j.ijresmar.2021.06.006

Ceesay, L. B. (2020). Building a high customer experience management organization: Toward customer-centricity. *Jindal Journal of Business Research, 9*(2), 162–175. https://doi.org/10.1177/2278682120968983

Cetin, G., & Dincer, F. I. (2014). Influence of customer experience on loyalty and word-of-mouth in hospitality operations. *Anatolia, 25*(2), 181–194. https://doi.org/10.1080/13032917.2013.841094

Creswell, J. W., & Creswell, J. D. (2017). *Research design: Qualitative, quantitative, and mixed methods approaches.* Sage publications.

De Keyser, A., Lemon, K. N., Klaus, P., & Keiningham, T. L. (2015). *A framework for understanding and managing the customer experience.* Working Paper No. 15-121. Marketing Science Institute, Cambridge, MA.

Eriksson, M., Bäckström, I., Ingelsson, P., & Åslund, A. (2018). Measuring customer value in commercial experiences. *Total Quality Management and Business Excellence, 29*(5), 618–632. https://doi.org/10.1080/14783363.2016.1224084

Eskiler, E., & Altunisik, R. (2019). *Fitness services and marketing.* Beta Publishing.

Eskiler, E., & Safak, F. (2022). Effect of customer experience quality on loyalty in fitness services. *Physical Culture and Sport, 94*(1), 21–34. https://doi.org/10.2478/pcssr-2022-0003

Ferraresi, M., & Schmitt, B. H. (2018). *Marketing esperienziale: come sviluppare l'esperienza di consumo.* FrancoAngeli.

Funk, D. (2017). Introducing a Sport Experience Design (SX) framework for sport consumer behaviour research. *Sport Management Review, 20*(20), 145–158. https://doi.org/10.1016/j.smr.2016.11.006

Gammelsæter, H. (2020). Sport is not industry: Bringing sport back to sport management. *European Sport Management Quarterly, 21*(2), 257–279. https://doi.org/10.1080/16184742.2020.1741013

Gao, L., Melero-Polo, I., & Sese, F. J. (2020). Customer equity drivers, customer experience quality, and customer profitability in banking services: The moderating role of social influence. *Journal of Service Research, 23*(2), 174–193. https://doi.org/10.1177/1094670519856119

García-Fernández, J., Gálvez-Ruiz, P., Sánchez-Oliver, A. J., Fernández-Gavira, J., Pitts, B. G., & Grimaldi-Puyana, M. (2020). An analysis of new social fitness activities: Loyalty in female and male CrossFit users. *Sport in Society*, *23*(2), 204–221. https://doi.org/10.1080/17430437.2019.1625332

García-Fernández, J., Valcarce-Torrente, M., Gálvez-Ruiz, P., & Mohammadi, S. (2022a). The challenges of digital transformation in the fitness industry in the world. In *The digital transformation of the fitness sector: A global perspective* (pp. 1–3). Emerald Publishing Limited.

García-Fernández, J., Valcarce-Torrente, M., Mohammadi, S., & Gálvez-Ruiz, P. (Eds.). (2022b). *The digital transformation of the fitness sector: A global perspective*. Emerald Publishing Limited.

Gwet, K. L. (2014). *Handbook of inter-rater reliability: The definitive guide to measuring the extent of agreement among raters*. Advanced Analytics, LLC.

Happ, E., Scholl-Grissemann, U., Peters, M., & Schnitzer, M. (2020). Insights into customer experience in sports retail stores. *International Journal of Sports Marketing & Sponsorship*, *22*(2), 312–329. https://doi.org/10.1108/IJSMS-12-2019-0137

Holbrook, M. B., & Hirschman, E. C. (1982). The experiential aspects of consumption: Consumer fantasies, feelings and fun. *Journal of Consumer Research*, *9*(2), 132–140. https://doi.org/10.1086/208906

Holmlund, M., Van Vaerenbergh, Y., Ciuchita, R., Ravald, A., Sarantopoulos, P., Ordenes, F. V., & Zaki, M. (2020). Customer experience management in the age of big data analytics: A strategic framework. *Journal of Business Research*, *116*, 356–365. https://doi.org/10.1016/j.jbusres.2006.01.008

Homburg, C., Jozić, D., & Kuehnl, C. (2017). Customer experience management: Toward implementing an evolving marketing concept. *Journal of the Academy of Marketing Science*, *45*(3), 377–401. https://doi.org/10.1007/s11747-015-0460-7

Izadi, B., Rouzfarakh, A., & Mahmoudian, A. (2023). Investigating the mediating role of functional and emotional value in relation to consumer experience and consumers' intention to repurchase (Case Study: Consumers of sports shops in Yasuj). *Consumer Behavior Studies Journal*, *9*(4), 44–68. https://doi.org/10.34785/J018.2022.015

Jaakkola, E., Helkkula, A., Aarikka-Stenroos, L., & Verleye, K. (2015). The co-creation experience from the customer perspective: Its measurement and determinants. *Journal of Service Management*. https://doi.org/10.1108/JOSM-09-2014-0254

Kranzbühler, A. M., Kleijnen, M. H. P., Morgan, R. E., & Teerling, M. (2018). The multilevel nature of customer experience research: An integrative review and research agenda. *International Journal of Management Reviews*, *20*(2), 433–456. https://doi.org/10.1111/ijmr.12140

Kuppelwieser, V. G., & Klaus, P. (2020). Measuring customer experience quality: The EXQ scale revisited. *Journal of Business Research*. https://doi.org/10.1016/j.jbusres.2020.01.042

Kwak, D. H., Kim, Y. K., & Hirt, E. R. (2011). Exploring the role of emotions on sport consumers' behavioral and cognitive responses to marketing stimuli. *European Sport Management Quarterly*, *11*(3), 225–250. https://doi.org/10.1080/16184742.2011.577792

Le, D., Scott, N., & Lohmann, G. (2019). Applying experiential marketing in selling tourism dreams. *Journal of Travel & Tourism Marketing*, *1*(16), 220–235. https://doi.org/10.1080/10548408.2018.1526158

Lemon, K., & Verhoef, P. (2016). Understanding customer experience throughout the customer journey. *Journal of Marketing, 80*(11), 69–96. https://doi.org/10.1509/jm. 15.0420

Lipkin, M., & Heinonen, K. (2022). Customer ecosystems: Exploring how ecosystem actors shape customer experience. *Journal of Services Marketing, 36*(9), 1–17. https://doi.org/10.1108/JSM-03-2021-0080

Mansoor, M., Awan, T. M., & Alobidyeen, B. (2020). Structure and measurement of customer experience management. *International Journal of Business and Administrative Studies, 6*(4), 171–182. https://dx.doi.org/10.20469/ijbas.6.10001-4

McColl-Kennedy, J. R., Zaki, M., Lemon, K. N., Urmetzer, F., & Neely, A. (2019). Gaining customer experience insights that matter. *Journal of Service Research, 22*(1), 8–26. https://doi.org/10.1177/1094670518812182

McCracken, G. D. (1988). *The long interview.* Sage.

McLean, G. J. (2017). Investigating the online customer experience – A B2B perspective. *Marketing Intelligence & Planning, 35*(5), 657–672. https://doi.org/10. 1108/MIP-12-2016-0222

Mohammadi, S., & Ghobadi, A. (2022). The Role of excitement in the reappearance of the spectators in football premier league matches with mediating role perceived quality and satisfaction of the event. *Consumer Behavior Studies Journal, 9*(1), 92–112. https://doi.org/10.34785/J018.2022.664

Mortimer, G., Fazel-e-Hasan, S. M., O'Donnell, K. A., & Strebel, J. (2018). Measuring the experience of off-price fashion shopping: Scale development and validation. *Journal of Fashion Marketing and Management, 22*(4), 454–475. https:// doi.org/10.1108/JFMM-01-2018-0005

O'Donnell, K. A., Strebel, J., & Mortimer, G. (2016). The thrill of victory: Women and sport shopping. *Journal of Retailing and Consumer Services, 28*, 240–251. https://doi.org/10.1016/j.jretconser.2015.10.005

Pardo-Jaramillo, S., Munoz-Villamizar, A., Osuna, I., & Roncancio, R. (2020). Mapping research on customer centricity and sustainable organizations. *Sustainability, 12*(19), 7908. https://doi.org/10.3390/su12197908

Rather, R. A. (2020). Customer experience and engagement in tourism destinations: The experiential marketing perspective. *Journal of Travel & Tourism Marketing, 37*(1), 15–32. https://doi.org/10.1080/10548408.2019.1686101

Roggeveen, A. L., Grewal, D., & Schweiger, E. B. (2020). The DAST framework for retail atmospherics: The impact of in- and out-of-store retail journey touchpoints on the customer experience. *Journal of Retailing, 96*(1), 128–137. https://doi.org/10. 1016/j.jretai.2019.11.002

Rossman, G. B., & Rallis, S. F. (2011). *Learning in the field: An introduction to qualitative research.* Sage.

Scott, W. A. (1955). Reliability of content analysis: The case of nominal scale coding. *Public Opinion Quarterly*, 321–325.

Shilbury, D., Westerbeek, H., Quick, S., Funk, D., & Karg, D. C. A. (2014). *Strategic sport marketing* (4th ed.). Allen & Unwin Academic.

Siani, M. G., Mohammadi, S., & Veisi, K. (2022). Digital Transformation in Iranian fitness centres. In *The digital transformation of the fitness sector: a global perspective* (pp. 159–164). Emerald Publishing Limited.

Skandalis, A., Byrom, J., & Banister, E. (2019). Experiential marketing and the changing nature of extraordinary experiences in post-postmodern consumer culture. *Journal of Business Research*, *97*, 43–50. https://doi.org/10.1016/j.jbusres. 2018.12.056

Ta, A. H., Aarikka-Stenroos, L., & Litovuo, L. (2022). Customer experience in circular economy: Experiential dimensions among consumers of reused and recycled clothes. *Sustainability*, *14*(1), 509. https://doi.org/10.3390/su14010509

Terblanche, N. S. (2018). Revisiting the supermarket in-store customer shopping experience. *Journal of Retailing and Consumer Services*, *40*, 48–59. https://doi.org/10.1016/j.jretconser.2017.09.004

Tivasuradej, Y. C. T., & Pham, N. (2019). Advancing customer experience practice and strategy in Thailand. *Asia Pacific Journal of Marketing and Logistics*, *31*(2), 327–343. https://doi.org/10.1108/APJML-09-2017-0220

Walls, A. R., Okumus, F., Wang, Y. R., & Kwun, D. J. W. (2011). An epistemological view of consumer experiences. *International Journal of Hospitality Management*, *30*(1), 10–21. https://doi.org/10.1016/j.ijhm.2010.03.008

Wiedmann, K. P., Labenz, F., Haase, J., & Hennigs, N. (2018). The power of experiential marketing: Exploring the causal relationships among multisensory marketing, brand experience, customer perceived value and brand strength. *Journal of Brand Management*, *25*(2), 101–118. https://doi.org/10.1057/s41262-017-0061-5

Yoshida, M., James, J. D., & Cronin, J. (2013). Sport event innovativeness: Conceptualization, measurement, and its impact on consumer behaviour. *Sport Management Review*, *16*(1), 68–84. https://doi.org/10.1016/j.smr.2012.03.003

Chapter 11

How Marketing and Design can Enhance Customer Experience in Hospitality by Meeting Their Evolving Needs

Michael Donald and Ashleigh Donald

Halo Business Consulting, UK

Abstract

With the continued rise of digital marketing, the opportunity for the hospitality industry to re-imagine and re-design processes and systems to create a seamless customer journey has never been bigger.

In this chapter, the authors look at how customer experience drives innovation and how our changing values, precipitated by social, economic and behavioural flux, mean that hospitality and tourism brands are creating new systems and processes.

The COVID-19 pandemic saw an influx of technology solutions that offered the service industry a multitude of platforms to capture the public's attention to drive both profit and guest experience. The authors have found that the pandemic accelerated trends, and customers have now become increasingly accustomed to instantaneous service. This chapter explores how technology has been leveraged to meet this behaviour and the guest expectations associated with it.

The authors have interviewed four hospitality leaders from various sectors of the hospitality industry to help identify and analyse customer and employee trends. These leaders included: Florence Alloing – Group General Manager at Georgian House in London; David Gardner – Managing Partner at 80 Days; Rob Flinter – General Manager of Park Plaza Waterloo in London and Andrea Shaw – Director at FM Recruitment. Each interviewee was presented with a questionnaire to explore their experiences regarding customer experience, guest expectations, technological advancement, recruitment and organisational values. The authors used a thematic method to identify trends and have presented these findings to support the

Marketing and Design in the Service Sector, 175–186
doi:10.1108/978-1-83797-276-020241012

article. All quotes from these interviews will be referenced (Donald & Donald, 2023).

Keywords: Customer experience; design; digital marketing; behaviour; personalisation; hospitality

The hospitality industry, with its inherent commitment to servicing some of the most fundamental customer needs, is a sector where customer centricity isn't merely a feature, but a defining characteristic. It is an industry where experience is the product and where each customer's satisfaction ultimately determines success. Yet, as we evolve through the digital age, an era underscored by an explosion of plentiful and readily available personal data, the line between sales and marketing has continued to blur and the curated customer journey starts earlier in the booking cycle than ever before. This gives businesses that understand their customers' needs, the opportunity to design experiences that engage their targeted audience, while reflecting their brand identity, from the outset.

A confluence of factors, including advancements in technology, the rise of the social media phenomenon and global shifts, such as the COVID-19 pandemic, have expedited this process (Shames & Calin, 2023). The impact of these changes has left indelible marks on the fabric of the hospitality industry, prompting a profound rethink of existing practices, systems and processes. However, each challenge begets opportunity. For the industry, it is the prospect to harness the forces of change, to reimagine, redesign and revitalise existing systems, thereby forging a more sophisticated, seamless and dynamic customer journey.

As the bedrock of any service industry, customer experience is a multifaceted entity, an amalgamation of multiple touchpoints that customers encounter throughout their journey. In the hospitality industry, it begins right from the initial research stage when potential guests peruse through different options. It continues through the booking process, the communication before arrival, during the actual experience and post-departure. Each of these stages presents an opportunity for the hospitality establishment to craft a memorable experience and forge a long-term relationship with the customer.

The dynamic nature of customer values and behaviours is fuelling a continuous flux across the social, economic and behavioural spectrum, necessitating continuous evolution within the hospitality industry in order to maintain trust with the customer (Calderon-Monge et al., 2020). To keep pace with the changing times, hospitality operators should adopt a proactive approach to anticipate emerging trends, understand evolving customer expectations and adapt their systems and processes accordingly. This philosophy should permeate every aspect of decision-making, from the choice of amenities and the design of the building and its interiors to the recruitment of employees and the execution of marketing strategies.

In this regard, the influence of digital marketing has been transformative. Unlike traditional marketing methods, which often rely on a blanket approach, digital marketing offers ways to reach potential customers with precision and personalisation that was previously unthinkable. It enables businesses to deliver the right message to the right people at the right time, thus significantly enhancing the effectiveness of their marketing efforts. Moreover, it opens up channels for two-way communication, allowing customers to engage with the brand, share their experiences and provide valuable feedback (Les Roches, 2023).

Similarly, design has emerged as a critical factor influencing customer experience. More than just the aesthetics of the interiors, it encapsulates the functionality and eco-credentials of the facilities, the usability of the website and mobile apps, the simplicity of the booking process and the smoothness of arrival and departure procedures. By focussing on design, the industry can not only provide a more enjoyable and comfortable experience to their customers but also differentiate themselves in an increasingly competitive market (Pereira, 2016).

In the face of the seismic changes brought about by the COVID-19 pandemic, technology has stepped up as a beacon of hope. From providing a safe and contactless experience to guests to offering personalised recommendations based on data analytics, technology has been at the forefront of efforts to enhance customer experience. It has emerged as a powerful tool to meet the growing expectations of today's tech-savvy guests, who demand instantaneous service, seamless experiences and a high level of personalisation.

At this juncture, the insights offered by both hospitality innovators and established brands can be invaluable. While new players bring fresh perspectives, disruptive technologies and innovative marketing strategies, traditional brands can contribute their vast experience, deep understanding of customer preferences and proven methods. By learning from each other, and by continuously adapting and innovating, the industry can pave the way for an exciting future.

This chapter delves into the evolution of customer experience in the hospitality industry, with a focus on the transformative influence of digital marketing and design. Drawing upon industry insights, practical examples and expert views, it explores how the industry can meet the evolving needs of customers to enhance their experience. To stimulate thought and inspire action, it presents a vision of a future where marketing, design and technology converge to create an enhanced, seamless and personalised customer journey.

The Paradigm Shift in Customer Experience

Historically, the hospitality sector has revolved around core amenities, ensuring guests are met with a cosy bed, a spotlessly clean environment, delectable dining and top-notch service. The emphasis largely rested on the period of a guest's stay. However, the digital age, underscored by the emergence of user-oriented platforms and rapid technological progress, has dramatically transformed our understanding of 'customer experience'. Florence Alloing, Group General Manager at Georgian House, comments 'There's an intensified emphasis on genuine experiences nowadays. Simply having a stellar product isn't the magnet for customers it once was' (Donald & Donald, 2023).

Customer experience today is a cumulation of every single point of interaction between the guest and the brand. This extends far beyond the boundaries of a hotel room, a restaurant, a bar or an event. The experience often kick-starts well before a decision to purchase is made, during the discovery phase. How a potential guest perceives a brand's digital presence – its website, social media platforms or even reviews on third-party sites – can deeply influence their decision-making process. A sleek, user-friendly and enlightening online footprint can be a game changer, potentially swaying guests to prefer one establishment over competitors.

The subsequent step, reservation, is equally pivotal. A booking system that is secure, straightforward and adaptable, catering to a myriad of guest preferences, can elevate the overall experience a notch higher. With cutting-edge analytics at their disposal, brands can now tailor offerings and suggestions, endowing guests with a heightened sense of exclusivity.

Of course, the essence of hospitality lies in the experience. Every facet, from the sense of arrival to the quality of the product and the efficiency and friendliness of service, has a lasting imprint on customers. Less pronounced details, such as unique interior design flourishes aligned to the sustainable use of resources, Wi-Fi quality, the ambience of the restaurant, the sounds and smells in the lobby and even the choice of complimentary bathroom products, come together to sculpt the comprehensive experience.

The post-stay phase, though signalling the end of a visit, lays the cornerstone for potential future engagements. Effective communication, through tailored offers, solicitations for feedback, and dynamic interactions on social media, can help build trust and develop a transient visitor into a loyal, lifelong brand ambassador (Kharouf et al., 2019).

But as with all industries, hospitality too cannot afford to remain static and the focus on collecting data, reviews and feedback from customers to continuously improve customer experience has become consistently more data-driven over the years. Florence adds 'We measure satisfaction with direct feedback surveys and online reviews. We consistently share with the team all reviews so we can all suggest business improvements. We analyse all the data we have available to get a sense of trends and evolution of customer expectations' (Donald & Donald, 2023). The kaleidoscope of customer values and behaviours is in perpetual motion. External forces, from socio-economic fluxes and global incidents to technological innovations and emerging lifestyles, perpetually mould guest expectations. The aftermath of the COVID-19 crisis proved as an excellent example as it underscored the necessity for adaptive booking policies, intensified hygiene protocols and minimal-contact services. Simultaneously, a burgeoning environmental awareness is steering guests towards eco-conscious establishments.

Confronted with such transformative dynamics, the hospitality realm remains undaunted. The sector is indefatigably recalibrating and rejuvenating its strategies, ensuring guest experiences are not just met but surpassed. The ultimate goal is evident: curate such an enchanting, immersive and unforgettable journey for guests that a brand distinctly stands out, even in an oversaturated market.

Digital Marketing and the Age of Personalisation

With the roots of digital marketing firmly embedded in the Internet revolution, this area of expertise has experienced an extraordinary evolution over the past two decades. This evolution has seen a shift in the hospitality industry's approach towards marketing itself. David Gardner, Managing Partner at 80 Days, a creative and digital *marketing* agency specialising in global *hospitality*, feels that in the pre-internet era, 'marketing was almost seen as a dirty battle, but once the early adopters started demonstrating the potential to communicate and share values differently, there was a shift to use the technology to design a better customer experience' (Donald & Donald, 2023). This shift isn't just about short-term advertising; it's about personalising the customer experience, forging genuine, lasting relationships and engaging customers on platforms that they feel most comfortable using while allowing your brand identity to shine.

In hospitality, design is not merely an aesthetic choice. It narrates a story, evokes emotions and promises an experience. A meticulously planned design caters to functional needs while ensuring guests feel a sense of comfort and belonging. David echoes Steve Krug's 'Don't Make Me Think: A Common-Sense Approach to Web Usability' and suggests that '"Don't make me think" is something that should be applied to everything in hospitality' (Donald & Donald, 2023). Just as a thoughtfully arranged bedroom or an attentive server allows a customer to relax, safe in the knowledge that everything they need is in hand, a streamlined, user-friendly website, optimised for search engines as much as for the target customer, serves as a primary digital touchpoint and sets the tone for potential customers' experiences.

For hotels especially, the evolution of the website has been driven by the change in customer habits, to the point that the best examples are now designed to curate the experience along the customer journey and guest preferences, just like their physical world counterparts. The first hotel websites felt somewhat inspired by the Yellow Pages, with little more than a phone number to call and a low-resolution photo to advertise the property. Now, with intense competition not just between different properties, but between different booking channels, websites need to add real value to users right from the start. David suggests that 'a good website will have certain touch points that are the same as all the competitors so that you just instinctively know where things are going to be. But then there has to be a level of differentiation and distinctiveness on top of that to infuse its brand character and make it memorable' (Donald & Donald, 2023).

Ultimately, unlike the broad strokes of traditional marketing, digital marketing is taking cues to target potential customers with an unprecedented level of personalisation. This is where a complex web of Search Engine Optimization (SEO), Search Engine Marketing (SEM), influencer outreach, social media campaigns, content creation and tailored email marketing can be weaved to design a digital marketing strategy that builds long-standing connections with customers.

In essence, the advent of digital marketing has not just changed the way the hospitality industry reaches out to its potential customers but also how it interacts with and retains its existing ones. This age of personalisation brings along a sense of individual attention and care, making each customer feel valued and unique. This undoubtedly paves the way for fostering stronger relationships, enhancing customer loyalty, and ultimately, driving sustainable growth in the hyper-competitive landscape of the hospitality industry.

Where Aesthetics Meets Functionality

In the intricate world of hospitality, design is not merely about eye-catching structures, well-thought-out room layouts or carefully selected colour palettes. Each element, from the furniture placement to the choice of art, crafts and immersive experience, often holds sway over a guest's perception and the overall experience. Hospitality design transcends visual allure, embodying usability, comfort and at times, a touch of local ethos that fosters a deeper emotional bond between the guest and the locale.

The aesthetic aspect of interior design, far from being mere ornamentation, is a calculated interplay of colours, lights, furniture and decor. It's about crafting a certain ambience, embodying a brand's ethos or narrating a unique story. Whether it's the initial wow factor of a grand hotel entrance, the calming tones of a guest room that promises relaxation or a restaurant's intricate decor that promises a unique dining experience, aesthetics play a pivotal role in evoking emotions and setting the stage for the guest's stay.

Yet, a visually stunning space that lacks practical utility would be an exercise in futility. A hotel's brilliance lies in its marriage of form and function. This encompasses designing layouts that epitomise convenience, opting for furniture that spells comfort, conceptualising communal zones that encourage social interaction and ensuring privacy when it's paramount. Modern design also leans heavily into technological integration – be it intuitive digital interfaces for room amenities, smart TV controls, robust Wi-Fi infrastructure or streamlined guest services. Ultimately, in an age of personalisation, the ability to adapt space to suit changing customer preferences on an individual basis.

We spoke to Rob Flinter, General Manager of the Park Plaza Waterloo and a hugely experienced hotelier who has led the refurbishment of numerous London hotels throughout his career. Rob suggests that there has been a distinct evolution of customer needs since the pandemic. The biggest change, perhaps unsurprisingly, is over an increased customer demand for flexibility. To customers, 'the promise of saving 5 or 10% on a non-refundable reservation a year in advance no longer holds the same value it once did'. With trends such as shared workspaces, digital nomads and the way we work still evolving, traditional office-based schedules face an uncertain future. Rob suggests that design trends are preparing themselves for this uncertainty the best way they can. He adds, 'The design of public space has witnessed a marked shift towards adaptability. Spaces today are becoming far less ostentatious, offering the ability to change use, style, and design swiftly' (Donald & Donald, 2023).

Deeply rooted in the fabric of memorable designs is the ability to capture the locale's essence. It might be manifested in using locally procured and sustainably-sourced materials, showcasing regional artwork, imbibing local architectural nuances or presenting indigenous culinary delights. Similarly to web design, these additional elements help reaffirm the brand identity and not only offer guests a richer, more authentic experience but also foster a unique connection with the destination.

Modern design in hospitality also resonates with the growing clarion call for sustainability. Today's discerning guests often look for establishments that champion eco-friendliness. Rob shares that 'customers are better informed than ever before. There has been a continued increase in demand for healthy, low-calorie options, questions about food provenance and green credentials are being inquired about more often' (Donald & Donald, 2023).

This ethos is reflected in the increasing adoption of renewable materials, energy-conserving installations, water-saving mechanisms and waste-reducing initiatives. Such features are not mere nods to contemporary values but are steps towards forging a sustainable future.

Hospitality design is a multifaceted entity that shapes memorable guest experiences. It's a delicate dance between visual splendour and utilitarian brilliance, a confluence of local charm and global comforts and a harmonious blend of sustainability and opulence. Brands that have taken the time and effort to get to know their guests and go on to seamlessly integrate these facets stand out in this industry, setting benchmarks for others to emulate.

Technology: The New Driving Force

When was the last time you pulled out an instruction manual for an iPhone? Apple is known not just for building beautiful products but for designing products that can be used intuitively. Technology in the hospitality industry, both guest-facing and behind-the-scenes, strives to achieve the same level of usability. The COVID-19 pandemic forced a hasty embrace of technology and automation, as hospitality venues worldwide sought to ensure customer safety while maintaining high-quality service. This shift towards technology isn't merely a reaction to a global crisis; it signals a more profound evolution in the sector. The burgeoning customer expectations for immediate, personalised service and seamless experiences have nudged technologies such as artificial intelligence (AI), virtual reality (VR), augmented reality (AR) and the Internet of Things (IoT) from the sidelines to the centre stage. However, the revolution unfolding in hospitality is not merely about incorporating high-tech gadgets or automated systems for the sake of novelty. Rather, it's about harnessing these cutting-edge technologies to understand and cater to guests' individual needs and delivering personalised service seamlessly to enhance their overall experience.

AI, with its vast array of applications, is proving to be a game-changer in the hospitality sector. From chatbots providing instant responses to customer queries and to AI-driven analytics facilitating hyper-personalised offers based on customer preferences, this technology is revolutionising customer engagement strategies. Machine learning, a subset of AI, can analyse large volumes of data to derive insightful trends, which can assist in understanding customer behaviour, predicting demand, optimising pricing and even personalising marketing communication.

VR and AR offer immersive and interactive experiences that can significantly enhance customer engagement. Venue can use VR technology to provide virtual tours of their properties, enabling potential customers to experience their offerings before making a booking. This can be particularly useful in attracting customers who value experiential decision-making. AR, meanwhile, can be used to augment the on-site experience, such as providing interactive show rounds, displaying restaurant menus with 3D images of dishes, or even creating immersive destination guides.

The IoT holds significant potential to heighten guest comfort and convenience. Smart rooms equipped with IoT devices can offer personalised experiences to guests, such as customising room temperature, lighting or even music based on their preferences. Moreover, IoT can also aid in enhancing operational efficiency, be it through energy management systems controlling lighting and heating based on occupancy, or predictive maintenance systems alerting employees about potential equipment failures.

Moreover, the widespread implementation of contactless technologies, fuelled by pandemic-induced safety concerns, is expected to continue, given the convenience they offer. Mobile check-ins, digital keys, contactless payments and mobile ordering are not only reducing physical contact but also empowering guests with greater control over their stay, thereby enhancing their experience.

Importantly, these technologies are not stand-alone solutions, but are increasingly interconnected, providing an integrated, seamless and personalised guest experience. A customer might use a mobile app for check-in, use voice commands to control room settings through a digital assistant, order room service through an in-app menu and receive personalised recommendations for local sightseeing based on their previous preferences.

The role of technology in the hospitality sector is rapidly evolving from a behind-the-scenes facilitator to a front-line enhancer of guest experiences. By harnessing these technologies, the hospitality industry is not only meeting the demands of a tech-savvy generation but is also paving the way for a future where digital convenience and personalised experiences go hand-in-hand.

The Dynamics of People Strategy and Customer Experience

In the hospitality sector, strategies to enhance customer experiences have always taken centre stage. Data-driven insights, trend identification and feedback-driven changes aim to elevate these external customer experiences. However, the internal dynamics, focussing on employee experiences, often take a backseat.

The recent transformative shifts in workplace dynamics, arguably, have been more profound than those impacting customers. As customers emerged from the cocoon of pandemic lockdowns, hungry for fresh and immersive travel experiences, many employees began championing their preference for more limited commuter-based travel. This tug-of-war of desires has reshaped how businesses operate.

In 2020, the abrupt shift to remote or hybrid working models wasn't a luxury but a necessity. These arrangements, which many enterprises previously brushed aside as impractical, now stood as the only viable solution. The outcomes were surprising. Industries discovered innovative pathways to maintain, and even boost, productivity. Operational costs diminished, and several enterprises warmed up to the idea of long-term hybrid work structures.

To delve deeper into this evolution, we engaged with Andrea Shaw, who is a Director at FM Recruitment, a London-based hospitality recruitment firm focussing on senior finance positions in the UK and international markets. Andrea shed light on the changing landscape of customer and employee expectations. 'Clients now expect a wider range of candidates to be presented in a faster period. They also crave more detailed information, predominantly in report format' (Donald & Donald, 2023) she states, highlighting the monumental shift towards an era of detailed, analytical insights.

Such insights have been instrumental for FM Recruitment, allowing them to recalibrate and remain at the forefront of work trends. A noteworthy transformation Andrea pointed out was the changing priorities of job seekers. 'As of 2023, the potential for hybrid working in any new job posting has now overtaken remuneration as the number one candidate query. Of course, salary will always be a crucial part of a candidate's decision-making process, but employers are more aware that salary alone will no longer be enough to attract top talent and the overall workplace culture will directly impact retention' (Donald & Donald, 2023).

The ensuing challenge? Employee retention. Andrea emphasises the vital role of organisational culture in not just attracting but also retaining talent. While the appeal of hybrid structures is undeniable, the ultimate decision often hinges on the company's broader ethos. How committed is an organisation to fostering a fair and inclusive work environment? Rob Flinter says 'We have had to look at the employee value proposition closely. We recognised some of the most immediate challenges that employees and potential employees faced and have re-evaluated some of the decisions we had previously made. For example, we have gone back to offering accommodation in central London for key roles which had disappeared years previously' (Donald & Donald, 2023).

This brings us to another critical element – the physical workspace. An employee's choice between a gloomy basement office with dated lighting fixtures and the comfort of their own home is clear-cut. Just as the design and ambience influence a guest's experience in the hospitality industry, it has an even more immediate impact on employee satisfaction. Supporting this, Andrea states, 'With the rise in mobile work preferences, many companies are transitioning from traditional office spaces to more flexible workspaces' (Donald & Donald, 2023).

Yet, this shift doesn't negate the need for privacy. Some work conversations necessitate discretion. Hence, while open, flexible spaces are in vogue, businesses must also provide private nooks, ensuring they can rapidly pivot based on evolving employee and client needs.

In essence, the pandemic has not just been about business survival but a period of introspection and evolution. As the hospitality industry navigates this new terrain, the intertwining of customer and employee experiences will be paramount. The success mantra? Adaptability, flexibility and a commitment to both external and internal stakeholders.

The Future of Marketing and Customer Experience

Looking into the future, the domains of marketing and customer experience within the hospitality industry appear to be on the precipice of exciting transformations. Driven by advanced technologies, changing consumer behaviours and the aftermath of the global pandemic, we are likely to witness further evolution in these arenas. Key concepts like personalised marketing, omnichannel experiences, sustainability, ethical practices and customer feedback as key performance metrics are poised to be instrumental in sculpting the landscape of tomorrow's hospitality industry.

Personalised marketing has already become the standard, but is expected to become even more pervasive in the future. With the advent and continuous advancement of technologies like AI and machine learning, hospitality brands will be able to refine their understanding of individual customers, tailoring marketing messages to resonate with their specific needs, preferences and behaviours. This degree of personalisation will enhance customer engagement, increase loyalty and ultimately drive revenue growth. Moreover, personalisation will not be confined to marketing messages but will extend to the entire customer experience, from personalised room settings and dining options to curated experiences and services.

Next on the horizon are omnichannel experiences. As consumers continue to engage with brands across multiple platforms – from websites and social media to mobile apps and physical locations – the demand for a seamless, integrated experience across all touchpoints will increase (Haynes, 2023). Hospitality brands will need to ensure consistency in their messaging, service quality and customer support across all channels. With the rising popularity of virtual and augmented reality, new channels may emerge that allow customers to interact with brands in more immersive and engaging ways.

The call for sustainability and ethical practices in hospitality is only going to get louder. Consumers are becoming increasingly conscious of the environmental and social impacts of their choices, including when it comes to travel and accommodation. Hospitality brands that can demonstrate a genuine commitment to sustainability – whether through eco-friendly operations, fairtrade and local sourcing, or community involvement – will likely find favour with this growing segment of conscious consumers. Marketing strategies will need to effectively communicate these efforts, making them an integral part of the brand's identity and value proposition.

Lastly, the importance of customer feedback as a key performance metric is set to grow. With online reviews and social media, customer opinions have never been more visible or influential. By actively seeking, analysing and acting upon customer feedback, hospitality businesses can improve their offerings, address pain points and enhance overall customer satisfaction. Advanced analytics will play a crucial role in understanding this feedback in more depth, revealing patterns and insights that can drive strategic decision-making.

In summary, the future of marketing and customer experience in the hospitality industry looks bright and dynamic. It promises to be an era where the customer truly sits at the heart of every strategy, where experiences are tailored and memorable and where brands stand for not just quality and comfort but also for the values they embody.

Discussion

The dynamic triad of marketing, design and technology is undeniably reshaping the hospitality industry. With its immense potential, it has not only redefined the traditional paradigms but has also paved the way for a future where the customer experience is the epicentre of all innovations and strategies.

In the face of continually shifting consumer needs and expectations, the industry mustn't merely react but proactively adapt and evolve. The hospitality industry's strength lies in its ability to be both resilient and flexible. This is evident in how it has navigated socio-economic fluctuations and unprecedented challenges like the recent global pandemic. Adapting to evolving customer needs is not simply about survival; it's about consistently aiming to exceed expectations, generate delight and inspire loyalty among customers.

Technology, with its ceaseless advancement, has emerged as a critical component of this adaptive mechanism. The accelerating integration of AI, VR, AR, IoT and machine learning is transforming how hospitality providers interact with and serve their customers. It is important to remember, however, that technology is not an end in itself. Rather, it serves as a sophisticated tool that, when used thoughtfully, can help understand customers on a deeper level, personalise their experiences and make their journeys more seamless and enjoyable.

Equally integral to the industry's evolution are innovative marketing and design strategies. The dawn of digital marketing has marked a shift from broad, mass-market campaigns towards more personalised, targeted communications. The use of customer data, coupled with powerful analytics, has enabled the creation of marketing strategies that resonate more effectively with individual consumers, fostering a stronger connection between brands and customers.

In the realm of design, the focus is shifting from mere aesthetics to an intricate blend of form and function. The design is now about creating spaces and experiences that not only delight the eye but also cater to the practical needs and cultural sensibilities of customers. This focus on experiential design contributes significantly to enhancing customer satisfaction and creating memorable experiences.

In conclusion, the intersection of marketing, design and technology offers immense potential to redefine and enhance the customer experience in the hospitality industry. By understanding and adapting to evolving customer needs, leveraging the power of technology and executing innovative marketing and design strategies, hospitality providers stand a greater chance of offering experiences that are not just satisfactory but truly personalised, engaging and memorable. This blend of innovation and adaptation is what will guide the industry into a future of unparalleled customer experiences, ensuring its growth and sustainability in the years to come.

References

Calderon-Monge, E., Pastor-Sanz, I., & Sendra Garcia, F. J. (2020). Analysis of sustainable consumer behavior as a business opportunity. *Journal of Business Research*, *120*, 74–81. https://www.sciencedirect.com/science/article/abs/pii/S0148296320304872?via%3Dihub

Donald and Donald. (2023). *Interviews conducted between the author and hospitality leaders to support this article.*

Haynes, R. (2023). *The digital experience: How to meet the rising expectations of hotel guests.* https://www.hospitalitynet.org/opinion/4115891.html

Kharouf, H., Sekhon, H., Fazal-e-Hasan, S. M., & Hickman, E., & Mortimer, G. (2019). The role of effective communication and trustworthiness in determining guests' loyalty. *Journal of Hospitality Marketing & Management.* https://doi.org/10.1080/19368623.2018.1505574

Les Roches. (2023). https://lesroches.edu/blog/hospitality-digital-marketing/

Pereira, N. (2016). *Design trends in the hospitality industry.* https://www.hoteliermiddleeast.com/business/28030-design-trends-in-the-hospitality-industry

Shames and Calin. (2023). *Blurred lines: Redefining traditional distribution systems definitions.* https://www.hospitalitynet.org/opinion/4119421.html

Index

Aesthetic experience, 13
Aesthetically pleasing, 8–9
Aesthetics, 8–9, 11–12, 59,
    180–181
Agile management, 70
Airbnb, 36
Ambiance, 36, 39, 168
Ambience, 22, 39–40
Ambient conditions, 39
Amusement parks, 64, 104
Ansoff model, 17
Anthropometric designs, 15–16
Architecture, 51–53
Artefacts, 39
Artificial intelligence (AI), 14–15, 181
    chatbots, 70
    riven algorithms, 103
Asia-Pacific (APAC) region,
    160–161
Atmosphere, 23–24, 26, 36–37
Atmospherics, 36–37
Augmented reality (AR) (see also
    Virtual reality (VR)), 4,
    68–69, 105, 107, 181
Authentic, 22–23, 26, 97
Authentic-seeking, 23
Authenticity, 22–24
Auto-ethnographic approach, 3
Automation technologies in hospitality
    industry, 71
    impact of, 72
    use of, 71–72

Background music, 26, 36–37
Behaviour, 176
Behavioural, 138–140
Big Data analysis, 84
Bitner's servicescape model, 39
Brand management, 154

Branding, 1
    importance of industrial design in,
      13–14
Businesses, 68

Café, 21
    bar culture, 27
    case studies, 25–30
    conceptual framework, 25
    data analysis, 30
    experiences, 23
    flaneurs, 25–26, 30
    Gainsborough, 27–28
    industry, 27
    Lincoln, 28–30
    Manchester's Northern Quarter,
      26–27
    methodology, 24–25
Challenges, 2, 8, 14–15, 87, 98, 157
Changing customs, 52
Chatbots, 66, 105, 181–182
Chi-square, 57
    goodness of fit test, 56
City-based hotels, 52–53
Classical music, 36–37
Co-creation, 66, 76–77
Coffee Republic, 21–22
Coffee shops, 22
Cognitive ergonomics, 15–16
Cognitive responses, 39, 42, 138,
    156–157
Color, 145–147
Color scheme, 145–147
Commercial spaces, 102
Communication, 4–5, 15–16, 84–85,
    149–150
Community spirit, 27
Competition, 67–68
Competitive market, 8, 65, 69, 177

Consumer behaviour, 13–14, 37,
    112–113, 154, 184
Consumer experience, 37–39, 106, 138,
    154
Consumer research, 1
Consumerism, 23
Consumption, 1, 22, 38, 55, 141
Content analysis, 5, 142–143
Context, 1–2
Correlation analysis, 87
Costa, 21–22
Counter culture, 25, 28–29
COVID-19 pandemic, 176, 181
Cradle-to-cradle design, 12
Creating experience, 138
Creativity, 8–9
Crisis, 2, 67–68
Crypto-assets, 112
Cryptocurrencies, 112
Cultural ergonomics, 15–16
Culture, 23, 30, 44, 67
Customer centricity, 9–10
Customer choice, 51–52
Customer engagement, 103, 148
Customer expectations, 14, 138–139,
    181
Customer experiences (CXs), 1, 36, 64,
    138–140, 154–155, 176
  aesthetics, 180–181
  AR, VR and IoT, 68–69
  automation technologies in
      hospitality industry, 71
  benefits of technology in hospitality,
      65–67
  co-creation, 76–77
  customer opinion of product worth,
      customer satisfaction and
      loyalty of customer, 75–76
  data analysis, 162–163
  definition, management and
      significance, 156–157
  delimitation of study, 78
  digital marketing and age of
      personalisation, 179–180
  dynamics of people strategy and,
      182–184

  enhancing through industrial
      design, 11–12
  in field of sports, 157–160
  future research recommendations,
      79
  game changer, 74
  importance in industrial design, 8–9
  innovation in hospitality industry
      leadership and services, 70
  innovation in processes, 72
  innovation in product and services,
      67
  innovation in product design, 68
  innovation in service design, 69–70
  latest hospitality technology trends,
      71
  latest technology and automation,
      70–71
  limitations of study, 77–78
  literature review, 67
  managerial implication of study, 79
  measuring and evaluating customer
      experience in, 13
  methodology, 160–163
  paradigm shift in, 177–178
  participants and procedure,
      161–162
  personalised services, 77
  practical applications, 168–169
  process innovation and service
      innovation, 67–68
  product design, 74–75
  research, 1
  research questions, 64–65
  results, 163
  security breach in hospitality
      industry, 73
  smart check-ins in hotels, 72–73
  in sports and recreational
      environments, 5
  in sports retail, 140–141
  technology, 181–182
  technology importance in
      hospitality industry, 65
  theoretical applications, 163–168
  theoretical framework, 156–160

validity and reliability of property
management system
software, 73–74
Customer journey, 156–157, 176
Customer needs, 1, 3–4, 15, 54,
149–150, 186
Customer opinion of product worth,
75–76
Customer psychology, 55
Customer satisfaction, 14–15, 36, 55,
75–76
musical variables impact on, 37–39
Customer-centred marketing,
ergonomics in, 15–17
Customer-centric service design, future
of industrial design for,
14–15
Customer-oriented services, 1
Customer's Booking Decision, 104
Customers benefit, 1
Customers' decision making, 30
Customer's emotions, 39
Customers' physical needs, 15–16
Cutting-edge, 64, 66, 70–71
Cybercriminals, 114
Cybersecurity, 66

Decision-making, 3, 14, 103, 178
Décor guest rooms, 109–110
Deep learning (DL), 14–15
Demographics, 8–9
Design, 8–9, 13–14, 177
Design aesthetics, 11–12
Design and space, 1
Design elements, 8–9, 11–12
Design hotels, 54
Design thinking (DT), 2–3, 9–10
Design–Atmosphere–Social–Test
model (DAST model),
139–140, 157–158
Designers, 8–9
Designscape, 1
Destination marketing organisation
(DMO), 104
Detox tourism, 4, 120, 122–123
Digital, 102, 121

Digital age, 14–15, 102
Digital detox, 120–121
Digital detox holiday (*see* Digital detox
tourism)
Digital detox tourism, 4, 120, 122–123
activities, 124–127
case studies, 127–133
methodology and results, 128–133
motivation factors, 123–124
Digital innovation, 2
Digital marketing, 176–177,
179–180
Digital modelling, 102
Digital technologies, 4, 14–15, 120
Digital-free tourism/holiday/travel (*see*
Digital detox tourism)
Digitalisation, 84, 120, 140
Disconfirmation paradigm, 12
Disconnected tourism (*see* Digital
detox tourism)
Drink, 102

E-commerce strategies, 89–96
E-marketing (*see* Online marketing)
Eco-design, 12
Eco-friendly building, 75
Economic, 5, 13, 141
Effectiveness, 12–13
Efficiency, 12–13
Electronic commerce, 71
Email newsletters, 66
Emotional, 1–3, 8, 39, 163
Emotional design, 11–12, 14–15
Emotional engagement, 2–3
Emotional reactions, 3
Empathy, 8–9
Engelab sports and recreational club in
Iran, 5
Enjoyable, 42, 77, 140, 177
Enjoyment, 39, 106, 158
Enqelab Sports Club, 160–161
Environmental, 12, 52–53, 157–158
Environmental awareness, 68
Environmental ergonomics, 15–16
Environmental psychology, 52–53, 55
Environmentally-conscious, 12

Ergonomics in customer-centred
   marketing, 15–17
Ethical practices, 5, 184
Ethnographic research, 24
European Union (EU), 112
Existential authenticity, 23
Experience design, 1–2, 54–55, 66
Experience-centric services, 1–2
Experiential marketing, 1, 47
Exterior, 1, 3–4, 46, 148–149
External design, 60
External environment, 2

Face-to-face communication, 55
Fashionable, 52–53
Fast music, 37–38
Fast-paced, 64, 66
Final template, 30–31
Flaneur, 23
Food, 102

Gainsborough, Café, 27–28
Game changer, 74
General Data Protection Regulation
   (GDPR), 66, 112
Genius loci, 23–24, 32
Genre, 38
Geographical location, 59
Guest accounts, 65
Guest experiences, 103
Guests, 54, 65
'Guests' expectations, 4

Head-mounted displays (HMDs), 110
Health, 4, 106–107, 124, 161
Healthcare, 1–2
Heritage building, 27–28
Hipster-ish, 26
Hospitality industry, 3, 5, 64, 102, 176
   automation technologies in, 71
   game changer, 74
   security breach in, 73
   technology importance in, 65
Hospitality technology, 71
Hotel architecture, 53
Hotel design, 51–52

   architecture and physical
      surroundings, 52–53
   customer psychology, 55
   development and trend for, 52
   findings, 56–58
   international hotels, 58–59
   managerial implications, 60
   methodology, 55–56
   product and service design, 53–54
   public preferences and aesthetics,
      59
Hotel lobby, 36
   findings, 41–44
   findings of interviews, 44
   importance of music within service
      environment, 39–40
   methodology, 41
   musical variables impact on
      customer satisfaction, 37–39
   musicscape, 37
   physical environment, 39
Hotel room design, 3–4
Housekeeping, 65
Housing, 102
Human-machine interactions, 84
Human–technology interactions, 114
Hypothesis, 84

In-depth interviews, 4
Inauthentic, 32
Industrial design, 8
   competitive advantage, 14
   design thinking and customer
      centricity, 9–10
   enhancing customer experience
      through, 11–12
   ergonomics in customer-centred
      marketing, 15–17
   future of industrial design for
      customer-centric service
      design, 14–15
   importance of customer experience
      in, 8–9
   importance of industrial design in
      marketing and branding,
      13–14

measuring and evaluating customer experience in industrial design, 13
product–service system approaches in, 10–11
service design in, 11
for sustainable customer experience, 12
for user experience, 12–13
Industrial Design Society of America (IDSA), 8–9
Industrial designers, 2–3, 8, 15–16
Initial template, 30
Innovation, 67, 84
in hospitality industry leadership and services, 70
marketing tools, 86
in processes, 72
in product and services, 67
in product design, 68
service, 67–68
in service design, 69–70
Instagram, 4, 84, 86–88, 96
Instantaneous service, 177
Intangible, 24, 105–106
Intentionally, 4
Interaction, 4–5, 40, 106, 140, 149–150, 178
Interdependency, 2–3
Interior, 1, 3–4, 46, 148–149
Internal and external environment, 1
Internal decoration, 51–52
Internal design, 60
Internal environment, 2
International hotels, 58–59
Internet marketing. (*see* Online marketing)
Internet of Things (IoT), 14–15, 68–69, 181
Interviews, 3–4, 41, 44, 88, 142, 161–162
Inventory management, 65
Iran, 4–5, 141–142, 160–161

Kanban, 70

Landscape, 3–4, 58–59, 98, 184
Latham hotel & resort, 53
Lean, 70
Lighting, 39, 54, 65, 148, 183
Lincoln, Café, 28–30
Lobbies, 36
Loyalty, 2–3, 8, 65, 159–160, 185
client, 77
of customer, 75–76

Machine learning (ML), 74
Macro-ergonomics, 15–16
Management by objective (MBO), 70
Manchester's Northern Quarter, Café, 26–27
Marketing, 10–11
importance of industrial design in, 13–14
managers, 154
strategies, 4–5, 84, 88, 185
Marketing 1.0, 85
Marketing 2.0, 85
Marketing 3.0, 85
Marketing 4.0, 85
Marketing 5.0, 85
MAXQDA 2020 software, 129
Media analytics, 70
Memorable, 1–3, 5, 36–37, 65, 168, 186
Metaverse
definition and explanation of, 107
inclusion and integration with VR, 107–108
Micro-ergonomics, 15–16
Mixed, 31
Mixed methods approach, 3
Mobile ordering, 70
Multilingual, 40
Music, 36–37, 40
Music background, 36–37
Musical variables impact on customer satisfaction, 37–39
genre, 38
tempo, 37–38
volume, 38
Musicscape, 37

Non-fungible tokens (NFTs), 112
NVivo, 142–143, 162–163

Offline spaces, 1
One-way ANOVA, 58
Online, 1, 3–4, 41, 84
Online brand communities, 70
Online interviews, 3, 41
Online marketing, 1, 4, 84
  characteristics of interviewed
    companies, 87
  findings, 88–98
  key extracts, 89–96
  literature review and development
    of research questions, 84–86
  methodology, 86–88
Online spaces, 1
Open coding, 88

Pandemic, 2, 105, 184
People strategy, 182–184
Personal experiences, 24, 158,
  182
Personalisation, 66, 179–180
Personalised services, 77
Physical environment, 39
Physical location, 184
Physical setting, 1–2
Place attachment, 22
Place identity, 3
Pleasure, 12–13, 39–40, 69
Poland, 4
Portofino Bay Hotel, 40
Positive experience, 11–12, 15–16, 77,
  168–169
Postmodern consumer culture, 154
Postmodern philosophy, 154
Process innovation, 67–68
Product and service design, 53–54
Product design, 74–75
  eco-friendly building, 75
  in-room entertainment, 74–75
Product hedonic value, 13
Product–service system (PSS), 2–3, 8
  approaches in industrial design,
    10–11

Property management system software,
  validity and reliability of,
  73–74
Psychological, 3–4, 15, 55, 131–132
Psychology, 55
Public preferences and aesthetics, 59
Purchasing intentions, 13
Purposive sampling, 41

Qualitative research, 4–5, 41, 124, 128,
  162–163
Quantitative research, 41
Questionnaires, 14, 41, 54

Recreational environments, 5
Recreational sports complexes,
  159–160
Recycling materials, 68
Restaurants, 109–110
Retail, 1, 36–37, 159–160
Returns on investment (ROI), 70
Robotics, 70
Robotics in hospitality, 104–105
Robots, 2, 105
Room reservations, 65

Satisfaction, 12–13, 44, 47, 59–60,
  176
Scoring questions, 55–56
Scrum, 70
Search Engine Marketing (SEM),
  179
Search Engine Optimization (SEO), 66,
  179
Security breach in hospitality industry,
  73
Self-expression, 4, 132
Sensory, 5, 138, 156–157
Service, 11
Service design (*see also* Product
  design), 1–3, 8
  in industrial design, 11
  process, 64
Service digitalisation, 2
Service environment, 36
  customer's point of view, 39–40

employees' and service providers'
point of view, 40
importance of music within, 39–40
Service experience, 2–3, 10–11, 55
Service innovation, 67–68
Service performance, 1, 140, 149
Service robots, 105
Service-dominant logic, 1
Services marketing, 1
Servicescape, 22, 36–37, 39
Servitisation, 3
Shabby chic, 26
Shape, 11–12, 139, 154–155
Shoppers, 36–37
Significance of personal, 24
Signs, 39
Slow tempo music, 37–38
Small and medium-sized enterprises
(SMEs), 84
Small companies, 4
'SmartStaySafety' operation, 105
Social bonding, 4, 131
Social impact assessments, 13–14
Social interactions, 1–2
Social life cycle assessments, 13–14
Social media, 66, 85
Sociological impressionism, 24
Sound, 22, 39, 157–158
Sound marketing, 36–37
South of the UK, 3, 41
Space, 1, 39, 41, 180
Spacescape, 1
Spiritually, 23
Sport retailers, 168
Sports customers, 159
Sports equipment retailers, 138–139
Sports industry, 155–156
Sports marketing, 164–167
Sports organisations, 155–156
Sports-recreational complexes,
research context–Iran and
establishment of, 160–161
Sportswear retail stores, 4–5
data analysis, 142–143
methodology, 141–143
participants and procedure, 142

research context, 141–142
results, 143–144
theoretical framework, 139–141
Sportswear stores, 138–139
Staff responsiveness to guest, 109–110
Stakeholders, 154–155
Starbucks, 21–22
Storytelling, 11–12
Strategic model, 154
Stress-free experience, 2
Structured interviews, 56
Subjective questions, 55–56
Surrounding environment, 23–24,
52–53, 59–60
Sustainability, 2–3, 12, 68
Sustainable, 1, 12, 103–104
Sustainable customer experience,
industrial design for, 12
Symbols, 39

Tangibles, 1
Technological, 65, 67, 88, 107, 177
Technology, 181–182
benefits, 65–67
importance, 65
Temperature, 22, 36–37, 39, 44
Template Analysis (TeA), 30
Tempo, 37–38, 47
Tensions, 36–37
Texture, 11–13
The internal and external environment,
1
Thematic analysis, 4, 162–163
Toronto Shangri-La Hotel lobby,
39–40
Total quality management (TQM), 70
Tourist experience, 120
'Tourists' demands, 53
Tripadvisor, 4, 120
21st century, 28, 84

Unique environments, 3
United Kingdom (UK), 3
Unplugged tourism (*see* Digital detox
tourism)
User experience (UX), 12–13

industrial design for, 12–13
User interface/user experience (UI/
    UX), 69
User-friendly, 8, 12–13, 69
'Users' satisfaction, 10–11
Utilitarian value, 13

Virtual assistants, 72
Virtual design (VD), 4, 102
    augmented reality, 105–107
    décor guest rooms, restaurants, staff
        responsiveness to guest,
        109–110
    definition, 102–103
    definition and explanation of
        metaverse, 107
    delimitation of study, 112–114
    future research recommendations,
        114
    in hospitality, 103–104

limitations of study, 110–112
managerial implication of study,
    114–115
metaverse inclusion and integration
    with VR, 107–108
robotics in hospitality, 104–105
VR, 104–105, 107
Virtual reality (VR), 4, 68–69,
    104–105, 107, 181
    metaverse inclusion and integration
        with, 107–108
Visual experience, 60
Volume, 38

Web Content Accessibility rules
    (WCAG), 108
Website, 66, 84, 104, 177, 184
Wellbeing, 126

YOTEL Boston, 105

Printed and bound by CPI Group (UK) Ltd, Croydon, CR0 4YY

19/11/2024

14595309-0001